Object-Oriented Programming in Turbo Pascal Disk

Save yourself the time and trouble of manual file entry. The optional disk contains all the source code used in **Object-Oriented Programming in Turbo Pascal**. It serves as a timesaver—a labor saving device that allows you to take a good look at the code, and to experiment and improve upon it as you see fit. Source code is available on 3-1/2 or 4-1/4 disk in MS-DOS format.

To Order: Return this coupon with your payment to **M&T Books**, 501 Galveston Drive, Redwood City, CA 94063 or **CALL TOLL-FREE 1-800-533-4372 (in CA 1-800-356-2002)**. Ask for Operator 7082.

YES! Please send me the Object-Oriented Programming with Turbo Pascal source code disk for $20.

CA residents add sales tax ___% __________

Total __________

____ **Check enclosed, payable to M&T Books.**

Charge my ____ VISA ____ MC ____ AmEx

Card no. ____________________ **Exp. Date** __________

Signature ____________________________

Name ____________________________

Address ____________________________

City ________________ **State** ______ **Zip** ________

Note: Prices subject to change without notice. Disks may be returned for replacement only if damaged upon receipt.

7082

NO POSTAGE
NECESSARY
IF MAILED
IN THE
UNITED STATES

BUSINESS REPLY MAIL
FIRST CLASS PERMIT 871 REDWOOD CITY CA

POSTAGE WILL BE PAID BY ADDRESSEE

M&T BOOKS
501 Galveston Drive
Redwood City CA 94063-9925

PLEASE FOLD ALONG LINE AND TAPE CLOSED

Object-Oriented Turbo Pascal

Object-Oriented Turbo Pascal

Alex Lane

M&T Publishing, Inc.
Redwood City, California

M&T Books
A Division of M&T Publishing, Inc.
501 Galveston Drive
Redwood City, CA 94063

Printed in the United States of America
First Edition published 1989

Limits of Liability and Disclaimer of Warranty

The Author and Publisher of this book have used their best efforts in preparing the book and the programs contained in it. These efforts include the development, research, and testing of the theories and programs to determine their effectiveness.

The Author and Publisher make no warranty of any kind, expressed or implied, with regard to these programs or the documentation contained in this book. The Author and Publisher shall not be liable in any event for incidental or consequential damages in connection with, or arising out of, the furnishing, performance, or use of these programs.

Library of Congress Cataloging in Publication Data

Lane, Alex.
Object-oriented Turbo Pascal / Alex Lane
p. cm.
1. Object-oriented programming 2. Pascal (Computer program language) 3. Turbo Pascal (Computer program) I. Title.
QA76.64.L36 1990
005.26'2--dc20

90-6013
CIP

ISBN 1-55851-109-1 $36.95 (book/disk)
ISBN 1-55851-087-7 $26.95 (book)
ISBN 1-55851-110-5 $20.00 (disk)

93 92 91 90 4 3 2 1

Project Editor: David Rosenthal

With love to my wife, Galina,
and my children, Andrew and Natalie

CONTENTS

ACKNOWLEDGMENTS

On the technical side, I'd like to thank Borland International for making Turbo Pascal 5.5 available to programmers, and to everyone at M&T Books, in particular Ellen Ablow, who had the faith to take on this project; Brenda McLaughlin, who supported and encouraged me; and David Rosenthal, who helped put it together.

I would be remiss, however, if I neglected to thank a number of people who also helped make this book possible, albeit indirectly. Thanks go to my grandparents, Vladimir and Elisabeth Voschinin, who inspired me, and my father, Carlos, who put printer's ink in my veins. Thanks to my parents, Ludwig and Natalie Furst, who nurtured me and gave me a solid foundation on which to stand. Thanks also to my friends, especially Catherine Faith Oppenheim, who encouraged me to write, my brother Steve, who helped me unearth my potential, and my brother Carlos, whose will and quiet humor are an inspiration. Prominent thanks to my family, who supported me patiently while I wrote this book.

Finally, I am grateful to everyone whose brain I picked, whose advice I pursued, and whose opinion I sought while writing this book. Thank you all.

WHY THIS BOOK IS FOR YOU

This book has been written to provide programmers with a practical introduction to object-oriented programming in Turbo Pascal 5.5. Object-oriented programming (OOP) is a methodology whose popularity is expanding as programmers learn they can write flexible, reusable software.

There's more to OOP, however, than learning a few new syntax rules. In this book, you'll gain insight not only into the mechanics of how OOP works in Turbo Pascal, but also into some of the basic issues that underlie object-oriented design. The text relies upon extensive explanations and numerous examples, and in the first part of the book, you'll be introduced to the elements of OOP in Turbo Pascal, including inheritance, methods, and virtual methods. Other topics include mouse programming and using the Turbo Debugger.

In the second part of the book, you'll examine several small applications that involve graphics, windowing, artificial intelligence, object-oriented databases, and graphics animation.

The book will be of general interest to programmers wanting to learn about object-oriented programming. The integration of OOP with graphics will be of particular interest to those wanting to take full advantage of the Borland Graphics Interface in Turbo Pascal 5.5. Also, engineers interested in applying object-oriented techniques to their needs will find the control system simulation useful. A basic familiarity with Turbo Pascal is assumed.

How to Order the Accompanying Disk

Save yourself the time and trouble of manual file entry. The optional disk contains all the source code used *Object-Oriented Turbo Pascal.* It serves as a timesaver — a labor-saving device that allows you to take a good look at the code, and to experiment and improve upon it as you see fit. The source code is available on 3-1/2" or 5-1/4" disk in MS-DOS format.

The disk is $20, plus sales tax if you are a California resident. Order by sending a check, or credit card numbert and expiration date, to:

Object-Oriented Turbo Pascal Disk
M&T Books
501 Galveston Drive
Redwood City, CA 94063

Or, you may order by calling our toll-free number between 8 A.M. and 5:00 P.M. Pacific Standard Time: 800/533-4372 (800/356-2002 in California). Ask for **Item #110-5**.

INTRODUCTION

A tremendous amount of enthusiasm and interest has been generated recently for a software engineering methodology called *object-oriented programming* (*OOP*). Computer magazines publish a steady stream of OOP-related articles. Seminars, symposia, and conferences on object-oriented design take place with increasing frequency. The fact you're reading this book is concrete evidence of this growing interest in object-oriented programming.

Before proceeding, let's clear up a few points. First of all, the term "object-oriented programming" is something of a misnomer; it's really more accurate to talk of "object-oriented design." Although programming and design are two separate activities, I have found them to be so interconnected that I tend to use both terms interchangeably throughout the book.

Like many performers who seem to rocket to fame overnight only after long years of preparation and audition, OOP has been around for a while. From its roots in the early '70s in the simulation language Simula, to its development in the Smalltalk environment, the object-oriented paradigm has developed largely outside the mainstream of computing. An offshoot of this development was the discovery that software objects were useful for general prototyping and application development, not just for simulation and research.

OOP started to gain recognition only a few years ago; today, OOP promises to be in the 1990s what "structured programming" was in the 1980s. However, the interest developed for OOP could not be sustained without the introduction of new object-oriented software products such as Turbo Pascal 5.5.

Why is OOP so popular? Well, object-oriented design is based on a simple observation: computer programs perform actions on objects. Leaving aside for the moment just what an "object" is, we may note that most conventional software is little more than a list of actions to be performed on certain data in a certain sequence. If you change the action or the type of data an action deals with, you change the program. OOP offers an opportunity to change the way data is manipulated by extending a program or adding to it, rather than changing it.

By concentrating on the data rather than on the actions, OOP represents a radical departure from conventional programming. To a certain extent, OOP is also incompatible with the top-down approach to structured programming that has held sway among mainstream software engineers for roughly the past decade. The top-down approach used in the development of conventional software concentrates on decomposing program requirements in a step-by-step fashion until the functions and procedures to be performed by a program are most suitable for solving the problem at hand. This may be contrasted with the object-oriented approach which, without going into detail at this point, tends to decompose problems into objects that store and manipulate information, exhibit a particular behavior, or both.

Like it or not, programming is a highly repetitive activity, involving frequent use of common themes such as sorting, searching, etc. Program modules that are developed for project X using the top-down approach will very likely have to be modified (some quite extensively) before they can be incorporated into project Y, which means going in and monkeying with source code. Objects, on the other hand, can often be modified without having to disturb the original code.

In order to maximize flexibility and reusability of software, the object-oriented approach structures the software around the objects rather than around the actions. In this way, software engineers can build software the same way hardware engineers build circuits, with the resulting ability to use proven, reusable, off-the-shelf components to build complex systems.

The enthusiasm and interest in OOP often turns into confusion and uncertainty as people start to actually study the subject in detail. One hurdle, at least prior to the release of Turbo Pascal 5.5, has been the lack of a popular programming language that permits an "easy entry" into OOP. For example, Smalltalk, which many consider to be the quintessential object-oriented language, has an all-or-nothing approach to OOP that presents a steep learning curve to the novice. On the other hand, with the introduction of object-oriented Turbo Pascal, the programmer can include as much (or as little) object-oriented code as he or she wants using a syntax that is very nearly identical to ordinary Turbo Pascal.

A more significant aspect of the confusion surrounding OOP is the lack of an exact definition of what OOP is. (Not that there isn't plenty of controversy on the issue, because everybody seems to have an opinion.) A healthy by-product of not having an OOP "standard" is the ease with which new ideas can be introduced and bounced around to see if they're worth anything. The object-oriented extensions in Turbo Pascal 5.5 are examples of such new ideas. An undesirable effect of this freedom is that object-oriented concepts are often implemented differently (if at all) in different environments, which basically means that prior experience with object-oriented languages such as Smalltalk or C++ will carry you only so far in learning about Turbo Pascal 5.5.

Another stumbling block to the successful understanding of OOP is getting used to looking at old concepts in a new, sometimes counterintuitive way. While at first some of the ideas behind OOP may seem contrary, just remember that if you stick with it long enough to overcome that initial conceptual "hump," you'll soon be wondering why you haven't been programming with objects all your life! Confronted with a programming or design assignment, you'll start to see ways of implementing the solution using objects. How long it takes to get over the hump is, in my mind, directly proportional to the amount of experience you have with conventional software. If you know a lot about conventional software, it might take a little while to grasp the essentials of object-oriented programming. Old mind-sets are a challenge to overcome, and OOP definitely challenges you to lay old habits aside. In part, the mission of this book is to get you over the hump as fast as possible.

The overall purpose of this book is to explain the concepts of object-oriented programming as they apply to Turbo Pascal, and to show how those concepts may be used in software development. It is divided into two parts, the first of which is a step-by-step introduction and explanation of how OOP is implemented in Turbo Pascal 5.5. We're going to take a pretty slow pace through these introductory chapters, providing enough detail to completely understand basic concepts such as inheritance, methods, polymorphism, and more. As we go along, I'll try to point out how these concepts work together, and show how they are used in design.

While the first part of the book demonstrates what objects can do, the second part shows how to use objects in your programs. We'll pay special attention to the specification of objects and their methods, as well as debugging using the Turbo Debugger that's been designed to work with Turbo Pascal 5.5. The focus of the second part of the book will be design. Rather than look at one application exhaustively, we'll look at applications in the three fields where OOP has gained enormous popularity: artificial intelligence (AI), databases, and graphics.

The hardware requirements for this book are pretty run-of-the-mill: an IBM-compatible computer with a CGA display is the minimum configuration, though I dare say you'll enjoy the graphics more if you have an EGA or VGA quality display connected to your machine. You'll also need a mouse for the graphics. By all means, go out and buy a mouse if you haven't already. They're cheap.

I'm assuming you're familiar with the fundamentals of Turbo Pascal, to the extent of perhaps having written several programs of medium complexity. I also assume that you have no background at all with

OOP. With that said, let's go on to explore object-oriented programming in Turbo Pascal.

1

INTRODUCTION TO OBJECTS

What Do We Mean by "Object-Oriented"?

A lot of people run up against a conceptual blank wall when first confronted with the term *object-oriented programming* (*OOP*). Since programming with "objects" doesn't strike any intuitive chords, some of the more resourceful newcomers to OOP might go after an answer through the back door by trying to figure out what other types of "oriented" programming there might be. Alas, there is no other style of programming with a name as descriptive as *object-oriented*. There are terms like *structured programming* and *top-down programming*, but these merely refer to a rigorous structuring of the design process. The fact is there is no analogous term to object-oriented, mostly because OOP is a departure from the mainstream of programming as it developed over the past several decades.

Traditionally, a computer program consists of a set of procedures that process data. This approach fits in well with the predominant architecture for modern computers known as the *von Neumann machine*. In this architecture (named after the mathematician John von Neumann), a central processing unit (CPU) is attached to a large collection of storage locations, collectively referred to as memory. Instructions are retrieved individually from memory and decoded by the CPU. Typically, these instructions cause data to be retrieved from memory, and then are processed and returned to memory (see Fig.

1.1). This basic scheme is true whether you program in assembly language or in a high-level language like Pascal. In each case, the emphasis is on the set of instructions (or program) that manipulate some sort of data. In writing the computer program, it is the programmer's responsibility to explicitly connect the various procedures to the data on which they operate.

Figure 1.1 — The von Neumann Architecture

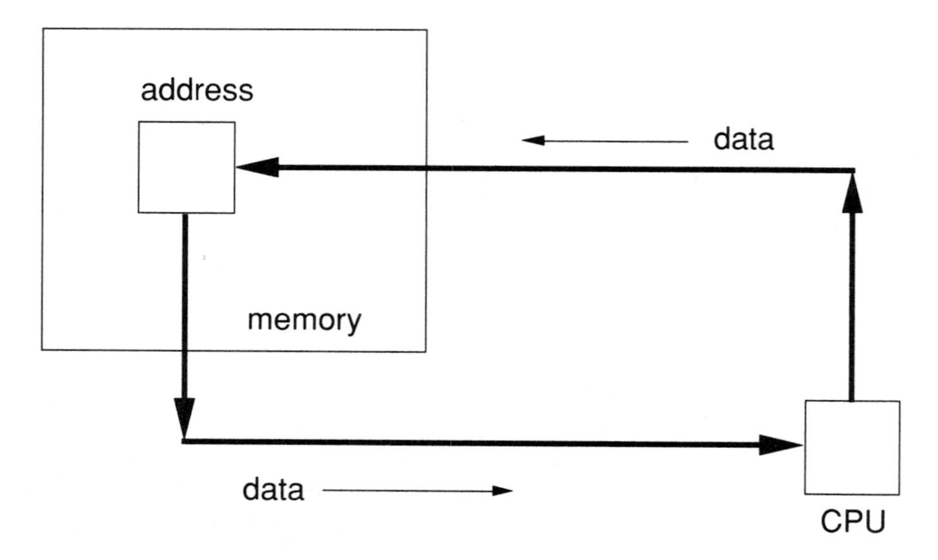

Virtually all of the software written since the start of the Computer Age has been written this way. Since this style of programming was the only way to do things, it was called, simply, *programming*. With the advent of OOP, traditional software can be retroactively described as *procedure-oriented* or *action-oriented* programming.

While this discussion may help to focus on the nature of conventional programming, it doesn't help in our quest to understand the "object" part of object-oriented programming. We have no choice but to tackle the definition of an object head on.

What is an Object?

In computer context, the word *object* has several uses that have nothing to do with OOP. As Turbo Pascal users, we know that source code is compiled into files called *object modules,* which are subsequently linked into an executable file. In the field of computer security, objects are entities in a computer system such as disks and processes that possess certain access rights to other parts of the system. Other uses of "object" are specifically designed to take advantage of its neutral, rather lackluster generality, as in the phrase, "Select an object on the screen using the mouse."

"Object" encompasses a broad spectrum of things and can denote everything or nothing. I'm an object, you're an object. This book is an object; so are its pages, the words on the page, the letters in the words, the ink in the letters, and so on. I can continue, but you get the idea: The world is filled with objects.

Objects in the real world have specific properties or attributes. Paper has color and weight, books have titles and prices, and people have names and shoe sizes. Of course, all three types of object — paper, book, and person — have countless other attributes as well. Generally, though, we focus only on those properties we feel are important in a given context, thereby creating *abstractions*.

Real objects also behave in a characteristic fashion. Cars speed up when you press the accelerator pedal. Dogs heel in response to a spoken command. Pizzas are delivered when you phone in your order to a pizzeria. Abstraction comes into play here as well, as we tend to focus selectively on behavior to fit our needs. If you pause to think about it, the pizza parlor undoubtedly pays taxes to the government and rent to the landlord. The point is, you as a customer probably never think about the pizzeria's tax bill or rent payment, focusing instead on attributes such as price, variety, and quality of the pizzas, and speed of delivery.

What is particularly important about object behavior is that you don't really need to know anything about the internals of an object to use it. Sticking with the pizzeria example, your only "interface" might consist of a voice on the phone and a delivery person at the door. The input to the pizzeria (called a *message* in OOP jargon) is the phone order. The output is (hopefully) a tasty, hot pie delivered to your door. You don't know (nor do you care to know) how many other workers are employed at the pizzeria, or the precise route taken by the delivery person to your front door.

So what does all this have to do with software? Software "objects" can mimic real-world objects by modeling their properties using variables. We can in effect create a model of a piece of paper by defining properties like color and weight. Any property we can identify in the real world can be modeled as a variable in an object.

Behavior can also be modeled in software objects by writing the appropriate functions and procedures and making them part of an object's structure (we'll get into some examples of this shortly). For now, our working definition of a software object is short:

> An "object" is a data structure in which data fields, functions, and procedures are locally defined.

Data Structures in Turbo Pascal

Let's briefly review some Turbo Pascal fundamentals regarding data types and variables.

Before using a variable in a Turbo Pascal program, you must declare it by specifying an identifier, or name, for the variable and stating its type. Turbo Pascal provides a set of basic scalar data types such as integer, char, boolean, etc., which may be grouped into more complex structures such as arrays, records, or objects.

Arrays

Arrays permit the convenient grouping of a prespecified number of items having the same data type. For example, the declaration

```
var
age : array[0..99] of integer;
```

provides us with a 100-element array named `age`. This type of data structure, though it offers convenient access to large amounts of data, is nevertheless not very flexible. In the example, each element of the array age contains only one integer. For more complex requirements, where we might, for example, want to store the name, address, city, state, and zip code as strings in a database, we can use multi-dimensional arrays, which look something like:

```
type
Fields = (Name, Address, City, State, Zip);

var
Database : array [1..100,Name..Zip] of string[20];
```

In this example, the enumerated type `Fields` defines an ordered set of values, the net effect of which is that the identifiers `Name`, `Address`, `City`, `State`, and `Zip` are declared as constants having the values 0 through 4, respectively. `Database` is then a two-dimensional array, as shown in Fig. 1.2.

This form of data structure works as long as all the fields can be represented as strings. In other cases, however, where one field is a string while another is an integer, this structure won't work unless you fiddle a lot with built-in Turbo Pascal functions like `Str()` and `Val()`. A more convenient alternative is to use a record or an object.

Figure 1.2 — A two-dimensional array of strings

	Name	Address	City	State	ZIP
1	'Alan Able'	'123 Main'	'Anytown'	'ME'	'00113'
2	Bebe Bord	'456 1st'	'Centerville'	'NJ'	'03092'
3	:	:	:	:	:
4	:	:	:	:	:
5	:	:	:	:	:
:					
:					
:					
100					

Records and objects in Pascal permit the programmer to define a data structure in terms of the basic Pascal data types and other user-defined record declarations. While there are significant differences between records and objects, there are also a few similarities pointed out in the next few paragraphs.

Records

A *record* consists of some number of components, called *fields*, each of which may be of a different type. For example, we could define record type called XYZ as in the following short program:

Listing 1-1

```
type
XYZ = record
      a : integer;
      b : real;
      c : string[32];
      end;

procedure Init( aa : integer; bb : real; cc : string;

                var Rec : XYZ);
begin
     with Rec do
     begin
        a := aa;
```

```
        b := bb;
        c := cc;
    end;
end;

var
R    :    XYZ;

begin

Init( 1234, 2.712, 'abcdefghijklmnopqrstuvwxyz', R);
writeln( 'The integer value is ', R.a );
writeln( 'The string value is "', R.c, '"' );
writeln( 'The real value is ', R.b );

end.
```

In this program, we declare a single variable, `R`, of type `XYZ`. The declaration for record type `XYZ` identifies an integer field called *a*, a real number field called `b`, and a string field called `c`. A schematic diagram of how this record is stored in memory is shown in Fig. 1.3. The procedure `Init` takes a set of parameter values and assigns them to the fields of a record of type `XYZ`, which is supplied as a variable parameter. The three `writeln` statements provide an opportunity to access the fields of `R` to show that this has, in fact, happened.

If you'll be dealing with several fields of a Pascal record within a block of statements, you can use the `with` statement, as we've done in the procedure Init. However, when you want to refer to a single field within a record, use what I call *dot notation* by writing the name of the record variable (`R` in this case), followed by a period and the name of the field you want, as in the statement

```
writeln( 'The integer value is ', R.a );
```

The field name must correspond to one of the field names in the type declaration.

Figure 1.3 — Schematic of XYZ Record R

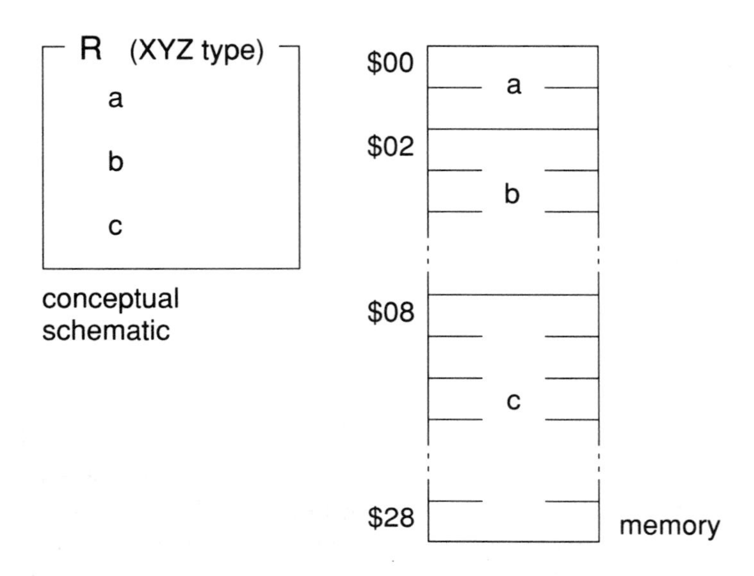

While all of the fields within a record declaration must have a unique name, the same field names may be used in other declarations, and they may represent fields of a different type. For example, the declarations

```
type
XYZ = record
       a : integer;
       b : real;
       c : string[32];
       end;

UVW = record
       a : real;
       b : integer;
       c : string[32];
       end;
```

are legal, despite the use of identical field names in two different records, and the use of `c` in both records to identify a 32-character string.

Objects

An object is declared in much the same way as a record. In fact, if you replace the word "record" in the type declaration in Listing 1-1 with the word "object," you'll find no change in the program's behavior. However, declaring the XYZ data type to be an object instead of a record allows us to make a seemingly minor change to the program, yet one with some pretty far-reaching consequences. Let's look at the following code:

Listing 1-2

```
type

XYZ = object
      a : integer;
      b : real;
      c : string[32];
      procedure Init( aa : integer; bb : real;
                      cc : string );
      end;

procedure XYZ.Init( aa : integer; bb : real;
                    cc : string );
begin
     a := aa;
     b := bb;
     c := cc;
end;

var
R    :    XYZ;

begin

R.Init( 1234, 2.712, 'abcdefghijklmnopqrstuvwxyz');
writeln( 'The integer value is ', R.a );
writeln( 'The string value is "', R.c, '"' );
writeln( 'The real value is ', R.b );

end.
```

Methods

The main difference between Listing 1-2 and 1-1 is the inclusion of the procedure `Init` as part of the object type declaration.

Let's break them out and look at them again. Here's the record type declaration:

```
type

XYZ = record
      a : integer;
      b : real;
      c : string[32];
      end;

procedure Init( ... );
begin
    ...
end;
```

In this case, the `XYZ` record and the `Init` procedure are completely separate of one another. Now, here's the object type declaration (with emphasis on the placement of the `Init` procedure):

```
type

XYZ = object
      a : integer;
      b : real;
      c : string[32];
      procedure Init( ... );
      end;

procedure XYZ.Init( ... );
begin
    ...
end;
```

The `Init` procedure has ceased to exist as a separate entity. It is still a procedure, but now it is an integral part of the `XYZ` object.

If we were to take a look at this object in memory, it would look something like Fig 1.4. Notice that the `XYZ` object from Listing 1-2 contains all the data fields of the `XYZ` record from Listing 1-1. In addition, the `XYZ` object includes a pointer to the procedure `Init` as part of its structure. If you were to declare more than one variable of type `XYZ`, you would find that, although each variable has its own region of memory reserved for field entries, all of them share a common pointer to the procedure `Init`. Furthermore, you would find it impossible to call this procedure without specifically involving an object of type `XYZ`. The ability to make functions and procedures part of a data structure is an important characteristic of objects. Historically, these functions and procedures are called *methods*.

Figure 1.4 — Schematic of XYZ Object R

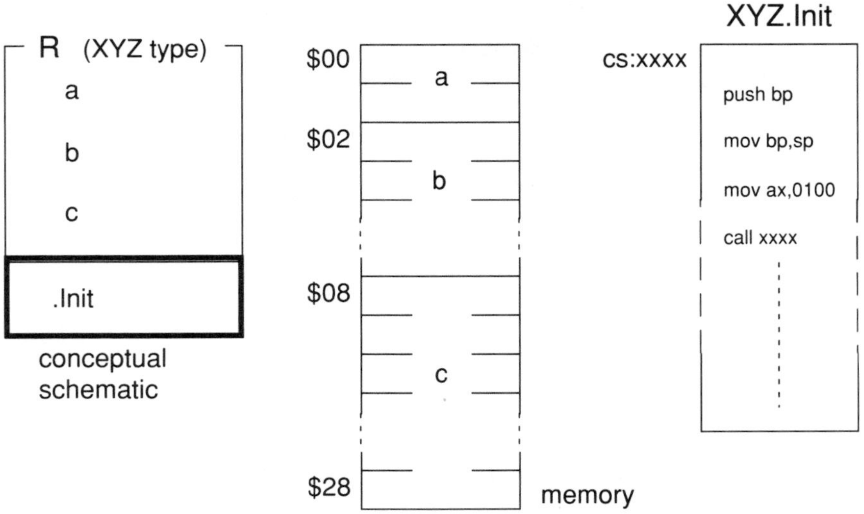

There are other changes that result from the inclusion of `Init` in the object type `XYZ`. First, the procedure is no longer referred to as plain old Init, as it was earlier. (If it were, the Turbo Pascal compiler would assume it was an ordinary procedure that had nothing at all to do with the object type XYZ.) The syntax XYZ.Init tells the compiler that this procedure is part of the XYZ object type. Notice that when we declare R to be a variable of type XYZ, we call the procedure using the same syntax as we would use to access a field of the object:

```
R.Init( 1234, 2.712, 'abcdefghijklmnopqrstuvwxyz');
```

Another difference you might notice is the absence of the XYZ object from the parameter list of XYZ.Init. At the same time, the code for XYZ.Init appears to use variables a, b, and c, without having declared them anywhere. These two features are related: First, you cannot call the XYZ.Init procedure unless you refer to an object of type XYZ (in this case, the variable R). Next, since you've already specified the object in the procedure call (R in the call to R.Init), Turbo Pascal allows you to manipulate all the fields of the XYZ object as if they were global variables. The general rule is: If you're in code that is part of an object's method, you can access the fields of that object without any ceremony. Otherwise, if you access the field of an object from code that is not part of the object's method, you must use the full dot notation.

Let's look at another example that's had a few things added.

Listing 1-3

```
{ Temperature }
{ -----------------------------------------------------
  Specification for Temperature class
  Variables:
            Value : real;
                  The value of the temperature object is
                  stored here as a real number.  The
                  temperature is stored in Celsius
                  degrees.

  Procedures:
            .PutTemp( T : real; DegType : char );
                  The value in T is stored in the Value
                  slot.  The value of DegType tells the
                  object the units of the temperature
                  being stored.  If the value of DegType
```

```
                    is not 'F' (Fahrenheit), the temperature
                    is stored in degrees Celsius.

  Functions:
            .GetTempC
                    Returns the temperature expressed in
                    Celsius.
            .GetTempF
                    Returns the temperature expressed in
                    Fahrenheit.
---------------------------------------------------------}
type

Temperature = object
            Value : real;
            procedure PutTemp( T : real; DegType : char );
            function GetTempC : real;
            function GetTempF : real;
            end;

procedure Temperature.PutTemp( T : real; DegType : char );
begin
     Value := T;
     if DegType = 'F' then
        Value := (T - 32) * 5/9;
end;


function Temperature.GetTempC : real;
begin
          GetTempC := Value;
end;

function Temperature.GetTempF : real;
begin
          GetTempF := (Value * 9/5) + 32;
end;


var
   A,B,C : Temperature;

begin
   A.PutTemp(32,'F');
   writeln('Temperature A is ', A.GetTempC:2:2, ' deg C');
   writeln('Temperature A is ', A.GetTempF:2:2, ' deg F');

   B.PutTemp(100,'F');
   writeln('Temperature B is ', B.GetTempC:2:2, ' deg C');
   writeln('Temperature B is ', B.GetTempF:2:2, ' deg F');
```

```
    C.PutTemp( -40,'F');
    writeln('Temperature C is ', C.GetTempC:2:2, ' deg C');
    writeln('Temperature C is ', C.GetTempF:2:2, ' deg F');

end.
```

Probably the first thing to jump out at you in Listing 1-3 is the comment labeled "Specification for Temperature class." Let's ignore the word "specification" for a minute and take a look at the word "class."

Classes

By and large, we'll use the terms *object type* and *class* interchangeably throughout the book. In traditional OOP parlance, a class is an abstraction that provides a template for objects, which are in turn called *instances* of the class. In Turbo Pascal, it is important to note that a declaration such as

```
Temperature = object
              Value : real;
              procedure PutTemp(T : real; DegType : char);
              function GetTempC : real;
              function GetTempF : real;
              end;
```

is not in itself an object, but merely a description of a template for an object. In Listing 1-3, the variables A, B, and C are instances of the class Temperature.

Specification

Specification of software is certainly not something unique to OOP. I include it here, however, as an expansion of the *protocol* or *interface* concept, which are traditional OOP terms that are used to describe the methods that are part of an object class. It is important to publish class specifications because it is often the only information available that tells you how to use the object. (If you'll recall, one of the advantages of OOP is not having to know anything about the internals of an object. This being the case, the specification is what tells you about the externals of the object.)

The specification for the `Temperature` class is pretty self-explanatory; it enumerates the variables associated with the fields of the `Temperature` class (in this case, there's only one real number, called `Value`), and then lists and explains the behavior of the procedure PutTemp and the functions `GetTempC` and `GetTempF`, which are part of the object definition for the `Temperature` class. A schematic diagram of what a `Temperature` object looks like in memory is shown in Fig. 1.5.

Figure 1.5 — Schematics of Temperature object A

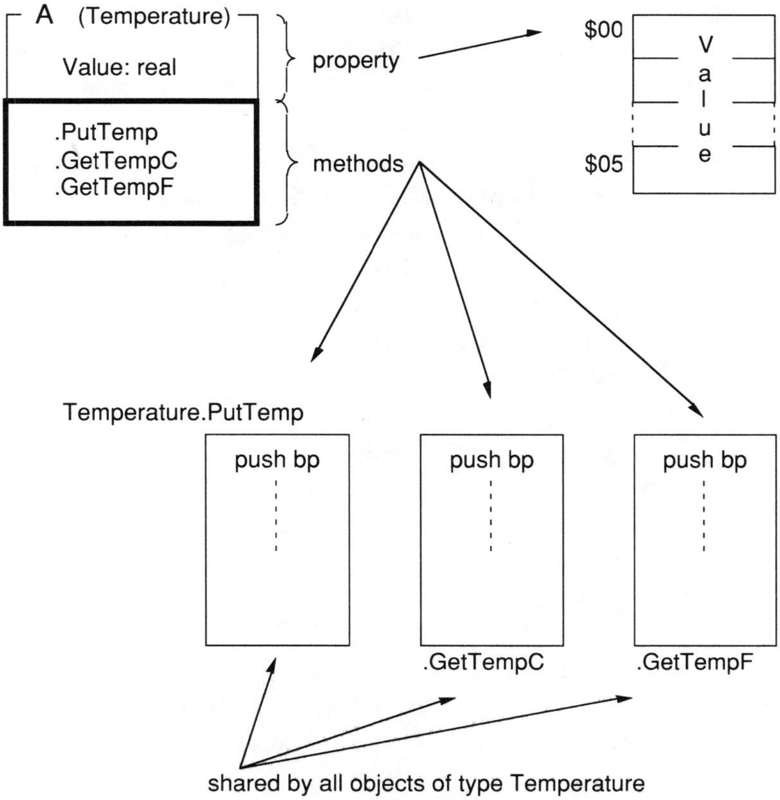

A (Temperature)
Value: real
.PutTemp
.GetTempC
.GetTempF
property
methods
$00
$05
V a l u e
Temperature.PutTemp
push bp
push bp
push bp
.GetTempC
.GetTempF
shared by all objects of type Temperature

The idea behind the `Temperature` class is the creation of an object that can supply a temperature value in either Celsius or Fahrenheit. (Recall that 32° Fahrenheit (deg F) corresponds to 0° Celsius (deg C) , and 212° F is equivalent to 100° C.)

Internally, the `Temperature` object stores a Celsius temperature. This is accomplished using the method `.PutTemp`. If the `DegType` parameter in the call to `.PutTemp` is F, the value of the `T` parameter is assumed to be a Fahrenheit temperature, which is converted to a Celsius value using the well-worn formula

C = (F-32)*5/9

(I should point out that in order to focus on the use of methods, the code for the method `.PutTemp` is not bulletproof and I would never dream of including it in production code. Note, however, that this inherent weakness is documented in the specification comments!)

The methods `.GetTempF` and `.GetTempC` are Pascal functions that allow other routines (sometimes called *clients*) to retrieve the value of the `Temperature` object either as a Fahrenheit or Celsius value, respectively. Most important, this retrieval can be done without knowing anything about how the value is stored inside the `Temperature` object. Notice also that by storing the value one way and then accessing it another (as in Listing 1-3, where the value of 32° F stored in `A` is immediately accessed as a Celsius temperature in the next line using the `.GetTempC` method), a program can convert temperatures without knowing the conversion formulas.

Postscript

The importance of supplying methods for storing and retrieving property values cannot be underestimated and will be examined in detail in Chapter 3, when we discuss issues of encapsulation.

Throughout the rest of the book, we will follow a few conventions of notation and nomenclature. First of all, all fields of an object, regardless of their data type, will be referred to as *properties*; analogously, all procedures and functions associated with an object type will be referred to as *methods*. All method names will be prefixed with a period when mentioned in the text.

Names for objects, properties, and methods will consist of run-together words with first letters capitalized, (for example, `ObjectName`). When we declare methods for an object type, we will almost always use the method name `.Init` to identify the method that initializes an instance of the object type (this procedure is called instantiation). We will try to consistently use the method names `.PutValue` and `.GetValue` to store and retrieve numeric values; `.PutStatus` and `.GetStatus` will store and retrieve boolean values.

Methods are one of the fundamental features of object-oriented Turbo Pascal. The ability to declare methods as part of an object definition is one of several major distinctions between objects and records. A more complete discussion of methods will be presented in Chapter 3.

For now, don't confuse method declarations with the ability to include procedural types in Turbo Pascal records. Recall that procedural types allow procedures and functions to be assigned to variables and passed as parameters. For example, we can try to imitate the object syntax in Listing 1-2 as follows:

Listing 1-4

```
{Imitating objects: how not to do it.}

type

string32 = string[32];

Proc = procedure( aa: integer; bb: real; cc : string;

                  var a : integer; var b : real; var c : string32 );
```

```
XYZ = record
      a : integer;
      b : real;
      c : string32;
      init : Proc;
      end;

{$F+}
procedure Init( aa : integer; bb : real; cc : string;
                var a : integer; var b : real;
                var c : string32 );
begin
     a := aa;
     b := bb;
     c := cc;
end;
{$F-}

var

R    :    XYZ;

begin

R.Init := Init;
R.Init( 1234, 2.71, 'This is a test', R.a, R.b, R.c);
writeln( 'The integer value is ', R.a );
writeln( 'The string value is "', R.c, '"' );
writeln( 'The real value is ', R.b );

end.
```

The purpose of this example is to show that yes, you can create an artificial object using non-OOP features of Turbo Pascal, but why bother? The result is awkward at best, and would be unusable in any sort of complex application. There is a place for procedural types, however, in object-oriented design, but that discussion must wait until we examine another remarkable way in which an object differs from a record: inheritance.

2

INHERITANCE

The ability to model an object using record-like fields (called *properties*) and built-in functions and procedures (called *methods*) is a pretty powerful tool in Turbo Pascal 5.5. Without inheritance, however, the ability to use objects would represent only a marginal enhancement to the language. If you've done some exploring on your own with the concepts introduced in the Chapter 1, you will have noticed that different classes frequently share many identical properties and methods, and that's an important discovery. Without the concept of inheritance, you'd be copying blocks of code from one class and modifying them for use in another, which is both laborious and inefficient. Inheritance eliminates the need for such duplication.

Much of our knowledge of the world is phrased in terms that are already familiar to us. We habitually describe new objects in terms of their similarity to known objects, while duly noting their difference. A penguin is an aquatic bird that does not fly. Free verse is poetry without rhyme or rhythm (called meter). A convertible is an automobile with a retractable roof.

Saying that "a penguin is an aquatic bird that does not fly" really says three things: First and most obvious, a penguin is a bird, which means it has the properties shared by all birds (that is, it is a warm-blooded, egg-laying animal with a backbone). Second, unlike most birds that have grasping feet, eat insects or plants, and spend their time on dry land, the penguin is aquatic (that is, it has webbed feet, eats fish, and swims in water). Finally, the fact that penguins don't fly helps distinguish them from other aquatic birds, such as pelicans, which do fly.

Figure 2.1 — Partial inheritance hierarchy for Birds

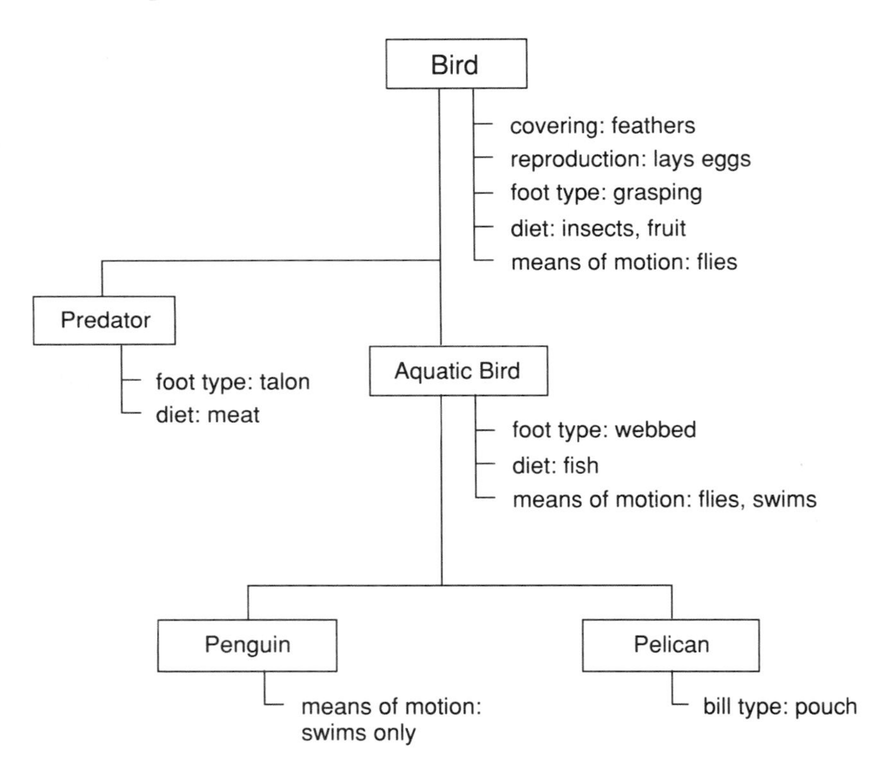

In object-oriented terms, we could posit an `AquaticBird` class (or object type in the Turbo Pascal idiom) that inherits the properties and methods of the `Bird` class (feathered, warm-blooded, egg-laying, etc.), substituting or adding new properties and methods (web-footed, swimming) as appropriate. In turn, the `Penguin` class inherits the properties and methods of the `AquaticBird` class, except it replaces the behavior "Flies" with "Does not fly." A diagram of this inheritance hierarchy is shown in Fig. 2.1. As we trace our way down the hierarchy in this figure, we go from the the general to the specific, adding more detail along the way.

When we develop a model for an object type, much of the success (or failure) of the design depends on how well we abstract the properties we want to model in our objects, and how we arrange them in a hierarchy of object types that inherit properties and methods from one another. Let's take a look at the method in the following example of students and faculty at a university.

Abstracting the Basics: the *Person* Object Type

Let's assume we want to model the student and faculty populations of a university community for the purpose of sending electronic mail (e-mail) over a campus-wide network. The first thing we would want to do is identify a set of properties and methods that apply to both students and faculty. We will abstract these properties and methods in an object type named `Person`. After a bit of brainstorming, we can come up with a list like the following (which is, by the way, not complete):

- name
- sex
- residence address
- campus e-mail address
- residence telephone
- date of birth
- social security number

All of the properties listed could find use in our program. For example, if the recipient of an e-mail message didn't read the message within a certain time period, our program could send the message to a person's residence using regular mail. Although we could devise a number of useful methods that utilize these properties, let's ignore all fields for the sake of simplicity except for name, sex, and the campus e-mail address, and specify only two methods for this abbreviated object type: our customary initialization procedure `.Init` and a procedure `.SendMsg`, which sends a message to a person's campus e-mail address (for our example, the message will be sent to the console screen). Listing 2-1 contains the object type declarations we'll need, as well as a short program that shows how the object types we've created behave. The output of the program is shown in Fig. 2.2.

Listing 2-1

```
program Listing 2_1;
type

SexType = (male, female);
String20 = string[20];

NameRec = record
           Last   : String20;
           Middle : String20;
           First  : String20;
           end;

Person = object
          Name  : NameRec;
          Sex   : SexType;
          Email : String20;
          procedure Init( FName, MName, LName : String20;
                           Gender : SexType;
                           E_mail : String20 );
          procedure SendMsg( Msg : string );
end;

procedure Person.Init( FName, MName, LName : String20;
                       Gender : SexType;
                       E_mail : String20 );
begin
     Name.First := FName;
     Name.Middle := MName;
     Name.Last := LName;
     Sex := Gender;
     Email := E_mail;
end;

procedure Person.SendMsg( Msg : string );
var
   Title : string[3];
begin
     if Sex = male then
        Title := 'Mr.'
     else
        Title := 'Ms.';
```

```
    writeln( 'TO: ', Title, ' ', Name.Last );
    writeln( 'ADDRESS: ', Email );
    writeln( '----------------------------------------');
    writeln( Msg );
    writeln;
end;

var

   JohnDoe    : Person;
   JaneDoe    : Person;
   NickGogol  : Person;

begin


    JohnDoe.Init( 'John', 'A.', 'Doe',   male, 'EM987' );
    JaneDoe.Init( 'Jane', 'A.', 'Doe', female, 'EM789' );
    NickGogol.Init( 'Nikolai', 'Vasilievich', 'Gogol',
                    male, 'DS000' );

    JohnDoe.SendMsg( 'Your library books are overdue.' );
    NickGogol.SendMsg(
         'The books you ordered are at the bookstore.');
    JaneDoe.SendMsg(
     'The physics midterm has been postponed two weeks.');

end.
```

Figure 2.2 — Output of Listing 2-1

```
C:\>LIST2-1

TO: Mr. Doe
Address: EM987
----------------------------------------
Your library books are overdue.

TO: Mr. Gogol
ADDRESS: DS000
----------------------------------------
The books you ordered are at the bookstore.

TO: Ms. Doe
ADDRESS: EM789
----------------------------------------
The physics midterm has been postponed two weeks.

C:\>
```

This is a very straightforward listing, with about the only notable point being the use of a record as a constituent of the Person object type. A composite view of the JaneDoe instance of the Person object type is shown in Fig. 2.3.

Figure 2.3 — Schematic of Person object JaneDoe

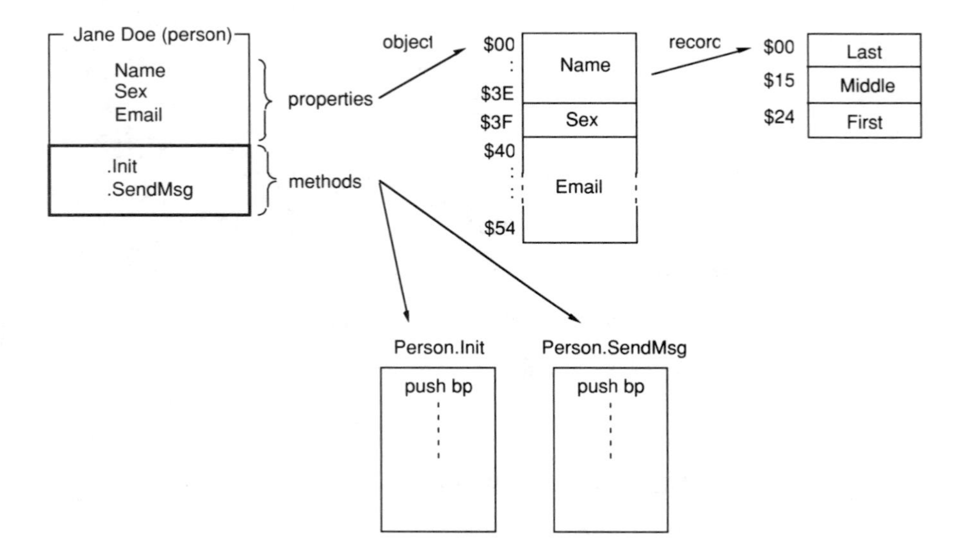

The Person object type and its associated methods in Listing 2-1 turn out to be useful for both students and faculty. Students could be, as in the example, informed of changes in schedule. Professors could be reminded of impending faculty meetings. Certainly a more sophisticated program would manage more than just sending a one-line message via e-mail, but the example makes the point.

The next step is to identify properties and methods that might be useful for students and faculty. We will then make the properties and methods of the Person object type available to the Student and Faculty object types through the mechanism of inheritance.

Building on the Person Object Type

Although both students and faculty will share a common set of properties and methods from the `Person` object type, each has properties (and associated methods) unique to themselves. For example, we can readily identify the following properties for the `Student` object type:

- major
- grade point average
- credits earned
- year of graduation
- class schedule

Along similar lines, faculty members might be distinguished by a different set of properties, such as:

- title
- salary
- department
- list of courses taught
- tenure status

Now, as noted at the beginning of the chapter, we could create a `Student` object type as follows: Enter the Turbo Pascal editor, mark the declaration of the `Person` object type with Ctrl-KB at the top and Ctrl-KK at the bottom, duplicate the block, and then replace *Person* with *Student* everywhere in the new block. We could then edit the block to include new properties and add procedure and function declarations for the new object type methods.

We could repeat the process to create a `Faculty` object type. There is a better way, as shown in Listing 2-2, where we implement a `Student` object type with only one additional property (grade point average, or `GPA`) and two additional methods (`.Init` and `.PutGPA`), and a `Faculty` object type with one additional property (`Title`), a new method (`.Init`), and a redefinition of the inherited method `.SendMsg`.

Listing 2-2

```
program Listing 2_2;
const

CumLaude = 3.2;
FailingGPA    = 2.0;

type

SexType = (male, female);
String20 = string[20];

NameRec = record
       Last   : String20;
       Middle : String20;
       First  : String20;
       end;

Person = object
      Name  : NameRec;
      Sex   : SexType;
      Email : String20;
      procedure Init( FName, MName, LName : String20;
                      Gender : SexType;
                      E_mail : String20 );
      procedure SendMsg( f : string );
      end;

Student = object(Person)
       GPA : real;
       procedure Init(FName, MName, LName : String20;
                      Gender : SexType;
                      E_mail : String20;
                      GradePointAvg : real );
       procedure PutGPA( NewGPA : real );
       end;

Faculty = object(Person)
       Title : String20;
       procedure Init(FName, MName, LName : String20;
                      Gender : SexType;
                      E_mail, FTitle : String20 );
       procedure SendMsg( Msg : string );
       end;

procedure Person.Init( FName, MName, LName : String20;
                       Gender : SexType;
                       E_mail : String20 );
begin
```

```
        Name.First := FName;
        Name.Middle := MName;
        Name.Last := LName;
        Sex := Gender;
        Email := E_mail;
end;

procedure Person.SendMsg( f : string );
var
        Title : string[3];
begin
        if Sex = male then
                Title := 'Mr.'
        else
                Title := 'Ms.';
        writeln( 'TO: ', Title, ' ', Name.Last );
        writeln( 'ADDRESS: ', Email );
        writeln( '----------------------------------------');
        writeln( f );
        writeln;
end;

procedure Student.Init( FName, MName, LName : String20;
                        Gender : SexType;
                        E_mail : String20;
                        GradePointAvg : real);
begin
        Person.Init( FName, MName, LName, Gender, E_mail );
        PutGPA( GradePointAvg );
end;

procedure Student.PutGPA( NewGPA : real );
begin
        GPA := NewGPA;
        if GPA >= CumLaude then
                SendMsg(
                 'Your GPA makes you eligible for the Dean''s List');
        if GPA <= FailingGPA then
                SendMsg(
                 'You are on academic probation owing to a low GPA.');
end;

procedure Faculty.Init( FName, MName, LName : String20;
                Gender : SexType;
                E_mail, FTitle : String20 );
begin
        Person.Init( FName, MName, LName, Gender, E_mail );
        Title := FTitle;
end;
```

```
procedure Faculty.SendMsg( Msg : string );
begin
     writeln( 'TO: ', Title, ' ', Name.Last );
     writeln( 'ADDRESS: ', Email );
     writeln( '----------------------------------------');
     writeln( Msg );
     writeln;
end;

var

     JohnDoe : Student;
     JaneDoe : Student;
     NickGogol : Faculty;

begin


JohnDoe.Init( 'John', 'A.', 'Doe',   male, 'EM987', 2.20);
JaneDoe.Init( 'Jane', 'A.', 'Doe', female, 'EM789', 3.24 );
NickGogol.Init( 'Nikolai', 'Vasilievich', 'Gogol',
                    male, 'DS000', 'Professor' );

JohnDoe.SendMsg( 'Your library books are overdue.' );
NickGogol.SendMsg(
      'The books you ordered are at the bookstore.');

JohnDoe.PutGPA( 1.97 );

end.
```

Aside from the object type declarations and the method definitions for the `Student` and `Faculty` classes, very little about the program has changed. In fact, the object type declaration and method definitions for the People class from Listing 2-1 have not changed at all! Later, you'll see how to package object type definitions into Turbo Pascal units, a technique that will help eliminate the need to go back and edit old files, thus enhancing the reusability of code and maintaining the integrity of developed code. The output of the program in Listing 2-2 is shown in Fig. 2.4.

Figure 2.4 — Output of Listing 2-2

```
C:\>LIST2-2

TO: Ms. Doe
Address: EM789
----------------------------------------
Your GPA makes you eligible for the Dean's List

TO: Mr. Doe
Address: EM987
----------------------------------------
Your library books are overdue.

TO: Professor Gogol
Address: DS000
----------------------------------------
The books you ordered are at the bookstore.

TO: Mr. Doe
Address: EM987
----------------------------------------
You are on academic probation owing to a low GPA.

C:\>
```

The Student objects JaneDoe and JohnDoe can execute the .SendMsg method because they inherit the method from the Person object type. Note that all the parameters passed in the call to Student.Init are immediately used in a call to the Person.Init method. As before, direct calls to .SendMsg generate the appropriate messages addressed to 'Mr. Doe' or 'Ms. Doe.' On the other hand, the Faculty object type has its own .SendMsg method that replaces or *overrides* the method in the Person object type. In Listing 2-2, this results in the addressing of the message to *Professor Gogol,* instead of to *Mr. Gogol.*

The new Student method .PutGPA does two things. First, it updates the contents of the GPA property of the Student object type. Second, it checks the GPA against high and low limits (declared as constants) and generates a congratulatory message if the GPA is above the high limit (as was done to Jane Doe during execution of the .Init procedure), or sends a warning message if it is below the low limit (as was done while updating John Doe's grade point average to 1.97).

The Syntax of Inheritance

If you want a declared object type to inherit the properties and methods of another, you include the name of the other class in parentheses right after the word *object* in the declaration, like this:

```
Student = object(Person)
...
```

This declaration says that the object type Student is a descendant type (sometimes called a derived class) of the object type Person, which means it inherits all the properties and methods of Person. This, in turn, makes Person the ancestor type (or base class) of Student. By the same token, Faculty is a descendant type of Person, which in turn, also becomes an ancestor type of Faculty. A composite of the JohnDoe instance of the Student object type is shown in Fig. 2.5. If you compare Figs. 2.3 and 2.5 you should see the Person object type nestled inside the Student object type.

Figure 2.5 — Schematic of Student object JohnDoe

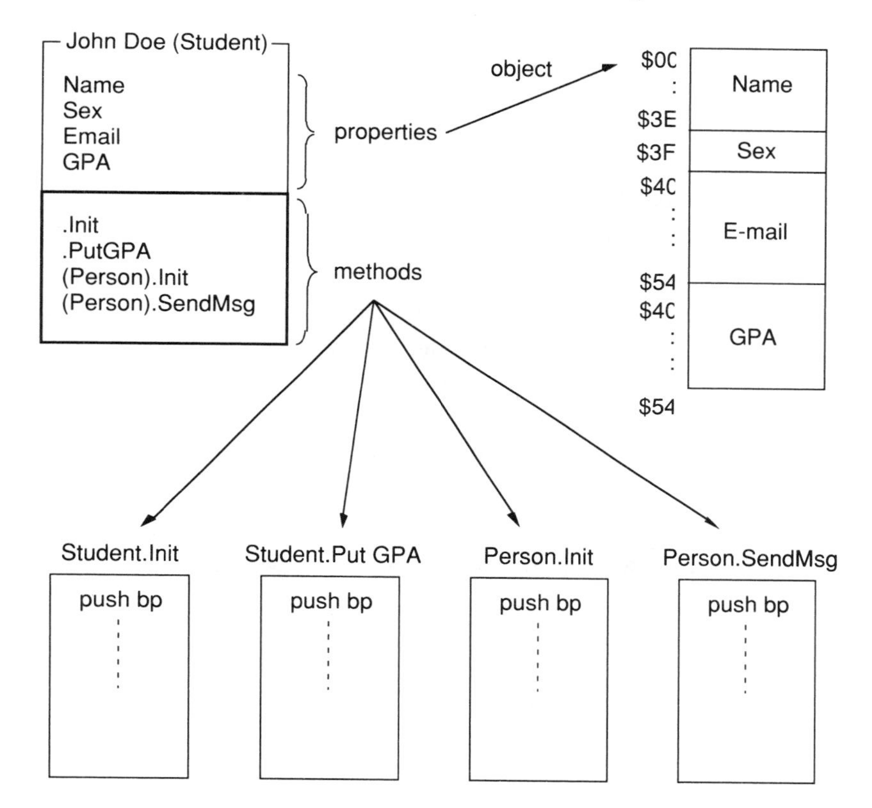

Design and Extension

The ability to inherit properties and methods makes it convenient to extend existing object types using derived classes, which means not having to go back and fiddle with code that has been debugged. In fact, in conjunction with a well-written specification for an object type, there is no need to even see the original source code, as we'll see in the following example taken from an industrial plant setting. As opposed to the previous examples, which are primarily illustrative, we will now design and implement a class hierarchy from scratch and write a short program to simulate an industrial plant.

Instruments in an industrial plant tell the operators in the plant control room whether the various machines in the plant are working correctly or not. The readings from these instruments are often used to cause certain things to happen when they should, and prevent other things from happening when they shouldn't.

Figure 2.6 shows a simplified schematic for a system that maintains pressure in a water distribution system. For our example, we'll let the water tank be a 200-foot high cylinder, 30 feet in diameter. To make things simple, we'll have the pump deliver 8000 gallons per minute (gpm) when it is on, regardless of other factors. The idea of this system is to regulate the water pressure between some high and low limit (as indicated by the respective pressure switches) by maintaining an adequate level in the water tank.

Figure 2.6 — Simple Control System

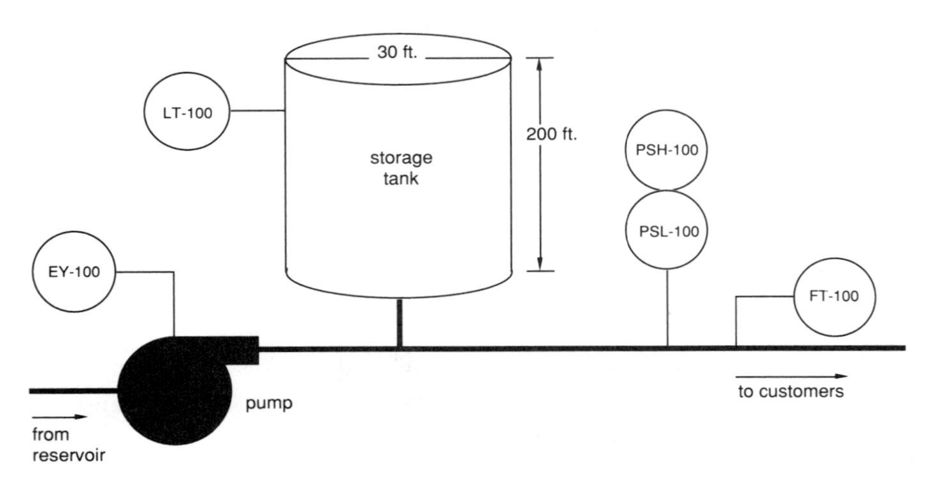

This is accomplished by turning the pump on when the pressure gets too low — that is, when the pressure dips below 60 pounds per square inch (psi). If the flow through the flowmeter is less than 8000 gpm, the action of the pump will eventually raise the water level in the tank, which means higher water pressure at ground level. When the level passes 173 feet, the water pressure will be high enough (75 psi) to turn the pump off. (The same principle is used in thermostats to regulate temperature in our homes.) If this combination of pumps and sensors does its job correctly, the residents served by the water main will have adequate pressure for washing dishes, taking showers, etc., and there will be enough water in reserve for emergency use, such as firefighting.

Modeling the Components of the System

Before attempting to model the components of the control system, we must decide what it is about them we want to model. Since we're going to be simulating the operation of the system, we need to model the operation of each component.

Digital Inputs

Each instrument in the system has an identifying label, called a tag number. The instrument with tag number PSL-100 is a pressure switch that turns on when it measures a pressure less than some specified minimum. Analogously, the instrument PSH-100 is a pressure switch that turns on when the measured pressure is greater than some set maximum. These switches are called digital inputs because the signal is either on or off (thus digital), and is sent from the real world into the control system for processing (hence input). These switches regulate the operation of the system.

For the purposes of our simulation, the following properties are sufficient:

- tag number
- pressure setpoint
- pressure reading
- status (ON or OFF)

Some people might want to include properties for storing the location of the instrument, the date it was last inspected, the name of the manufacturer, the model number, etc., but remember that we want to design objects that will help us simulate the system. The other properties have their place (probably in a maintenance database), but are not appropriate for our application.

How does the switch behave? For one thing, switches are on-off devices, so they can be represented digitally. Furthermore, signals are typically input from their physical location (which, wherever it is, is generally called "the field") to a control system. We will abstract the digital input characteristics of a switch in an object type called `DInput` (see Listing 2-3), with properties `Setpoint` and `Reading`. The `Reading` simply stores the current system pressure reading. For the low pressure switch, the `Setpoint` is the pressure reading below which the switch closes. Since we'll want to be able to enter a new setpoint, we should note that as a method (which we'll call `.PutSetpoint`).

Another method (`.PutReading`, which is abstracted under the `DInput` descendant type `LoSwitch`) updates the pressure reading in the system. Whenever the pressure reading falls to or below the low-pressure setpoint, the status of the instrument changes to ON; otherwise, its value is OFF. (There is an analogous `.PutReading` method for the `HiSwitch` descendant type of `DInput`. The reason for this will become clear in Chapter 5, when we discuss virtual methods.)

Finally, despite the fact that the `Status` property is directly accessible from a `Digital` object type from anywhere in the program, we will nevertheless have a method (`.GetStatus`) that returns the value of `Status`, indicating whether the switch is ON or OFF. Part of the reason (aside from the fact it is a good object-oriented design habit to develop) is that the status of the switch will be output to the screen whenever `.GetStatus` is called, so we can monitor its state continuously.

Digital Outputs

Like the switches in the previous section, the signal EY-100 (which controls the pump) is either on or off. However, this signal is sent from the control system to the motor that turns the pump. When EY-100 is on, the pump is on (which, you'll recall, means that 8000 gpm is flowing into the system); when EY-100 is off, the pump is off and there is no flow. The `Pump` object type will inherit the `.GetStatus` method from the `Digital` object type through the `DOutput` object type (see Listing 2-3), so that the operating status is printed to the screen every time we call this method to determine whether the pump is running or not.

Listing 2-3

```
program PumpControl; {Listing 2-3}

uses Crt; { for KeyPressed }

const

ON   = true;
OFF  = false;
MinR = 0;          { Minimum number of counts in an analog input }
MaxR = 4095;       { Maximum number of counts in an analog input }

var
    f : text;  {predefined file type}

type

Resolution = 0..4095;  { Range for analog input }
String12 = string[12];

Tag = object
      TagNumber : String12;
      procedure Init( ATag : String12 );
      end;

Digital = object(Tag)
          Status : boolean;
          procedure Init( ATag : String12; AStatus : boolean );
          procedure PutStatus( AStatus : boolean );
          function GetStatus : boolean;
          end;
```

```
Analog = object(Tag)
        Value : Resolution;
        ZeroVal : real;
        MaxVal  : real;
        Slope   : real;
        procedure Init( ATag : String12; AValue : Resolution;
                        Min, Max : real );
        procedure PutValue( AValue : real );
        function GetValue : real;
        end;

DOutput = object(Digital)
          end;

Pump = object(DOutput)
       FlowRate : real;
       procedure Init( ATag : String12; AStatus : boolean;
                       AFlow : real );
       function Flow : real;
       end;

Dinput = object(Digital)
             Setpoint  : real;
             Reading   : real;
             procedure PutSetpoint( NewSetpoint : real );
             end;

HiSwitch = object(Dinput)
           procedure Init( ATag : string;
                           ASetpoint : real;
                           AReading : real);
           procedure PutReading( NewReading : real );
           end;

LoSwitch = object(Dinput)
           procedure Init( ATag : string;
                           ASetpoint : real;
                           AReading : real);
           procedure PutReading( NewReading : real );
           end;

procedure Tag.Init( ATag : String12 );
begin
     TagNumber := ATag;
end;

procedure Digital.Init( ATag : String12; AStatus : boolean );
begin
     Tag.Init( ATag );
     Status := AStatus;
end;
```

```
procedure Digital.PutStatus( AStatus : boolean );
begin
     Status := AStatus;
end;

function Digital.GetStatus : boolean;
begin
     if Status = on then
        writeln( f, TagNumber, ' is ON.' )
     else
        writeln( f, TagNumber, ' is OFF.' );
     GetStatus := Status;
end;

procedure Pump.Init( ATag : String12; AStatus : boolean;
                     AFlow : real );
begin
     Digital.Init( ATag, AStatus );
     FlowRate := AFlow;
end;

function Pump.Flow : real;
begin
     if Status = true then
        Flow := FlowRate
     else
        Flow := 0;
end;

procedure Analog.Init( ATag : String12;
                       AValue : Resolution;
                       Min, Max : real );
begin
     Tag.Init( ATag );
     Value := AValue;
     MaxVal := Max;
     ZeroVal := Min;
     Slope := (Max-Min)/(MaxR-MinR);
end;

procedure Analog.PutValue( AValue : real );
begin
     if AValue > MaxVal then
        AVAlue := MaxVal
     else
        if AValue < ZeroVal then
           AValue := ZeroVal;
     Value := Round((AValue - ZeroVal)/Slope);
end;
```

```
function Analog.GetValue : real;
begin
     GetValue := Slope*Value + ZeroVal;
end;

procedure Dinput.PutSetpoint( NewSetpoint : real );
begin
     Setpoint := NewSetpoint;
end;

procedure LoSwitch.Init( ATag : string;
                         ASetpoint : real;
                         AReading : real);
begin
     Tag.Init( ATag );
     DInput.PutSetpoint( ASetpoint );
     PutReading( AReading );
end;

procedure LoSwitch.PutReading( NewReading : real );
begin
     Reading := NewReading;
     if Reading <= Setpoint then
        Status := true
     else
        Status := false;
end;

procedure HiSwitch.Init( ATag : string;
                         ASetpoint : real;
                         AReading : real);
begin
     Tag.Init( ATag );
     Dinput.PutSetpoint( ASetpoint );
     PutReading( AReading );
end;

procedure HiSwitch.PutReading( NewReading : real );
begin
     Reading := NewReading;
     if Reading >= Setpoint then
        Status := true
     else
        Status := false;
end;

{ HtToPSI converts a height (of a column of water) into a
  pressure.  The math is pretty simple:  A column of water
  2.31 feet high exerts a force of one pound per square inch at
  the bottom. }
```

```
function HtToPSI( Height : real ) : real;
begin
     HtToPSI := Height/2.31;
end;

{ FlowToDeltaHt converts a flow into (or out of) our system into
  a change in height in the tank.
  The math is as follows:  Divide the flow, in gpm, by 7.48
  gal/cu.ft. to get the number of cubic feet pumped per minute.
  Divide this number by the volume of 1 vertical foot of the
  tank, which is the radius squared times 'pi' (15*15*3.1416). }

function FlowToDeltaHt( Flow : real ) : real;
begin
     FlowToDeltaHt := Flow/(7.48 * 706) ;
end;

var
   LT100,
   FT100   : Analog;
   PSL100 : LoSwitch;
   PSH100 : HiSwitch;
   EY100  : Pump;
   time   : integer;

begin

{ If no file name is passed to the program, then ParamStr(1)
  will be the null string, which will cause Assign to output
  to the standard output (the screen).  If a file name is
  passed, the output will be saved in the file for later
  reference. }

     Assign( f, ParamStr(1) );
     Rewrite( f );

     LT100.Init( 'LT100', 512, 50, 250 );
     FT100.Init( 'FT100', 2048, 0, 10000 );
     PSL100.Init( 'PSL100', 60, HtToPSI(LT100.GetValue) );
     PSH100.Init( 'PSH100', 75, HtToPSI(LT100.GetValue) );
     EY100.Init( 'EY100', off, 8000);
     time := 0;

     repeat

     Inc( time );  { increment the time }
{ First, adjust the reading in LT-100 by reducing the level in
  LT100.Value by an amount corresponding to the flow out of the
  system.  We do this by fetching the value of FT100, converting
  it to a height in the tank, and subtracting from the actual
  height... }
```

```
     LT100.PutValue( LT100.GetValue -
                         FlowToDeltaHt(FT100.GetValue) );

{ We take the result and update the switches }
     PSL100.PutReading( HtToPSI(LT100.GetValue) );
     PSH100.PutReading( HtToPSI(LT100.GetValue) );

{Let's publish the level in the tank...}
     writeln( f, 'Level in tank is ', LT100.GetValue:2:2,
                              ' feet at minute ', time );

{ If the pressure is too low, turn on the pump }
     if PSL100.GetStatus = on then
        EY100.PutStatus( ON );
{ If the pressure is too high, turn off the pump }
     if PSH100.GetStatus = on then
        EY100.PutStatus( OFF );

{ Adjust the level in the tank to
  account for however much flow is provided by the pump.  As
  before, we use the function FlowToDeltaHt to do the conversion
  for us, and then add... }
     LT100.PutValue( LT100.GetValue + FlowToDeltaHt( EY100.Flow ));

     until KeyPressed;
     Close( f );
end.
```

The raison d'être of the `DOutput` object type is to be a place marker for possible future enhancements. In such a case, after you add suitable properties and methods to `DOutput`, they will be automatically inherited by its descendant types.

The `Pump` type has a `FlowRate` property and a related method called `.Flow`. `FlowRate` holds the volume of water (in gallons) delivered per minute when the pump is on; the `.Flow` method is a Turbo Pascal function that returns the number stored in `FlowRate` if the pump is on, or zero if the pump is off.

Again, this seemingly roundabout route to fetch numbers from objects has a reason: For those of you who know something about pumps, you've long ago realized that the behavior of our simulated pump is vastly oversimplified. You could replace the `Pump` object type definition here with one of your own. And as long as other parts of the program got the pump flow by using the `.Flow` method, not a single line of that other code would have to be touched!

On other fronts, the `Pump` object type also inherits the `.PutStatus` method from the `Digital` object type, which will allow us to set the output either ON or OFF, thus indirectly controlling the flow into the system.

Analog Inputs

The signals LT-100 (which shows level in the tank) and FT-100 (which shows flow through a meter) that are input to the control system are not on/off digital signals, but analog signals in the milliamp range. This current is sent into the analog side of an analog-to-digital converter, and typically comes out the other end as a 12-bit number between 0 and 4095, which correspond to the lowest and highest readings obtainable from the instrument. For example, if the level indicator's range is from 100 to 200 feet, then a reading of 2048 means that the level in the tank is 150 feet.

As described here, these signals have no behavior, but in our simulation, they will supply information for other parts of the system to work, so we'll need a `Value` property to hold the value and a couple of "standard" methods (`.PutValue` and `.GetValue`) to supply an interface between the quantity stored in the `Value` property and other objects in the system.

The issue here is this: As explained earlier, raw data arrives from the instrument in the field as a number of counts between 0 and 4095. Other objects in the system, however, are interested in numbers that represent engineering units such as feet, psi, gpm, etc. Therefore, analog inputs must have a `.PutValue` method that permits us to store, say, 2048 counts in the level object, and a `.GetValue` method that lets us retrieve 150 feet when the need arises. This is somewhat similar to the example in the previous chapter where temperatures could be retrieved in either Celsius or Fahrenheit degrees.

The `Analog` object type, in addition to having a `Value` property in which to store the count, also has the properties:

ZeroVal. Stores the engineering units corresponding to 0 counts

MaxVal. Stores the engineering units corresponding to (in our case) 4095 counts

Slope. Used by the `.GetValue` method to convert the count in `Value` into a real number representing engineering units, see Figure 2.7

Figure 2.7 — Converting counts into engineering units

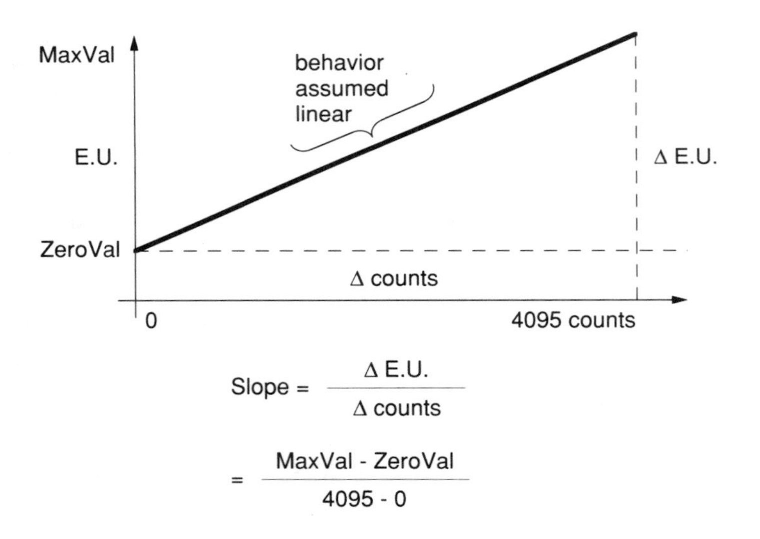

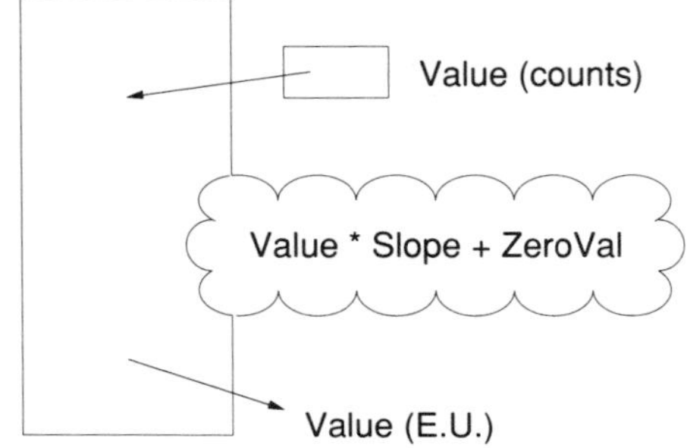

The Object Type Hierarchy

Based on the above discussion, we can plot out a usable object type hierarchy for the objects in Fig. 2.6. This hierarchy, which has the `Tag` object type as its root, is shown in Fig. 2.8. The `Tag` type has only one property, a `TagNumber` string, which we will use to identify all instruments.

Figure 2.8 — Tag object type hierarchy

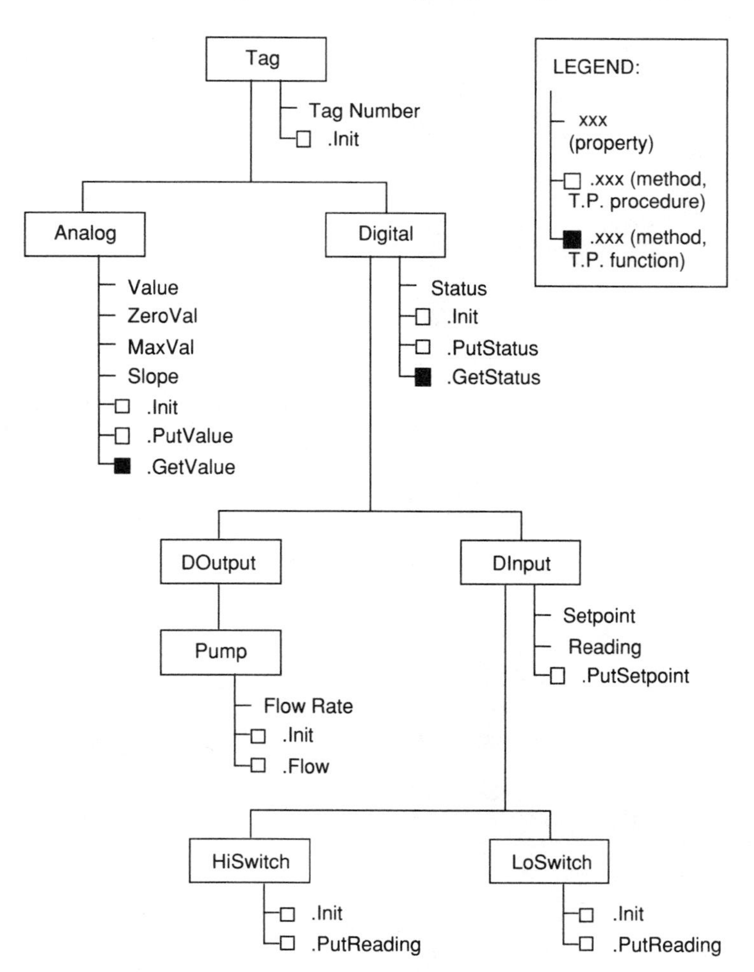

3

MORE ON METHODS

Having been introduced to methods and inheritance, you now have a good foundation on which to start using OOP techniques in your Turbo Pascal code. In this chapter, we'll take a more detailed look at methods, including the packaging of methods into units and the extension of methods.

Units

A Turbo Pascal unit is a collection of constants, data types (including object types), variables, procedures, and functions. It is, in effect, a library of declarations you can use in your programs simply by naming them in a `uses` statement. For example, in Listing 2-3, we have the line

```
uses Crt;
```

This line allows us to use any of the functions declared in the standard Turbo Pascal unit `Crt` (in particular, the function `KeyPressed`, which pauses the display before exiting the program).

Although you can develop a unit from scratch using the appropriate unit syntax (shown in Figure 3.1), many people find it convenient to create a unit from a completed, debugged program by making the appropriate modifications to the structure of the program.

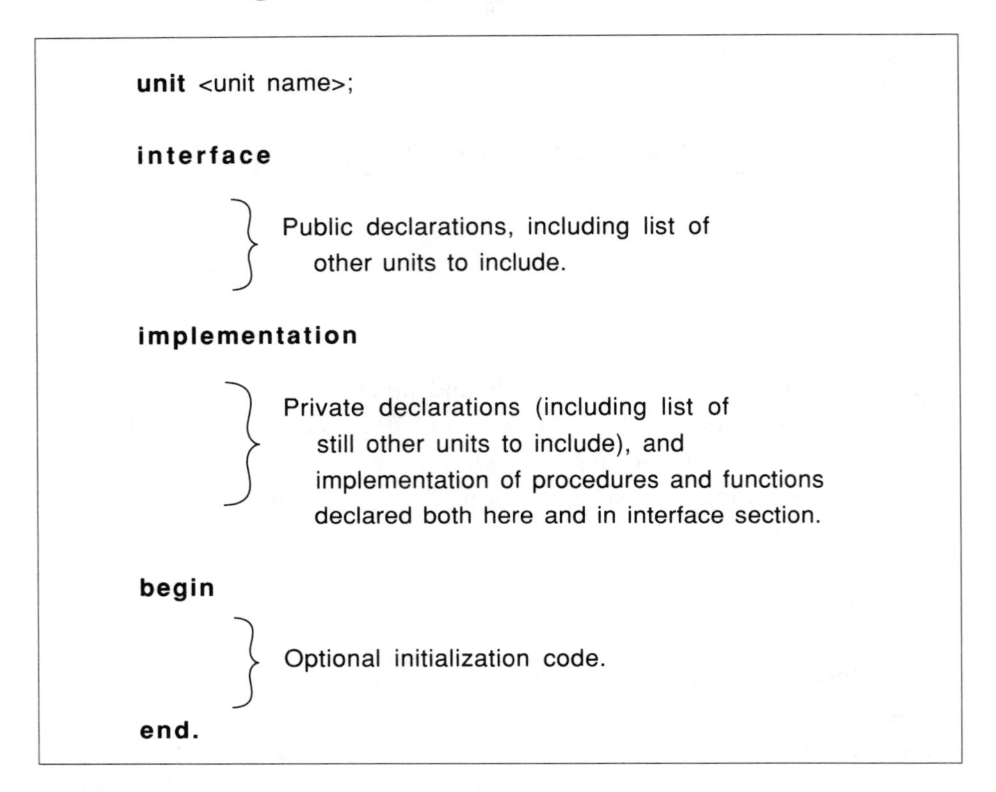

Figure 3.1 — Syntax for Turbo Pascal unit

Basically, what you do is delete the main part of the program (the begin/end block at the end of the code) and then reorganize the data and object type declarations to form the *interface* section of the unit and the function and procedure code into the *implementation* section. As an example of creating a unit from a program, I've taken the `Tag` object type hierarchy developed in Listing 2-3 and created a package called `Tags`. The resulting unit, with a couple of enhancements, is shown in Listing 3-1. It should be saved and compiled as `TAGS.PAS`.

Listing 3-1

```
{ Unit: Tags

Utilization notes:

1. If no file name is supplied on the command line, the
   program will print output to the screen.  If a file
   name is supplied, the output will be directed to the
   file.

2. The object 'Quiet' controls program output
   (including the opening and closing of output files.)
   The procedure Quiet.On will turn output off and close
   the output file, if one is specified.  Subsequent calls
   to the procedure Quiet.Off will turn output back on and
   append it to f.  The default status of Quiet is ON.

3. Users wanting to write to a file must first
   make sure Quiet is Off, and direct output to
   the file f, as in the following example.

     if Quiet.IsOff then
         writeln( f, 'Put your string here' );

4. Programs using this unit should, at the end of the program,
   explicitly make a call to Quiet.On to make sure all files are
   closed.
  }

{ Specification for Tags class **************************

  Variables:
            TagNumber : String12;
            Stores a tag number of up to 12 characters.

  Procedures:
            .Init( ATag : String12 );
            ATag is stored in TagNumber.

  Descendant object types:
            Digital
            Analog              }

{ Specification for Digital class ***********************

  Variables:
            Status : boolean;
            Indicates whether digital object is ON or OFF.
            ON denotes TRUE; OFF, FALSE.
```

```
  Procedures:
            .Init( ATag : String12; AStatus : boolean );
            ATag is stored in TagNumber; AStatus is stored
            in Status.

            .PutStatus( AStatus : boolean );
            Sets Status to AStatus.

  Functions:
            .GetStatus : boolean;
            Returns ON or OFF status of object.
            If variable 'Quiet' (boolean) is ON, then
            Status is not printed to screen; otherwise
            the Status and TagNumber are printed to
            the screen.

  Descendant object types:
            DInput
            DOutput          }

{ Specification for Analog class *************************
  Variables:
            Value : Resolution;
            Value must have a value between 0 and 4095.

            ZeroVal : real;
            Engineering unit value corresponding to a Value
            of 0.

            MaxVal : real;
            Engineering unit value corresponding to a Value
            of 4095.

            Slope : real;
            A number calculated from the equation:
                (MaxVal-ZeroVal)/(4095-0).

  Procedures:
            .Init( ATag : String12; AValue : Resolution;
            Min, Max : real );
            Storage as follows:
                ATag -> TagNumber
                AValue -> Value
                Min -> ZeroVal
                Max -> MaxVal

            .PutValue( AValue : real );
            Converts AValue engineering units into counts
            (between 0 and 4095) and stores in Value.
```

```
  Functions:
            .GetValue : real;
            Converts and returns the counts in Value to
            engineering units.

  Descendant types:
            None.        }

{ Specification for DInput class ************************

  Variables:
            Setpoint : real;
            Contains a value at which something happens.

            Reading : real;
            Contains an number that is compared to the
            setpoint.

  Procedures:
            .PutSetpoint( NewSetpoint : real );
            Sets Setpoint to NewSetpoint.

            NOTE: .Init procedure is packaged with
                 descendant classes.

  Descendant object types:
            HiSwitch
            LoSwitch          }

{ Specification for DOutput class ***********************

    NO VARIABLES, NO PROCEDURES, NO FUNCTIONS
    (see descendant object type)

  Descendant object types:
            Pump         }

{ Specification for HiSwitch class **********************

  Procedures:
            .Init(( ATag : string;
                    ASetpoint : real;
                    AReading : real);
            Storage as follows:
              ATag -> TagNumber
              ASetpoint -> Setpoint
            The value of AReading is stored in Reading
            using the .PutReading method.

            .PutReading( NewReading : real);
            Store NewReading in Reading.  Set Status to
```

```
           ON if Reading >= Setpoint.

  Descendant object types:
None.       }

{ Specification for LoSwitch class ************************

  Procedures:
           .Init(( ATag : string;
                   ASetpoint : real;
                   AReading : real);
           Storage as follows:
             ATag -> TagNumber
             ASetpoint -> Setpoint
           The value of AReading is stored in Reading
           using the .PutReading method.

           .PutReading( NewReading : real);
           Store NewReading in Reading.  Set Status to
           ON if Reading <= Setpoint.

  Descendant object types:
None.       }

{ Specification for Pump class *************************

  Variables:
           FlowRate : real;
           A number representing gpm flow when pump is
           ON.  NOTE: THIS IS A *VERY* ROUGH APPROXIMATION
           OF PUMP BEHAVIOR!

  Procedures:
           .Init( ATag : String12; AStatus : boolean;
                  AFlow : real );
           Storage as follows:
                  ATag -> TagNumber
                  AStatus -> Status
                  AFlow -> FlowRate

  Functions:
           .Flow : real;
           Returns the value stored in FlowRate.

  Descendant object types:
           None.       }
```

```
unit Tags;

interface

uses Crt; { for KeyPressed }

const

ON  = true;
OFF = false;
MinR = 0;        { Min number of counts in an analog input }
MaxR = 4095;     { Maximum number of counts in an analog input }

var
    f : text;  {predefined file type}

type

Resolution = 0..4095;  { Range for analog input }
String12 = string[12];


Tag = object
      TagNumber : String12;
      procedure Init( ATag : String12 );
      end;

Digital = object(Tag)
          Status : boolean;
          procedure Init( ATag : String12; AStatus : boolean );
          procedure PutStatus( AStatus : boolean );
          function GetStatus : boolean;
          end;

Analog = object(Tag)
         Value : Resolution;
         ZeroVal : real;
         MaxVal : real;
         Slope  : real;
         procedure Init( ATag : String12; AValue : Resolution;
                         Min, Max : real );
         procedure PutValue( AValue : real );
         function GetValue : real;
         end;

DOutput = object(Digital)
          end;

Pump = object(DOutput)
       FlowRate : real;
       procedure Init( ATag : String12; AStatus : boolean;
```

```
                     AFlow : real );
       function Flow : real;
       end;


DInput = object(Digital)
            Setpoint  : real;
            Reading   : real;
            procedure PutSetpoint( NewSetpoint : real );
            end;

HiSwitch = object(DInput)
           procedure Init( ATag : string;
                           ASetpoint : real;
                           AReading : real);
           procedure PutReading( NewReading : real );
           end;

LoSwitch = object(DInput)
           procedure Init( ATag : string;
                           ASetpoint : real;
                           AReading : real);
           procedure PutReading( NewReading : real );
           end;

FSwitch = object
          State : boolean;
          procedure Init( InitState : boolean );
          procedure On;
          procedure Off;
          function IsOn : boolean;
          function IsOff : boolean;
          end;


function HtToPSI( Height : real ) : real;

function FlowToDeltaHt( Flow : real ) : real;

var
   Quiet : FSwitch;

implementation

procedure Tag.Init( ATag : String12 );
begin
     TagNumber := ATag;
end;
```

```
procedure Digital.Init( ATag : String12; AStatus : boolean);
begin
     Tag.Init( ATag );
     Status := AStatus;
end;

procedure Digital.PutStatus( AStatus : boolean );
begin
     Status := AStatus;
end;

function Digital.GetStatus : boolean;
begin
     if (Status = ON) and (Quiet.IsOff) then
        writeln( f, TagNumber, ' is ON.' )
     else
        if (Quiet.IsOff) then
           writeln( f, TagNumber, ' is OFF.' );
     GetStatus := Status;
end;

procedure Pump.Init( ATag : String12; AStatus : boolean;
                     AFlow : real );
begin
     Digital.Init( ATag, AStatus );
     FlowRate := AFlow;
end;

function Pump.Flow : real;
begin
     if Status = true then
        Flow := FlowRate
     else
        Flow := 0;
end;

procedure Analog.Init( ATag : String12;
                       AValue : Resolution;
                       Min, Max : real );
begin
     Tag.Init( ATag );
     Value := AValue;
     MaxVal := Max;
     ZeroVal := Min;
     Slope := (Max-Min)/(MaxR-MinR);
end;

procedure Analog.PutValue( AValue : real );
begin
     if AValue > MaxVal then
        AValue := MaxVal
```

```
     else
        if AValue < ZeroVal then
           AValue := ZeroVal;
     Value := Round((AValue - ZeroVal)/Slope);
end;

function Analog.GetValue : real;
begin
     GetValue := Slope*Value + ZeroVal;
end;

procedure DInput.PutSetpoint( NewSetpoint : real );
begin
     Setpoint := NewSetpoint;
end;

procedure LoSwitch.Init( ATag : string;
                         ASetpoint : real;
                         AReading : real);
begin
     Tag.Init( ATag );
     DInput.PutSetpoint( ASetpoint );
     PutReading( AReading );
end;

procedure LoSwitch.PutReading( NewReading : real );
begin
     Reading := NewReading;
     if Reading <= Setpoint then
        Status := true
     else
        Status := false;
end;

procedure HiSwitch.Init( ATag : string;
                         ASetpoint : real;
                         AReading : real);
begin
     Tag.Init( ATag );
     DInput.PutSetpoint( ASetpoint );
     PutReading( AReading );
end;

procedure HiSwitch.PutReading( NewReading : real );
begin
     Reading := NewReading;
     if Reading >= Setpoint then
        Status := true
     else
        Status := false;
end;
```

```
procedure FSwitch.Init( InitState : boolean );
begin
     State := InitState;
     if State = false then   { If we want output}
        Rewrite( f )        { Open file f }
     else
        begin
        Rewrite( f );       { Open file f }
        Close( f );         { and close it }
        end;
end;

procedure FSwitch.On;
begin
     if State = false then
        begin
        State := true;
        Close( f );
        end;
end;

procedure FSwitch.Off;
begin
     if State = true then
        begin
        State := false;
        Append( f );
        end;
end;

function FSwitch.IsOn : boolean;
begin
     if State = true then
        IsOn := true
     else
        IsOn := false;
end;

function FSwitch.Isoff : boolean;
begin
     IsOff := not IsOn;
end;

{ HtToPSI converts a height (of a column of water) into a
  pressure.
  The math is pretty simple:  A column of water 2.31 feet
  high exerts a force of one pound per square inch at the
  bottom. }

function HtToPSI( Height : real ) : real;
begin
```

```
    HtToPSI := Height/2.31;
end;

{ FlowToDeltaHt converts a flow into (or out of) our system
  into a change in height in the tank.
  The math is as follows:  Divide the flow, in gpm, by 7.48
  gal/cu.ft. to get the number of cubic feet pumped per minute.
  Divide this number by the volume of 1 vertical foot of the
  tank, which is the radius squared times 'pi' (15*15*3.1416). }

function FlowToDeltaHt( Flow : real ) : real;
begin
    FlowToDeltaHt := Flow/(7.48 * 706) ;
end;

{ initialization code }
begin

Assign( f, ParamStr(1) );

Quiet.Init(OFF);

end.
```

As you can see, converting the program is fairly straightforward. The first thing you do is think of an appropriate name for the unit (`Tags` in our case) and then save the file under that name! (This is easy to do in the Turbo Pascal Integrated Development Environment. You press F10 to activate the menu bar, followed by F (for FILE), then W (for Write To), after which you enter the new name and you're done.) This is a very important step, because if the unit name and the file name are not the same, you'll get a compiler error. The rest is about as straightforward. You put the lines

```
unit Tags;

interface
```

at the beginning of the file, delete the program portion that begins with the variable definitions for LT100, etc., and place the keyword *implementation* between the last object type declaration and the first method description. Finally, after the last method description there is a begin/end block for initialization code. Often, this block is empty, but in our unit we want the `Quiet` variable (which determines whether status reports are generated by `Digital` objects) to be ON, thus enabling the reports by default.

One subtle addition to the unit is a pair of what look to be one-line function declarations. These declarations appear in the interface portion of the unit so that the functions `HtToPSI` and `FlowToDeltaHt` are accessible from outside the unit. If the two declarations are left out of the interface part, the unit will compile without error, but the two functions will be callable only from the other procedures and functions in the implementation section of the unit.

The code in the `Tags` unit contains all the information a program needs to use the `Tag` and descendant object types. The specification portion of the unit is not required by the Turbo Pascal syntax, but may be considered nearly as important as the code. Sure, we've all heard the standard sermon on writing good documentation, but here, it's more than just good programming practice. The specification contains all the information a programmer will need to be able to use the unit, particularly in those cases where the source code of the unit is not available. If you want to enhance the *encapsulation* of the objects and prevent users of your units from directly accessing the properties (variables) in your object types, you can completely leave out references to the actual property names in the specification, thus requiring users to interact with objects via methods.

Encapsulation is a word often used in OOP. Objects encapsulate data with an associated set of procedures and functions that manipulate the data. Encapsulation is closely related to the concept of data hiding, in which the internal object structure is inaccessible from outside the object. Basically, it means that the user of an object type is aware of only those methods and properties that are necessary to use it. Turbo Pascal does not enforce data hiding, so we must discipline ourselves to act as if data were hidden.

One enhancement to the unit is the encapsulation (to a great degree) of the file I/O information. A special `FSwitch` object type has been declared along with a variable of that type named Quiet. When the status property of Quiet is ON, the file f (a text file type declared in the interface section of the unit) is closed and no further output is directed to it. When Quiet is OFF, the file f is reopened, and output resumes. The only thing the programmer needs to know about file I/O in this unit is stated in the utilization notes at the beginning of the specification.

Once you've packaged object type definitions into a unit, you must compile it into a .TPU file before you can use it in another program. Compilation is simple and can be performed from the Turbo Pascal environment by typing Alt-C (which brings up the compilation menu), followed by M (for Make). Listing 3-2 is a revamped version of Listing 2-3, shortened greatly by using the Tags unit (and removing comments, to save space). There is also a line of code that shows how the manipulation of the Quiet object affects program output. Output with the line commented and uncommented appears in Fig. 3.2a and 3.2b, respectively.

Listing 3-2

```
program Listing3_2;

uses Tags, Crt;

var
   LT100,
   FT100  : Analog;
   PSL100 : LoSwitch;
   PSH100 : HiSwitch;
   EY100  : Pump;
   time   : integer;

begin

     LT100.Init( 'LT100', 512, 50, 250 );
     FT100.Init( 'FT100', 2048, 0, 10000 );
     PSL100.Init( 'PSL100', 60, HtToPSI(LT100.GetValue) );
     PSH100.Init( 'PSH100', 75, HtToPSI(LT100.GetValue) );
     EY100.Init( 'EY100', off, 8000);
     time := 0;

     repeat
```

```
    Inc( time );  { increment the time }
    LT100.PutValue( LT100.GetValue - FlowToDeltaHt(FT100.GetValue) );

    PSL100.PutReading( HtToPSI(LT100.GetValue) );
    PSH100.PutReading( HtToPSI(LT100.GetValue) );

    if Quiet.IsOff then
       writeln( f, 'Level is ', LT100.GetValue:2:2, ' ft at minute ', time );

    if PSL100.GetStatus = on then
       EY100.PutStatus( ON );
    if PSH100.GetStatus = on then
       EY100.PutStatus( OFF );

    LT100.PutValue( LT100.GetValue + FlowToDeltaHt(EY100.Flow ));

{ if the next line of code is not commented out, you'll see only
  reports for even values of time; otherwise, reports for each
  time value will be printed. }

{    if (time mod 2 = 0) then Quiet.On else Quiet.Off;      }

    until KeyPressed;
    Quiet.On;
end.
```

Figure 3.2a — Output of Listing 3-2

```
Level is 74.08 ft at minute 1
PSL100 is ON.
PSH100 is OFF.
EY100 is ON.
Level is 74.66 ft at minute 2
PSL100 is ON.
PSH100 is OFF.
EY100 is ON.
Level is 75.25 ft at minute 3
PSL100 is ON.
PSH100 is OFF.
EY100 is ON.
Level is 75.84 ft at minute 4
PSL100 is ON.
PSH100 is OFF.
EY100 is ON.
Level is 76.42 ft at minute 5
PSL100 is ON.
PSH100 is OFF.
EY100 is ON.
```

Figure 3.2b — Output of Listing 3-2 with 'Quiet' turned ON during odd times after time = 1

```
Level is 74.08 ft at minute 1
PSL100 is ON.
PSH100 is OFF.
EY100 is ON.
Level is 74.66 ft at minute 2
PSL100 is ON.
PSH100 is OFF.
EY100 is ON.
Level is 75.84 ft at minute 4
PSL100 is ON.
PSH100 is OFF.
EY100 is ON.
Level is 77.01 ft at minute 6
PSL100 is ON.
PSH100 is OFF.
EY100 is ON.
Level is 78.18 ft at minute 8
PSL100 is ON.
PSH100 is OFF.
EY100 is ON.
```

Extending Object Types

One of the advertised strengths of OOP is the ability to extend existing objects with a minimum of fuss and bother. To show you what that means, let's extend the `Tags` unit by coming up with a more realistic model for a pump.

NewPump

If you haven't hung around pumps a lot, our model of pump behavior might not sound all that unrealistic. If we plot a graph of pressure versus flow, we get something that looks like Fig. 3.3a. What this basically says is that no matter what the pressure, the flow coming out of the pump remains the same. Real pumps have pressure-flow curves that look more like Fig. 3.3b. Notice how the flow increases as the pressure in the system decreases, and vice versa.

Figure 3.3a — Flow relation for Pump object type

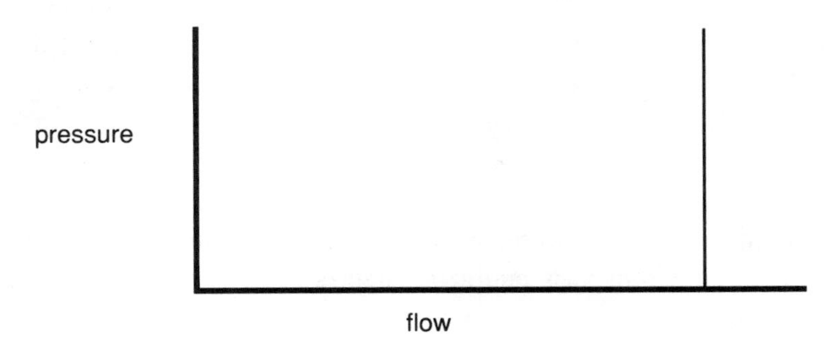

Figure 3.3b — Flow relation for NewPump object type

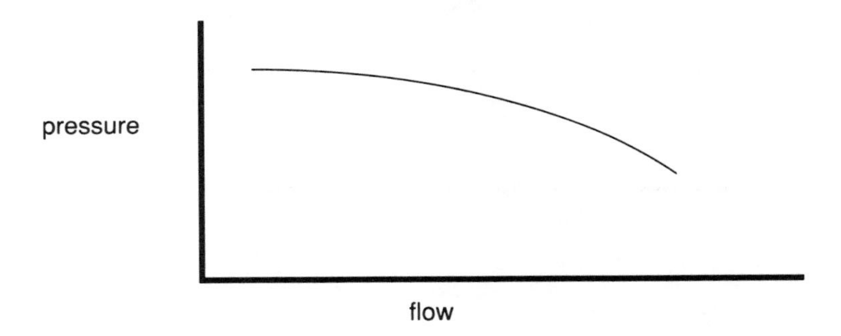

Determining Behavior

Let's see what happens in our simulated control system when we replace the pump that's there with a new object type we'll call `NewPump`. We will approximate the behavior of this new object type with a quadratic curve — that is, pressure varies with the square of the flow. This means that the pressure-flow curve will be a parabola having the equation:

$$Pressure = MaxPressure - K*Flow^2$$

where MaxPressure is the pressure at the pump discharge with no flow in the system (Flow = 0), and K is a constant. We can determine K by specifying two operating points for the pump: 9000 gpm at a pressure of 65 psi, and 4000 gpm at a pressure of 75 psi. Once we have K, we can determine MaxPressure. (Figure 3.4 shows the math for these two steps.)

Figure 3.4 — Determining K and MaxPressure from two operating points

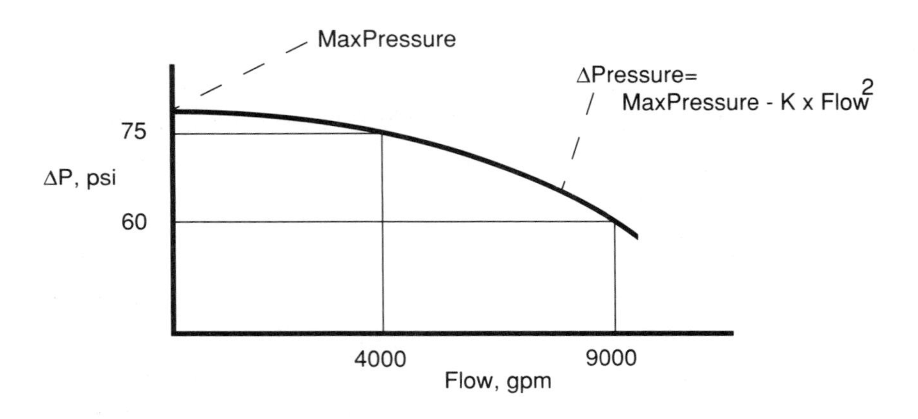

$$75 = \text{MaxPressure} - K\,(4000)^2$$
$$60 = \text{MaxPressure} - K\,(9000)^2$$
$$K\,(9000^2 - 4000^2) = 75 - 60$$

$$K = \frac{15}{65 \times 10^6} = 2.31 \times 10^{-7}$$

$$\text{MaxPressure} = 75 + (2.31 \times 10^{-7})\,(4000)^2$$
$$= 78.7 \text{ psi}$$

Determining Properties

In light of the discussion so far, it's clear we'll need properties for maximum pressure and scaling factor. As a design comment, you could in theory make `NewPump` a descendant type of `Pump` and use the property `FlowRate` to store the maximum pressure (after all, both are real numbers!). That way, you'd only have to create a descendant with a property for scaling factor, etc. This is bad programming practice, and poor design methodology. If you absolutely insist on making `NewPump` a descendant type of `Pump`, go back and redesign the code for `Pump` in the original unit. However, you should (as we will do here) resist the temptation to be cute and create a separate type if necessary. It will save you a small fortune in aspirin in the long haul. In our example, we will make `NewPump` a descendant of the `DOutput` type. If we design it correctly, the interface for both the `Pump` and `NewPump` object types will be substantially the same.

If our pump is going to calculate its discharge flow based on current pressure, we'll have to find a way to feed that pressure to the `NewPump` object. Our problem is this: how are we going to do it? Since we'll need to find the current pressure every time we make a call to the function `.Flow` (the function currently being used in Listing 3-2 to return pump flow), we could simply change the function declaration to include a parameter and pass in the current pressure as the parameter.

The only problem with this is that it will require us to go through our source code and change every reference we make to `.Flow` to `.Flow( APressureValue)`, which for our small program is not too big a deal, but could be cumbersome for larger programs. Isn't there a way to get the information without changing the calling convention for the method `.Flow`? There is, and the result is presented in Listing 3-3 for the unit `NewTags`.

Listing 3-3

```
unit NewTags;

interface

uses Tags, Crt;

type

PFunc = function : real;
pPFunc = ^PFunc;

NewPump = object(DOutput)
          MaxPressure : real;
          ScalingFactor : real;
          GetPressureDemon : PFunc;
          procedure Init( ATag : String12; AStatus : boolean;
                          MaxP, Scale : real;
                          PressFunction : pPFunc );
          function Flow : real;
          end;

implementation

procedure NewPump.Init( ATag : String12; AStatus : boolean;
                          MaxP, Scale : real;
                          PressFunction: pPFunc );
begin
     Digital.Init( ATag,AStatus);
     MaxPressure := maxP;
     Scalingfactor := Scale;
     @GetPressureDemon := PressFunction;
end;

function NewPump.Flow : real;
begin
     if Status = true then
        Flow := Sqrt( (MaxPressure -GetPressureDemon)/ScalingFactor )
     else
        Flow := 0;
end;

{ Initialization code }
begin
{ None.}
end.
```

Notice first of all that the third property of our NewPump object type, GetPressureDemon, is of type PFunc, which (as a preceding declaration tells us) is a procedural type denoting a function with no parameters returning a real value. This combined property/function behaves in the manner of what in object-oriented circles is called a *demon*.

A demon (sometimes spelled daemon) is a function that is not invoked explicitly, but runs only when something happens. In our code, the function GetPressureDemon is only called when the .Flow method is called, and then only if the .Status is ON. Demons do things behind the scenes. Returning to our example of the pizza parlor from Chapter 1, imagine there is a small, friendly demon watching the cheese tray, and every time the chef reaches into the tray for a handful of cheese, the demon checks to make sure there is enough cheese left for another pie. As long as there is sufficient cheese, the demon remains silent. If the cheese gets short, the demon bounces over to the refrigerator, fetches more cheese, returns, fills the tray, and resumes watching.

Calling the GetPressureDemon from the .Flow method allows .Flow to remain a parameterless function. The address of the function to execute whenever the current pressure is needed is passed to the NewPump object as a pointer to the PFunc type, which is stored in the GetPressureDemon property.

The only obligation this arrangement imposes is the need to declare a parameterless function that returns a real value (preferably the value of the current pressure!). Furthermore, in accordance with the Turbo Pascal rules for procedural variables, the compiled function must be called using a far pointer. This is done by bracketing the function with the compilation flags {$F+} and {$F-} above and below the function declaration, respectively. A version of our control system simulation that makes use of the NewPump object type is presented in Listing 3-4.

Listing 3-4

```
program Listing3_4;

uses Tags, Crt, NewTags;

var
   LT100,
   FT100  : Analog;
   PSL100 : LoSwitch;
   PSH100 : HiSwitch;
   EY100  : NewPump;
   time   : integer;

{ The following function is used by the NewPump object.
  Since it is used with a procedural variable, far calls
  must be forced for compilation. }
{$F+}
function SystemPressure : real;
begin
     SystemPressure := HtToPSI(LT100.GetValue);
end;
{$F-}

begin

     LT100.Init( 'LT100', 512, 50, 250 );
     FT100.Init( 'FT100', 2048, 0, 10000 );
     PSL100.Init( 'PSL100', 60, SystemPressure );
     PSH100.Init( 'PSH100', 75, SystemPressure );
     EY100.Init( 'EY100', off, 100, 4.8e-7, @SystemPressure);
     time := 0;

     repeat

     Inc( time );  { increment the time }
     LT100.PutValue( LT100.GetValue - FlowToDeltaHt(FT100.GetValue) );

     PSL100.PutReading( SystemPressure );
     PSH100.PutReading( SystemPressure );

     if Quiet.IsOff then
        writeln( f, 'Level is ', LT100.GetValue:2:2,
                                          ' ft at minute ', time);

     if PSL100.GetStatus = on then
        EY100.PutStatus( ON );
     if PSH100.GetStatus = on then
        EY100.PutStatus( OFF );
     LT100.PutValue( LT100.GetValue +
```

```
                    FlowToDeltaHt( EY100.Flow ));

    until KeyPressed;
    Quiet.On;
end.
```

Postscript

In this chapter, we've looked at encapsulating object type declarations into Turbo Pascal units and extending those units without having to modify existing code. We've also seen how we can dynamically attach functions called demons to an object structure. By now, if you've been following along faithfully, you're probably wondering if there is a better way to view the operation of our simulated control system instead of digging through files full of numbers and words. There is, and in the next chapter we'll look at a graphics object type for drawing plots, and discuss the issues involved in its design.

4

OBJECTS IN GRAPHICS

Up to now, the emphasis of the material in this book has been on the mechanics of using the object-oriented features of Turbo Pascal, with little attention devoted to the manner in which information is output to the user. Although we saw in the previous chapter how an object could be used to control output from a program, the output from our simulation program gives you very little idea of how the various parts of the system behave. If you wanted to see what really happens in the system, you'd take the output file and sit down with a piece of graph paper and plot out the points for the various parameters of interest; tedious work at best. Why do that by hand when there is a computer in front of us?

In the first part of this chapter, we'll take a look at the issues involved in designing a graphics object type for plotting graphs and then present code for the `Plot` object type, which will allow us to draw x-y plots from our simulated control system on the screen.

Plot

Graphic objects (and here I use the word in its generic, non-OOP sense) lend themselves particularly well to encapsulation in object type definitions, and doing graphics programming in non-OOP systems has an almost-but-not-quite object-oriented feel about it. The graph is a fertile example for illustrating object-oriented design using graphics.

There are, of course, many different types of graphs, but probably by far the most common is the x-y plot, as shown in Fig. 4.1. The most basic characteristics of the plot are the following:

Title. If you don't know what it represents, it doesn't matter what it looks like. Probably the most important part of a plot is its title.

Axes. A plot is defined by two perpendicular axes, represented by lines at the bottom and the left of the plot area. The horizontal line is traditionally called the x axis; the vertical line, the y axis.

Scales. There is a scale on each axis, represented by numbers at both ends of each axis, and usually by additional numbers and tick marks along the axis for reference purposes.

Axis Labels. The labels on each axis describe the nature of the numbers on the scale. This tells the viewer basically what it is he or she is looking at.

Graphs. There are one or more graphs (often called *curves* in technical circles, even if they consist of line segments) in the area bounded by the axes.

One of the most popular uses for plots is to track the behavior of some parameter versus time, which is what we'll do with our simulation. In time plots, time is traditionally plotted on the x axis, and the parameter is plotted on the y axis.

Figure 4.1 — The x-y plot

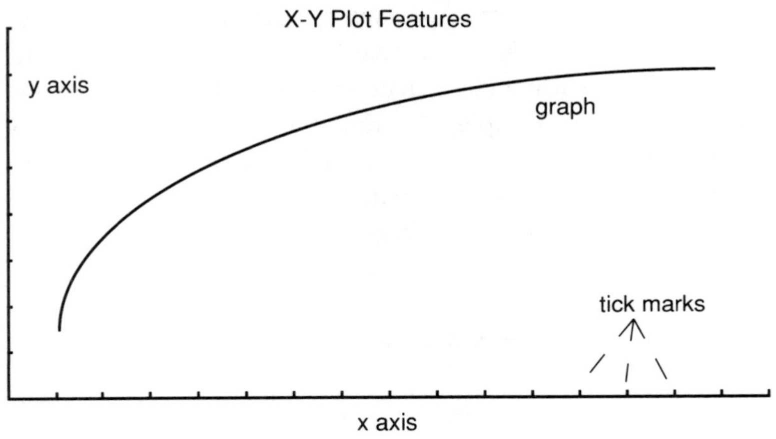

X-Y Plot Features

y axis

graph

tick marks

x axis

Properties

The list of items we'll need to know about a graph to include in an object type declaration is pretty hefty, even for moderately flexible plotting schemes. Things like the title and labels for both axes are fairly straightforward. We will let Turbo Pascal select both the text style and size for us; our object type will be able to cope with a variety of text sizes. Next, we'll need maximum and minimum values for each axis, and since these numbers are not restricted to the domain of integers, we'll use real numbers to store these values. We'll also need scaling factors for both the x and the y axis, so that we can represent a range of 0 to 100,000 as simply 0 to 100 (and store the fact that values need to be divided by a scaling factor of 100 prior to plotting).

The rest of the information we'll need will basically help with the housekeeping associated with the graph. Perhaps the most basic set of numbers will be the coordinates of the Turbo Pascal viewport. A viewport is a specific rectangular region of the graphics screen, as shown in Fig. 4.2. It is established by calling the procedure `SetViewPort` with parameters that identify the left, right, top, and bottom limits of the viewport, as well as a flag that indicates whether graphics are cut off, of "clipped" at the boundaries of the viewport. One of the most important characteristics of a viewport is that once a viewport is set using the `SetViewport` procedure, all graphics commands use a coordinate system that is local to the viewport. In Fig. 4.3, for example, we show the outline of two viewports, and arrows show the coordinate (20,10) for each. This makes it easy to draw inside the viewport and relieves the programmer of the need to constantly change frames of reference.

Figure 4.2 — A viewport

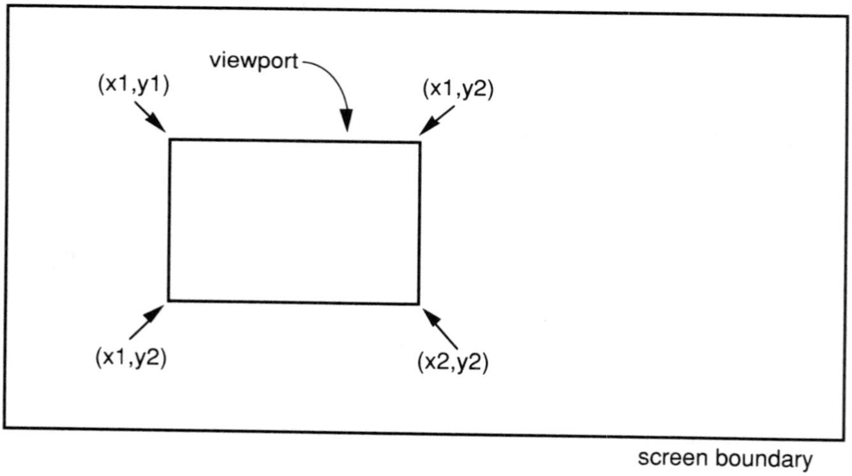

viewport
(x1,y1)
(x1,y2)
(x1,y2)
(x2,y2)
screen boundary

Figure 4.3 — The coordinate (20,10) for two viewports

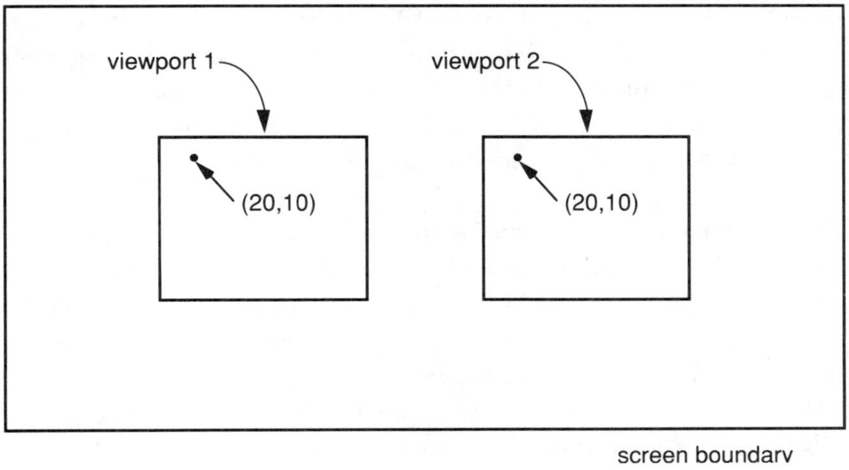

Another set of numbers we'll need to store describe the width and number of decimal places to use when using the `Str` procedure to convert numbers to strings (recall that a call to `Str( 4.3:1:2, s )` returns the string '4.30' in `s`). This comes in handy when you want a scale to read 0 to 1 (instead of 0.00 to 1.00) or to move the vertical y axis left or right inside a viewport (so as to align the y axes of two graphs placed one above the other).

Other information that will come in handy can be calculated and stored for future use during initialization of the object. For example, we can find the difference between the maximum and minimum for each axis, and then store the difference for each in its own property. Knowing how high and how wide the labels and the numbers on the axis scales are (thanks to the Turbo Pascal `TextHeight` and `TextWidth` functions), we can determine the endpoints of the x and the y axis. We can store the viewport coordinates of the point where the x and the y axis come together (also called the origin), and store the length (in pixels) of the x and y axes.

The object type we're contemplating here isn't too "smart" in that it doesn't know how to manipulate, update, or search for data (a descendant object type might do that!). We're going to make the assumption that a series of data points will be handed to the object for plotting, and therefore, all the object need do is remember the last point received from "outside," and simply draw a line from the old point to the new point, provided the flag `PlotEnabled` is true.

Although what we've described will probably do as a minimum, let's go further and design some additional basic functions. We should have the ability to place a dotted line vertically or horizontally anywhere in the plot. This capability allows us to show high or low limits, or if placed at regular intervals, to form a grid. Analogously, we should be able to place a number anywhere along the horizontal or vertical axes. Again, this allows us to denote limits, or label a scale. Finally, we should be able to place small tick marks on either axis.

We now have enough information to build a fairly flexible object type that gives us some basic capabilities. Once we get the `Plot` object type encapsulated into a unit, we'll be able to smoothly integrate it into our simulation and see what goes on in the system.

The code for the Plot object type is presented in Listing 4-1 as a unit. It should be saved and compiled as PLOTDATA.PAS. There are no surprises in the code, except that the `.Init` method for the object type is much longer than what we have been accustomed to seeing. Once we have initialized a `Plot` object, we can identify limits, place numbers along the aces, and send it data to plot using the `.AddPoint` method.

Listing 4-1

```
{ Unit : PLOTDATA

  Utilization notes:

1. For information purposes only, there is a 4-pixel
   border between the edge of a plot viewport and the
   actual area occupied by the plot.
```

```
2. The .Init method fills the rectangle formed by the
   viewport in blue.  Axes, labels, etc. are white.
}
{ Specification for Plot class ***************************

  Variables:
            x1 : integer;
            Coordinate (global) of the left edge of the
            Plot object's viewport.

            x2 : integer;
            Coordinate (global) of the right edge of the
            Plot object's viewport.

            y1 : integer;
            Coordinate (global) of the top edge of the
            Plot object's viewport.

            y2 : integer;
            Coordinate (global) of the bottom edge of the
            Plot object's viewport.

            Mnx : real;
            Minimum x axis scale value.

            Mny : real;
            Minimum y axis scale value.

            Mxx : real;
            Maximum y axis scale value.

            Mxy : real;
            Maximum y axis scale value.

            XW : integer;
            Width value for x-axis scale.
            Refer to Turbo Pascal description
            of Str function.

            XD : integer;
            Number of decimal places for x-axis scale.
            Refer to Turbo Pascal description
            of Str function.

            YW : integer;
            Width value for y-axis scale.
            Refer to Turbo Pascal description
            of Str function.

            YD : integer;
            Number of decimal places for y-axis scale.
```

```
Refer to Turbo Pascal description
of Str function.

XSFac : real;
Scaling factor for x axis.

YSFac : real;
Scaling factor for y axis.

XLabel : string;
Label for x axis.

YLabel : string;
Label for y axis.

PlotTitle : string
Title for plot.

OldPoint : Point;
Object type that stores the local viewport
coordinates of the last point plotted.
Set to (0,0,FALSE) during initialization.

OriginX : integer;
Viewport x coord of origin.

OriginY : integer;
Viewport y coord of origin.

MaxXAxis : integer;
Viewport x coordinate of the maximum x-axis
endpoint.

MaxYAxis : integer;
Viewport y coordinate of the maximum y-axis
endpoint.

DeltaXAxis : integer;
Equal to MaxXAxis - OriginX.

DeltaYAxis : integer;
Equal to OriginY - MaxYAxis.

DeltaX : real;
Equal to Mxx - Mnx.

DeltaY : real;
Equal to Mxy - Mny.
```

```
        PlotEnabled : boolean;
        If true, line is drawn between OldPoint
        and new data point in .AddPoint method.

Procedures:
        .Init( miny, maxy, ysf, minx, maxx, xsf : real;
               lft, rt, tp, btm,
               wx, dx, wy, dy : integer;
               xlbl, ylbl : string; penbl : boolean );
        Store all viewport parameters, maxima and minima
        for both axes.  Store width and number of decimal
        places for both axes, and whether to connect first
        point to origin (penbl).  Calculate all "deltas,"
        set viewport with border, draw axes, labels and
        maximum and minimum scale values.

        .AddPoint( x, y : real );
        Figure out where in the plot area the new point
        is located, and draw a line between the point
        stored in OldPoint and the new point.

        .DrawVGridLine( y : real );
        Given a value on the y axis, a dotted
        horizontal line is drawn at value y.

        .DrawHGridLine( x : real );
        Given a value on the x axis, a dotted
        vertical line is drawn at value x.

        .PlaceXAxisValue( r : real);
        Places the number r at value r on the x axis
        after applying scaling factor (XSFac).  Number
        is displayed XW spaces wide, with WD decimal
        places.

        .PlaceYAxisValue( r : real);
        Places the number r at value r on the y axis
        after applying scaling factor (YSFac).  Number
        is displayed YW spaces wide, with YD decimal
        places.

        .DrawTickMark( x, y : integer );
        Given x and y coordinates (local to viewport)
        color pixels at (x,y), (x+1,y), (x, y+1), and
        (x+1,y+1).


Descendant object types:
        None.              }
```

```
unit PlotData;

interface

uses Graph, Crt, Points;

const

LBuf = 4;        {left border "buffer"}
RBuf = 4;        {right border}
TBuf = 4;        {top border}
BBuf = 4;        {bottom border}
left = 3;
right = 1;
top = 0;
bottom = 2;

type

Plot = object
       x1, x2, y1, y2 : integer; { viewport left, right, top, bottom }
       Mnx, Mny, Mxx, Mxy : real; { min/max x min/max y }
       XW,XD,YW,YD : integer;
       XSFac, YSFac : real;
       XLabel : string;
       YLabel : string;
       PlotTitle : string;
       OldPoint : Point; { last point plotted }
       OriginX : integer; { viewport x coord of origin }
       OriginY : integer; { viewport y coord of origin }
       MaxXAxis : integer;
       MaxYAxis : integer;
       DeltaXAxis : integer;
       DeltaYAxis : integer;
       DeltaX : real;
       DeltaY : real;
       PlotEnabled : boolean;
       procedure Init( miny, maxy, ysf, minx, maxx, xsf : real;
                       lft, rt, tp, btm,
                       wx, dx, wy, dy : integer;
                       ptitle, xlbl, ylbl : string;
                       penbl : boolean );
       procedure AddPoint( x, y : real );
       procedure DrawHGridLine( y : real );
       procedure DrawVGridLine( x : real );
       procedure PlaceXAxisValue( r : real );
       procedure PlaceYAxisValue( r : real );
       procedure DrawTickMark( x, y : integer );
       end;

implementation
```

```
procedure Plot.Init( miny, maxy, ysf, minx, maxx, xsf : real;
                     lft, rt, tp, btm,
                     wx, dx, wy, dy : integer;
                     ptitle, xlbl, ylbl : string;
                     penbl : boolean );
var

LBorder, THeight : integer;
VP : ViewPortType;
TST : TextSettingsType;
s : array[0..3] of string[11];
begin
     XW := wx;      XD := dx;
     YW := wy;      YD := dy;
     XSFac := xsf;
     YSFac := ysf;
     Xlabel := xlbl;
     Ylabel := ylbl;
     PlotTitle := ptitle;
     x1 := lft;
     x2 := rt;
     y1 := tp;
     y2 := btm;
     Mnx := minx*xsf;
     Mxx := maxx*xsf;
     Mny := miny*ysf;
     Mxy := maxy*ysf;
     DeltaX := Mxx - Mnx;
     DeltaY := Mxy - Mny;
     Str( maxx:XW:XD, s[right]);
     Str( maxy:YW:YD, s[top]);
     Str( minx:XW:XD, s[left]);
     Str( miny:YW:YD, s[bottom]);
     THeight := TextHeight(s[0]);
     if TextWidth( s[top] ) < TextWidth( s[bottom]) then
        LBorder := TextWidth(s[bottom])
     else
        LBorder := TextWidth(s[top]);

     SetViewPort( lft, tp, rt, btm, true);
     if GraphResult = grError then
       OutTextXY(0,0,'Input error to SetViewPort in Plot.Init');
     GetViewSettings( VP );
     with VP do
     begin
          { next line is for color monitors }
          SetFillStyle( SolidFill, blue );
          { next line is for monochrome monitors }
          { SetFillStyle( SolidFill, black ); }
          Rectangle(0,0,x2-x1, y2-y1);
          FloodFill( 1,1, GetMaxColor );
```

```
          OriginY := y2-y1-2*(BBuf+THeight);
          OriginX := LBuf+LBorder+THeight;
          MaxYAxis := TBuf+(3*THeight div 2);
          MaxXAxis := x2-x1-RBuf-(TextWidth(s[right]) div 2);
          DeltaXAxis := MaxXAxis - OriginX;
          DeltaYAxis := OriginY - MaxYAxis;

          GetTextSettings( TST );
          with TST do
          begin
               Line( OriginX, MaxYAxis, OriginX, OriginY);
               SetTextJustify(RightText, BottomText);
               MoveTo(OriginX, OriginY);
               OutText(s[bottom]);
               MoveTo(OriginX,TBuf+(2*THeight));
               OutText(s[top]);

               Line( OriginX, OriginY,MaxXAxis,OriginY);
               SetTextJustify(CenterText, BottomText);
               MoveTo(OriginX, y2-y1-BBuf-THeight);
               OutText(s[left]);
               MoveTo( MaxXAxis, y2-y1-BBuf-THeight);
               OutText(s[right]);

               MoveTo(OriginX+DeltaXAxis div 2, y2-y1-BBuf);
               OutText( XLabel );
               SetTextStyle( Font, VertDir, CharSize );
               MoveTo( LBuf+(THeight div 2),
                       OriginY-(DeltaYAxis div 2) );
               SetTextJustify( CenterText, CenterText );
               OutText(YLabel);
               SetTextStyle( Font, Direction, CharSize );
               MoveTo( (x2-x1) div 2, TBuf+(THeight div 2));
               OutText(PlotTitle);
               SetTextJustify( Horiz, Vert );
          end;
     end;
     OldPoint.Init(OriginX,OriginY);
     PlotEnabled := Penbl;
end;

procedure Plot.AddPoint( x, y : real );
var
   VP : ViewPortType;
   px, py : integer;
begin
     GetViewSettings( VP );
     SetViewPort( x1, y1, x2, y2, true );
     px := OriginX+Round(((x-mnx)/DeltaX)*DeltaXAxis);
     py := OriginY-Round(((y-mny)/DeltaY)*DeltaYAxis);
     if (x >= mnx) and
```

```
        (x <= mxx) and
        (y >= mny) and
        (y <= mxy) then
          begin
          with OldPoint do
               begin
               if PlotEnabled then
                  line( OldPoint.X, OldPoint.Y, px, py );
               OldPoint.Init( px, py );
               PlotEnabled := true;
               end;
          end;
     with VP do
          SetViewPort( x1, y1, x2, y2, true );
end;

procedure Plot.DrawHGridLine( y : real );
var
   VP : ViewPortType;
   LST : LineSettingsType;
   py : integer;
begin
     GetViewSettings( VP );
     SetViewPort( x1, y1, x2, y2, true );
     if (y > mny) and (y < mxy) then
        begin
        py := OriginY-Round(((y-mny)/DeltaY)*DeltaYAxis);
        GetLineSettings( LST );
        with LST do
             begin
             SetLineStyle( DottedLn, Pattern, NormWidth );
             Line( OriginX, py, MaxXAxis, py );
             SetLineStyle( LineStyle, Pattern, Thickness );
             end;
        end;
     with VP do
          SetViewPort( x1, y1, x2, y2, true );
end;

procedure Plot.DrawVGridLine( x : real );
var
   VP : ViewPortType;
   LST : LineSettingsType;
   px : integer;
begin
     GetViewSettings( VP );
     SetViewPort( x1, y1, x2, y2, true );
     if (x > mnx) and (x < mxx) then
        begin
        px := OriginX+Round(((x-mnx)/DeltaX)*DeltaXAxis);
        GetLineSettings( LST );
```

```
          with LST do
               begin
               SetLineStyle( DottedLn, Pattern, NormWidth );
               Line( px, OriginY, px, MaxYAxis );
               SetLineStyle( LineStyle, Pattern, Thickness );
               end;
          end;
       with VP do
            SetViewPort( x1, y1, x2, y2, true );
end;

procedure Plot.DrawTickMark( x, y : integer );
var
   VP : ViewPortType;
begin
     GetViewSettings( VP );
     SetViewPort( x1, y1, x2, y2, true );
     PutPixel( x, y, GetColor );
     PutPixel( x+1, y, GetColor );
     PutPixel( x, y+1, GetColor );
     PutPixel( x+1, y+1, GetColor );
     with VP do
          SetViewPort( x1, y1, x2, y2, true );
end;

procedure Plot.PlaceXAxisValue( r : real );
var
   VP : ViewPortType;
   TST : TextSettingsType;
   px : integer;
   s  : string;
begin
     GetViewSettings( VP );
     SetViewPort( x1, y1, x2, y2, true );
     if (r > mnx) and (r < mxx) then
        begin
        GetTextSettings( TST );
        Str( (r/XSFac):XW:XD, s );
        px := OriginX+Round(((r-mnx)/DeltaX)*DeltaXAxis);
        SetTextJustify( CenterText, BottomText);
        MoveTo( px, y2-y1-BBuf-TextHeight(s));
        OutText(s);
        with TST do
             SetTextJustify( Horiz, Vert );
        DrawTickMark( px, OriginY-1 );
        end;
     with VP do
          SetViewPort( x1, y1, x2, y2, true );
end;
```

```
procedure Plot.PlaceYAxisValue( r : real );
var
   VP : ViewPortType;
   TST : TextSettingsType;
   py : integer;
   s  : string;
begin
     GetViewSettings( VP );
     SetViewPort( x1, y1, x2, y2, true );
     if (r > mny) and (r < mxy) then
        begin
        GetTextSettings( TST );
        Str( (r/YSFac):YW:YD, s );
        py := OriginY-Round(((r-mny)/DeltaY)*DeltaYAxis);
        SetTextJustify( RightText, CenterText);
        MoveTo( OriginX, py );
        OutText(s);
        with TST do
            SetTextJustify( Horiz, Vert );
        DrawTickMark( OriginX+1, py-1 );
        end;
     with VP do
         SetViewPort( x1, y1, x2, y2, true );
end;

{ Initialization code }
begin

{ None }

end.
```

Listing 4-2 tests all the features of the PlotData unit by creating a single graph in the middle of the screen and displaying the performance curve of the pump we created in the previous chapter for the NewPump object type. The output of Listing 4-2 is shown in Fig. 4.4.

Listing 4-2

```
program Listing4_2;

uses Graph, Crt, PlotData;

var
   Plot1 : Plot;
   LB, RB, TB, BB : integer;
   GraphDriver, GraphMode : integer;
   i : integer;
   tmp : real;

begin

     GraphDriver := Detect;
     InitGraph( GraphDriver, GraphMode, '' );
     Graph.SetColor( white );

     { border of 50 }
     LB := 50;
     RB := GetMaxX - LB;
     TB := 50;
     BB := GetMaxY - TB;

     Plot1.Init( 0, 90, 1, 0, 11, 1000,
                 LB, RB, TB, BB, 1, 1, 1, 1,
                 'Pump Performance Curve',
                 'Flow, gpm (x 1000)', 'Pressure, psi',
                 false);

     { draw the limits, label them }
     Plot1.DrawVGridLine( 9000 );
     Plot1.DrawVGridLine( 4000 );
     Plot1.DrawHGridLine( 75 );
     Plot1.DrawHGridLine( 60 );
     Plot1.PlaceXAxisValue( 9000 );
     Plot1.PlaceXAxisvalue( 4000 );
     Plot1.PlaceYAxisValue( 60 );
     Plot1.PlaceYAxisValue( 75 );
     { done! setting up graph }

     for i := 0 to 70 do
         begin
         { plot
               pressure = MaxPressure - K * Flow ^2
           where
               MaxPressure = 78.7
               K = 2.3 e -7
         }
```

```
        tmp := 3000+(100*i);
        Plot1.AddPoint( tmp, 78.7-(tmp*tmp*2.3e-7) );
        end;

    repeat until KeyPressed;
    RestoreCRTMode;
end.
```

Figure 4.4 — Performance curve of NewPump object (output of Listing 4-2)

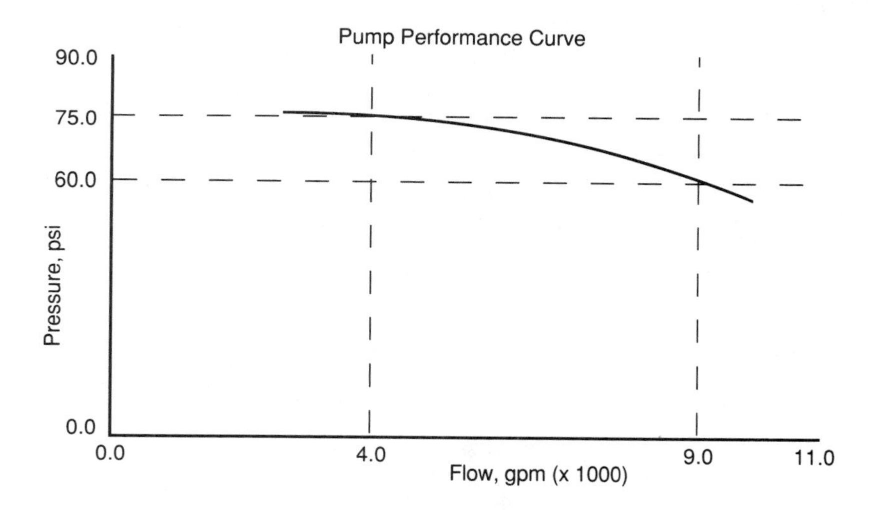

It should be pretty easy to integrate graphics into the control system simulation we developed a couple of chapters ago. To make things interesting, we'll also add a simple function consisting of a number of nested `if` statements that will cause the flow measured by FT100 (the flow meter measuring the water leaving the tank headed for distribution) to change over time. This will simulate the varying water usage that occurs over a day's time.

To get a good feel for what goes on in the system, we'll look at three plots. The first plot will show system pressure over time (we'll look at a full day, or 1440 minutes). The second plot will show the discharge flow from the pump, which will look like a series of peaks and sharp valleys. The points at which the flow becomes zero correspond to the pump turning off. The third plot will show the flow through FT100 out of the system. The code for this version of the simulation is presented in Listing 4-3, and the output is shown in Fig. 4.5.

Listing 4-3

```
program Listing4_3;

uses Tags, Crt, Graph, NewTags, PlotData;

var
   LT100,
   FT100  : Analog;
   PSL100 : LoSwitch;
   PSH100 : HiSwitch;
   EY100  : NewPump;
   time   : integer;
   SPress, PFlow, SFlow : Plot;
   GraphDriver, GraphMode : integer;
   Slice : integer;

{$F+}
function SystemPressure : real;
begin
     SystemPressure := HtToPSI(LT100.GetValue);
end;
{$F-}

procedure SetNewFlowRate( i : integer );
begin
     if i > 1400 then FT100.PutValue(4000)
     else
     if i > 1000 then FT100.PutValue(500)
     else
     if i > 800 then FT100.PutValue(3000)
     else
     if i > 620 then FT100.PutValue(6600)
     else
     if i > 480 then FT100.PutValue(8600)
     else
     if i > 240 then FT100.PutValue(7000)
     else
     if i > 120 then FT100.PutValue(4000)
```

```
     else
     if i > 60 then FT100.PutValue(5000);
end;

begin

     GraphDriver := Detect;
     InitGraph( GraphDriver, GraphMode, '' );
     Graph.SetColor( white );

     Slice := GetMaxY div 6;

     SPress.Init( 40, 100, 1,
                  0, 1440, 1,
                  50,GetMaxX-50,0,2*Slice-20,
                  0,0,1,2,
                  'SystemPressure vs. Time', 't, min', 'psi',
                  false );
     PFlow.Init( 0, 100, 100,
                  0, 1440, 1,
                  50,GetMaxX-50,2*Slice,4*Slice-20,
                  0,0,1,2,
                  'Pump Discharge Flow vs. Time', 't, min',
                  'gpm (x100)',
                  false );
     SFlow.Init( 0,100, 100,
                  0,1440, 1,
                  50,GetMaxX-50,4*Slice,6*Slice-20,
                  0,0,1,2,
                  'System Flow vs. Time', 't, min', 'gpm (x100)',
                  false);

     SPress.DrawHGridLine( 60 );
     SPress.DrawHGridLine( 75 );
     SPress.PlaceYAxisValue( 60 );
     SPress.PlaceYAxisValue( 75 );

     Quiet.On;  { to shut up the Digitals }
     LT100.Init( 'LT100', 2048, 50, 250 );
     FT100.Init( 'FT100', 2048, 0, 10000 );
     PSL100.Init( 'PSL100', 60, SystemPressure );
     PSH100.Init( 'PSH100', 75, SystemPressure );
     EY100.Init( 'EY100', off, 100, 4.8e-7, @SystemPressure);

     for time := 0 to 1440 do
          begin
          { adjust level for water leaving tank }
        LT100.PutValue( LT100.GetValue -
                            FlowToDeltaHt(FT100.GetValue) );
          { figure out PSL and PSH readings }
```

```
      PSL100.PutReading( SystemPressure );
      PSH100.PutReading( SystemPressure );

      if PSL100.GetStatus = on then
         EY100.PutStatus( ON );
      if PSH100.GetStatus = on then
         EY100.PutStatus( OFF );
      LT100.PutValue( LT100.GetValue +
                          FlowToDeltaHt( EY100.Flow ));

      SPress.AddPoint( time, SystemPressure );
      PFlow.AddPoint( time, EY100.Flow );
      SFlow.AddPoint( time, FT100.GetValue );

      SetNewFlowRate( time );
   end;

   repeat until KeyPressed;
   RestoreCRTMode;
end.
```

Figure 4.5 — Plot outputs from Listing 4-3

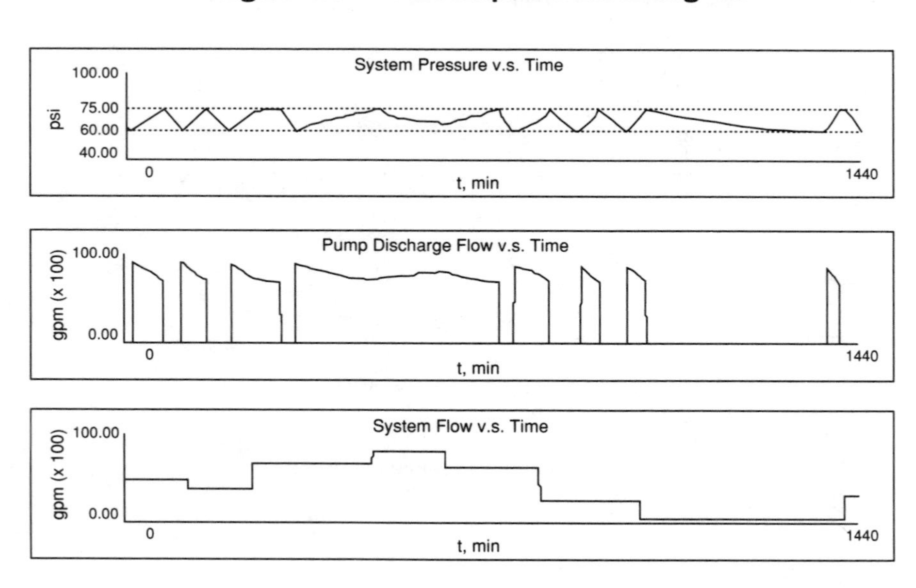

Postscript

There are a lot of possibilities for enhancement of the basic plot object type presented in this chapter. One could propose a descendant class that had the ability to open a data file, search for a particular starting point, and display the data at that point in the file. Another idea might be to write a method (probably implemented in assembly language) to allow scrolling of data within the plot area. Feel free to experiment and redesign the code.

In the next chapter, we'll tackle one of the more complicated concepts in OOP, yet one which pays rich dividends in programming flexibility: polymorphism using virtual methods.

5

VIRTUAL METHODS

I have always felt uneasy about the word "virtual." So many things in the computer field are virtual. We have virtual memory, virtual terminals, virtual windows; you get the picture. What does virtual mean? The *American Heritage Dictionary* defines the word like this:

> **vir-tu-al** *adj*. Existing or resulting in essence or effect though not in actual fact, form, or name: the virtual extinction of the buffalo.

Buffalo aside, saying something is virtual is a little like saying "it is and it isn't." A procedure that calls a virtual method doesn't have all the information it needs to make the call, and won't have that information until run time. If this sounds confusing, don't worry, just keep reading. Understanding comes as a result of letting the concept sink in.

Methods Calling Methods

Within a Turbo Pascal object method, it is not unusual to find calls to other methods (we've seen this often enough in the listings in this book). Most of the time, object behavior is straightforward enough for the compiler to be able to determine what code must eventually be executed, and so the appropriate addresses are inserted into the executable program. Sometimes, however, letting the compiler figure out everything in advance is not what we want at all. What we need (and what virtual methods provide) is a way for the compiler to do its work, while allowing the determination of what code to run to be postponed until later, when the program is run.

I can imagine some of you raising your eyebrows at the idea of the Turbo Pascal compiler leaving undone something as important as figuring out what function to call at a certain point in the program. How this is done is really beside the point: the mechanics of what happens inside the compiler is actually pretty complicated. We need only be concerned with the effects of how virtual methods are implemented.

The Elf and the VirtualElf

To better visualize what's going on, imagine an object type we'll call an `Elf`. Objects of type `Elf` specialize in running small errands to a fictitious grocery store. Each `Elf` object has a name (which we'll supply in an `.Init` procedure) and two methods. The first method, named `.GoShopping`, simply calls the second method, named `.ShopScript`. The method `.ShopScript` prints a brief summary of what happens when the `Elf` goes shopping for us. `Elf` objects are not very flexible; in fact, every time they go to the store, they buy eggs and milk, whether we need them or not. Listing 5-1 presents a short Turbo Pascal program that implements the `Elf` object type's behavior, and the program output is shown in Fig. 5.1.

Listing 5-1

```
program Listing5_1;

type

Elf = object
      Name : string;
      constructor Init( Monicker : string );
      procedure ShopScript;
      procedure GoShopping;
      end;
```

```
constructor Elf.Init( Monicker : string );
begin
     Name := Monicker;
end;

procedure Elf.ShopScript;
begin
     writeln( '<Door slams as ', Name, ' leaves>');
     writeln( '<long pause.......>' );
     writeln( '<Door slams as ', Name, ' returns>');
     writeln( Name, ': I went to the store and bought milk and eggs.');
end;

procedure Elf.GoShopping;
begin
     ShopScript;
end;


var
   Jay : Elf;

begin
     Jay.Init( 'JAY' );

     Jay.GoShopping;
end.
```

Figure 5.1 — Output of Listing 5-1

```
<Door slams as JAY leaves>
<long pause.......>
<Door slams as JAY returns>
JAY: I went to the store and bought milk and eggs
```

Now let's imagine a second object type we'll call a `VirtualElf`. Like `Elf`, a `VirtualElf` has a name, and the same two methods. A `VirtualElf` behaves differently in that he calls us from the store to find out what we want him to buy. We will take advantage of the existing code for the `Elf` object type and make the `VirtualElf` a descendant type that inherits the `Name` property and the `.Init` and `.GoShopping` methods, while supplying its own `.ShopScript` method (which overrides that of the `Elf` object type). The code for the VirtualElf is shown in Listing 5-2, and sample output is shown in Figure 5.2.

Listing 5-2

```
program Listing5_2;


type

Elf = object
      Name : string;
      constructor Init( Monicker : string );
      procedure ShopScript; { virtual;}
      procedure GoShopping;
      end;

VirtualElf = object( Elf )
             procedure ShopScript; { virtual; }
             end;

constructor Elf.Init( Monicker : string );
begin
     Name := Monicker;
end;

procedure Elf.ShopScript;
begin
     writeln( '<Door slams as ', Name, ' leaves>');
     writeln( '<long pause.......>' );
     writeln( '<Door slams as ', Name, ' returns>');
     writeln( Name, ': I went to the store and bought milk and eggs.');
end;

procedure Elf.GoShopping;
begin
     ShopScript;
end;

procedure VirtualElf.ShopScript;
var
   ShoppingList : string;
begin
     writeln( Name, ': When I get to the store, I''ll call you.');
     writeln( '<Door slams as ', Name, ' leaves>');
     writeln( '<pause.......>' );
     writeln( 'PHONE: Brrring!');
     writeln( '<pick up phone>' );
     writeln( 'YOU: Hello?' );
```

```
    writeln( Name, ': Hi. What do you want me to buy?' );
    write( 'YOU (enter something): ');
    readln( ShoppingList );
    writeln( Name, ': Gotcha. Bye.');
    writeln( '<hang up phone>' );
    writeln( '<pause.......>' );
    writeln( '<Door slams as ', Name, ' returns>');
    writeln( Name, ': As you requested, I bought: ', ShoppingList );
end;

var
   Jay : Elf;
   Ray : VirtualElf;

begin
    Jay.Init( 'JAY' );
    Ray.Init( 'RAY' );

    Jay.GoShopping;
    Ray.GoShopping;
end.
```

Figure 5.2 — Output of Listing 5-2

```
<Door slams as JAY leaves>
<long pause.......>
<Door slams as JAY returns>
JAY: I went to the store and bought milk and eggs
<Door slams as RAY leaves>
<long pause.......>
<Door slams as RAY returns>
RAY: I went to the store and bought milk and eggs
```

Now, we would expect the `VirtualElf` object to execute its own version of `.ShopScript`, but contrary to our expectations, both Jay (our `Elf` object) and Ray (our `VirtualElf`) behave in exactly the same manner! Let's take a look at Fig. 5.3 to see what happened.

We've learned that when a descendant object type inherits a method from an ancestor, calling the inherited method starts execution of the ancestor's compiled method (as opposed to a copy of the method. This is shown in Fig. 5.3a. The code for the method `Elf.GoShopping` starts at a certain address, call it X. When the

`.ShopScript` method is called, execution jumps to a specific address: that of `Elf.ShopScript`, call it Y.

Figure 5.3a — What occurs when VirtualElf.GoShopping is called with Early Binding

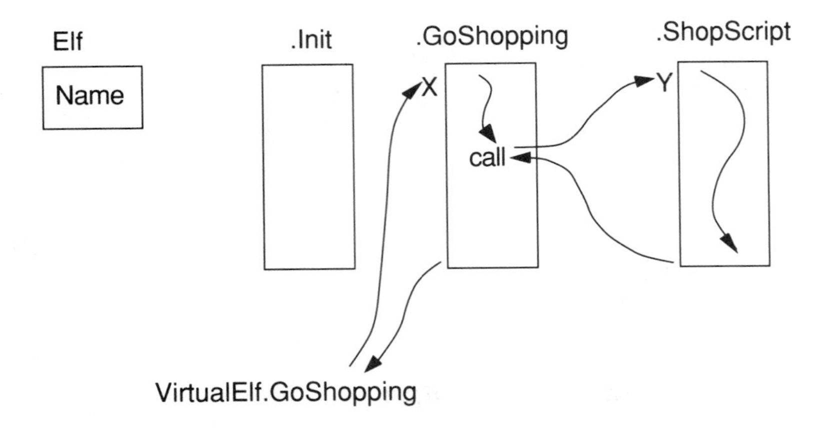

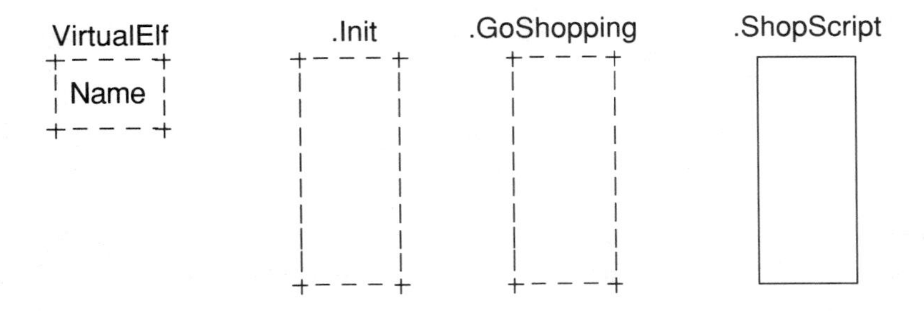

Note: Properties and methods shown with dotted outlines are inherited.

Figure 5.3b — What occurs when VirtualElf.GoShopping is called with Late Binding

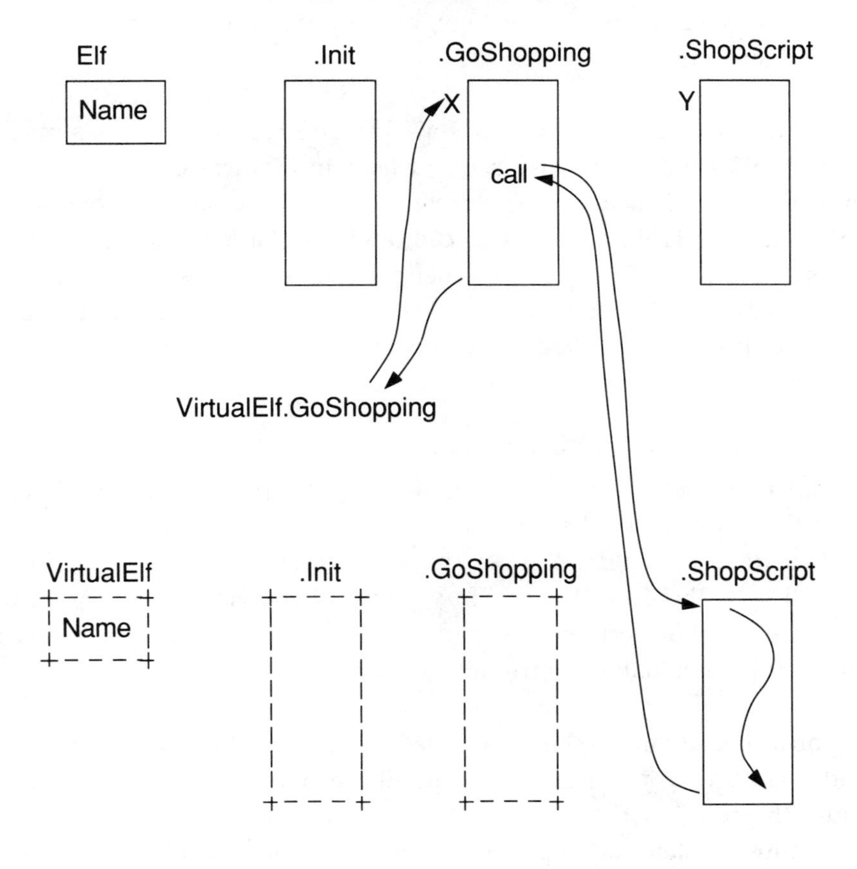

Note: Properties and methods shown with dotted outlines are inherited.

Recall that when the program is compiled, references to any procedure or function addresses must be resolved at the time of compilation (also called compile time, for short) so that the code may be properly processed. This means that when the code for `Elf.GoShopping` was compiled, Turbo Pascal determined the address of `Elf.ShopScript` and inserted it to the code. (This insertion is often called "binding," and since it occurs at compile time — as opposed to run time — it is called "early binding." By analogy, binding that occurs at run time is called "late binding.")

If you look at the assembly code for `Elf.GoShopping` (for example, using the Turbo Debugger discussed later in the next chapter), you'll find that the call to the procedure `.ShopScript` specifies one and only one permissible address to call, and that happens to be the address of `Elf.ShopScript`. So, when the procedure `Jay.GoShopping` is called, execution starts at the address of the inherited `Elf.GoShopping` method, which always calls `Elf.ShopScript` and returns.

What we want, of course, is for the method `Elf.GoShopping` to recognize that it should call the `.ShopScript` procedure associated with the object that called it in the first place. If `Jay.GoShopping` is executing, it should call `Jay.ShopScript`; if `Ray.GoShopping` is executing, it should call `Ray.ShopScript`. In other words, we want to be able to hold off specifying the address of the procedure to execute until we actually get around to calling it!

If you thing about it, this is a little like the situation with our `Elf` and `VirtualElf` object types: the Elf behaves in only one way because the code for the `.ShopScript` method was written that way; everything is laid out up front in order to do his job. The same method for the `VirtualElf`, on the other hand, is flexible enough to be able to accept input at run time, thus allowing the "behavior" of the elf to be modified at run time despite the code for executing `VirtualElf.ShopScript` being every bit as "cast in concrete" as that for `Elf.ShopScript`. While the `Elf` depends on "early binding," the `VirtualElf` utilizes "late binding" and becomes more useful in the process.

Analogously, by declaring a method to be virtual, it is compiled in such a way that the identification of which method to run is held off until later, when the program is run.

Virtual Syntax

There are a couple of syntactic changes that must be implemented before we can make use of virtual methods. First, every instance of an object type must be initialized using a special procedure called a *constructor*. The net effect of using a constructor is the creation of a 16-bit field, called a Virtual Method Table (VMT) field, in the object type (see Figure 5.4 for a comparison of the Elf object type both without and with virtual methods). Since we've gotten in the habit of defining a procedure called .Init for nearly every object type we've defined so far, all we really have to remember to do is declare .Init to be a constructor instead of a procedure. The rest of the code (for initializing properties, for example) remains the same.

Figure 5.4 — Comparison of Elf declared with and without virtual method

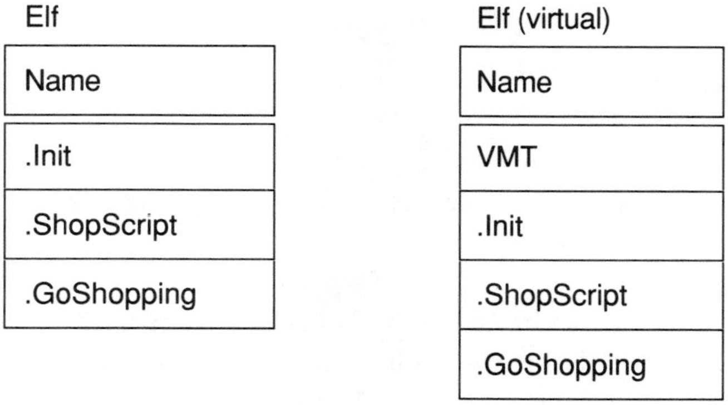

Elf	Elf (virtual)
Name	Name
.Init	VMT
.ShopScript	.Init
.GoShopping	.ShopScript
	.GoShopping

The second change we must make is the inclusion of the keyword virtual at the end of the line that declares a virtual method. If we change the lines that declare the method .ShopScript for both the Elf and VirtualElf object types in Listing 5-2 to read:

```
procedure ShopScript; virtual;
```

the problem we saw in the output in Figure 5.2 disappears. The output of the modified Listing 5-2 (LIST5-2A.PAS on the disk) is presented in Figure 5.5.

Figure 5.5 — Output of modified Listing 5-2

```
<Door slams as JAY leaves>
<long pause.......>
<Door slams as JAY returns>
JAY: I went to the store and bought milk and eggs
<Door slams as RAY leaves>
<pause.......>
PHONE: Brrring!
<pick up phone>
YOU: Hello?
RAY: Hi.  What do you want me to buy?
YOU (enter something): champagne, caviar, and bon-bons
RAY: Gotcha. Bye.
<hang up phone>
<Door slams as RAY returns>
RAY: As you requested, I bought champagne, caviar, and bon-bons.
```

Getting Practical

While the `Elf` and `VirtualElf` object types may be of use to us for illustration of the difference between ordinary and virtual behavior, they do lack practicality.

We first mentioned virtual methods back in Chapter 2 in the discussion of the methods for the digital inputs that we later packaged into the `Tags` unit in Listing 3-1. In Listing 5-3, we present the specific portions of that code that could benefit from the introduction of virtual methods.

Listing 5-3

```
{ Declarations from the interface section of Listing 3-1 }

DInput = object(Digital)
            Setpoint  : real;
            Reading   : real;
            procedure PutSetpoint( NewSetpoint : real );
            end;

HiSwitch = object(DInput)
           procedure Init( ATag : string;
                           ASetpoint : real;
                           AReading : real);
           procedure PutReading( NewReading : real );
           end;

LoSwitch = object(DInput)
           procedure Init( ATag : string;
                           ASetpoint : real;
                           AReading : real);
           procedure PutReading( NewReading : real );
           end;

{ Procedure definitions from the implementation section of Listing
3-1 }

procedure LoSwitch.Init( ATag : string;
                         ASetpoint : real;
                         AReading : real);
begin
     Tag.Init( ATag );
     DInput.PutSetpoint( ASetpoint );
     PutReading( AReading );
end;

procedure LoSwitch.PutReading( NewReading : real );
begin
     Reading := NewReading;
     if Reading <= Setpoint then
        Status := true
     else
        Status := false;
end;

procedure HiSwitch.Init( ATag : string;
                         ASetpoint : real;
                         AReading : real);
begin
     Tag.Init( ATag );
```

```
     DInput.PutSetpoint( ASetpoint );
     PutReading( AReading );
end;

procedure HiSwitch.PutReading( NewReading : real );
begin
     Reading := NewReading;
     if Reading >= Setpoint then
        Status := true
     else
        Status := false;
end;
```

The first thing that jumps out at us about this listing fragment is the fact that the code for both LoSwitch.Init and HiSwitch.Init is identical. Both methods call the same (inherited) Tag.Init method and the same (inherited) DInput.PutSetpoint method. Only each respective .PutReading method is different and that (assuming that virtual methods didn't exist) is what forces the .Init methods in Listing 3-1 to be part of the LoSwitch and HiSwitch object types.

If you didn't know what you now know about virtual methods, you might think that both .Init methods could be abstracted, or combined into one method belonging to the DInput object type. The code fragments in Listing 5-4 do this. Notice that now, neither the LoSwitch nor the HiSwitch object type has an .Init method and the DInput object type has a .PutReading method defined for it. We've included a writeln call in DInput.PutReading for purposes of illustration.

Listing 5-4

```
{ Declarations from the interface section of Listing 3-1 }

DInput = object(Digital)
           Setpoint  : real;
           Reading   : real;
           procedure Init( ATag : string;
                           ASetpoint : real;
                           AReading : real);
```

```
            procedure PutReading( NewReading : real );
                {should be virtual; }
            procedure PutSetpoint( NewSetpoint : real );
            end;

HiSwitch = object(DInput)
           procedure PutReading( NewReading : real );
                {should be virtual; }
           end;

LoSwitch = object(DInput)
           procedure PutReading( NewReading : real );
                {should be virtual; }

           end;


{ Procedure definitions from the implementation section of Listing 3-1 }

procedure DInput.Init( ATag : string;
                       ASetpoint : real;
                       AReading : real);
begin
     Tag.Init( ATag );
     DInput.PutSetpoint( ASetpoint );
     PutReading( AReading );
end;

procedure DInput.PutReading( NewReading : real );
begin
     writeln( 'If this prints, .PutReading should be virtual!' );
end;

procedure LoSwitch.PutReading( NewReading : real );
begin
     Reading := NewReading;
     if Reading <= Setpoint then
        Status := true
     else
        Status := false;
end;

{procedure HiSwitch.Init( ATag : string;
            ASetpoint : real;
            AReading : real); }  { DELETED! }

procedure HiSwitch.PutReading( NewReading : real );
begin
     Reading := NewReading;
     if Reading >= Setpoint then
        Status := true
```

```
      else
         Status := false;
end;
```

Listing 5-5 provides a short test program to see what results our modifications obtained; output is shown in Figure 5.6. If you run the program, you'll notice that the `DInput.PutReading` method was executed twice; once for the `LS` object, again for the `HS` object. In light of our earlier discussion, this behavior was to be expected: when it came time to call the `.PutReading` method, `DInput` called its own version instead of that of its descendants.

Figure 5.6 — Output of Listing 5-5 without virtual methods in NewTags unit

```
If this prints, .PutReading should be virtual!
If this prints, .PutReading should be virtual!
Tag1: Setpoint = 3.40; Reading = 0.00
Tag2: Setpoint = 6.70; Reading = 0.00
```

Now uncomment the keyword virtual for the `.PutReading` method, change `.Init` from a procedure to a constructor, and recompile and rerun Listing 5-5. You should get output that looks like Figure 5.7. Note that now, the `LS` and `HS` objects are correctly instantiated, which is a result of declaring `.PutReading` to be virtual.

Listing 5-5

```
program Listing5_5;

uses NewTags;   { Tags modified to abstract .Init method in
                  DInput type and make .PutReading virtual.}

var
   HS : HiSwitch;
   LS : LoSwitch;
begin
     HS.Init('Tag1', 3.4, 2.1 );
     LS.Init('Tag2', 6.7, 10.2 );
     writeln( HS.TagNumber, ': Setpoint = ', HS.Setpoint:2:2,
              '; Reading = ', HS.Reading:2:2 );
     writeln( LS.TagNumber, ': Setpoint = ', LS.Setpoint:2:2,
              '; Reading = ', LS.Reading:2:2 );
end.
```

Figure 5.7 — Output of Listing 5-5 with virtual methods in NewTags unit

```
Tag1: Setpoint = 3.40; Reading = 2.10
Tag2: Setpoint = 6.70; Reading = 10.20
```

Virtual by Design

You might get the impression from the previous discussion that determining whether or not a method needs to be declared as virtual is a somewhat trial-and-error affair. It can be, of course, but doesn't have to be. How can we tell whether a method needs to be virtual (and consequently, whether an object type must have a constructor)?

A telltale indicator is whether there is interaction between an inherited and an overridden method in a descendant object type. Notice how, in the Elf/VirtualElf program, the method `.GoShopping` (inherited) called `.ShopScript` (overridden), and how, in the Tags example, the method `.Init` (inherited) called `.PutReading` (overridden). Let's do one more example, and see this interaction at work again.

We are given the task of writing a program to conjugate the present tense of the three main groups of French verbs: those that end in *ir*, in *er*, and in *re*. (If you are unfamiliar with the conjugation of French verbs, consider the following paragraph to be the specification for a rather esoteric string manipulation.)

Consider three classes of strings ending in *ir*, *er*, and *re*. We define six types of operations on these strings: FPS, SPS, TPS, FPP, SPP, TPP.

For each class of string, we remove the last two letters (*ir*, *er*, or *re*) and, depending on the operation, append a string in accordance with the following table:

	String to append for class ending in:		
Operation	**-ir**	**-er**	**-re**
FPS	'is'	'e'	's'
SPS	'is'	'es'	's'
TPS	'it'	'e'	' ' (blank)
FPP	'issons'	'ons'	'ons'
SPP	'issez'	'ez'	'ez'
TPP	'issent'	'ent'	'ent '

Let's look at some issues related to the design the object types we'll use in the program shown in Listing 5-6. First, since the verb endings won't change, we can declare them as arrays of constants, one for each type of verb. We will have a base object type called `Verb`, which will have a property that holds the general form of the verb (we'll call this property by its grammatical name, which is `Infinitive`), and another property (which we'll call the `Root`) to hold the infinitive with the last two letters truncated. In addition to an `.Init` method for instance instantiation, we'll also need a method `.ConjugateVerb` that prints all six possible forms of the verb in the present tense. To make things a bit flexible, the method `.ConjugateVerb` will call a method `.VerbForm` that actually concatenates the `Root` and the appropriate ending, depending on the type of verb. We now have the combination of an inherited method calling an overridden method, so thus, `.VerbForm` should be declared as a virtual method. The output of Listing 5-6 is shown in Fig. 5.8.

Listing 5-6

```
program Listing5_6;

type

Person = ( fps, sps, tps, fpp, spp, tpp );
Ending = array[fps..tpp] of string;
```

```
const
ER_Nominative : Ending
                    = ( 'e', 'es', 'e', 'ons', 'ez', 'ent' );
IR_Nominative : Ending
                    = ( 'is', 'is', 'it', 'issons', 'issez', 'issent');
RE_Nominative : Ending
                    = ( 's', 's', '', 'ons', 'ez', 'ent');

type
Verb = object
       Infinitive : string;
       Root       : string;
       constructor Init( TheVerb : string );
       function VerbForm( E : Person ) : string; virtual;
       procedure ConjugateVerb;
       end;

RE_Verb = object( Verb )
          function VerbForm( E : Person ) : string; virtual;
          end;


IR_Verb = object( Verb )
          function VerbForm( E : Person ) : string; virtual;
          end;

ER_Verb = object( Verb )
          function VerbForm( E : Person ) : string; virtual;
          end;

constructor Verb.Init( TheVerb : string );
begin
     Infinitive := TheVerb;
     Root := Copy( TheVerb, 1, (Length(TheVerb) - 2) );
end;

{ This function is needed to be able to compile the .ConjugateVerb
  method }
function Verb.VerbForm( E: Person ) : string;
begin
     VerbForm := '';
end;

function ER_Verb.VerbForm( E : Person ) : string;
begin
     VerbForm := Concat( Root, ER_Nominative[E] )
end;

function IR_Verb.VerbForm( E : Person ) : string;
begin
     VerbForm := Concat( Root, IR_Nominative[E] )
end;

function RE_Verb.VerbForm( E : Person ) : string;
begin
     VerbForm := Concat( Root, RE_Nominative[E] )
```

```
end;

procedure Verb.ConjugateVerb;
begin
     writeln( 'Conjugation of the verb ', Infinitive, ':' );
     writeln( 'je ', VerbForm( fps ) );
     writeln( 'tu ', VerbForm( sps ) );
     writeln( 'il ', VerbForm( tps ) );
     writeln( 'nous ', VerbForm( fpp ) );
     writeln( 'vous ', VerbForm( spp ) );
     writeln( 'ils ', VerbForm( tpp ) );
end;

var
   repondre : RE_Verb;
   finir    : IR_Verb;
   manquer  : ER_Verb;
begin
     repondre.Init( 'repondre' );
     finir.Init( 'finir' );
     manquer.Init( 'manquer' );

     repondre.ConjugateVerb;
     finir.ConjugateVerb;
     manquer.ConjugateVerb;

end.
```

Figure 5.8 — Output of Listing 5-6

```
Conjugation of the verb repondre:
je reponds
tu reponds
il repond
nous reponds
vous repondez
ils repondent
Conjugation of the verb finir:
je finis
tu finis
il finit
nous finissons
vous finissez
ils finissent
Conjugation of the verb manquer:
je manque
tu manques
il manque
nous manquons
vous manquez
ils manquent
```

Now admittedly, we could have designed (with some clumsiness) `.ConjugateVerb` in such a way that it did not call any other methods, so that each type of verb had its own unique version of `.ConjugateVerb`. However, by breaking things up the way we have, we can easily extend our program to accommodate verbs that do not conform to the rules implemented in Listing 5-6. For example, Listing 5-7 introduces the irregular verb object type, which doesn't follow the rules described above for ordinary verbs.

Listing 5-7

```
program Listing5_7;

uses FrenchVb;  { Listing5_6 converted to a unit. }

type

IrregularVerb = object( Verb )
                PresentTense: Ending;
                constructor Init( Inf, FPSin, SPSin, TPSin,
                                  FPPlu, SPPlu, TPPlu : string );
                function VerbForm( E : Person ) : string; virtual;
                end;

constructor IrregularVerb.Init;
begin
     Verb.Init( 'etre' );
     PresentTense[fps] := FPSin;
     PresentTense[sps] := SPSin;
     PresentTense[tps] := TPSin;
     PresentTense[fpp] := FPPlu;
     PresentTense[spp] := SPPlu;
     PresentTense[tpp] := TPPlu;
end;

function IrregularVerb.VerbForm( E : Person ) : string;
begin
     VerbForm := PresentTense[ E ];
end;

var
   repondre : RE_Verb;
   finir    : IR_Verb;
   manquer  : ER_Verb;
   aller    : IrregularVerb;
```

```
begin
     repondre.Init( 'repondre' );
     finir.Init( 'finir' );
     manquer.Init( 'manquer' );
     aller.Init( 'aller', 'vais', 'vas', 'va', 'allons', ''allez', 'vont');

     repondre.ConjugateVerb;
     finir.ConjugateVerb;
     manquer.ConjugateVerb;
     aller.ConjugateVerb;

end.
```

Running Listing 5-7 requires converting Listing 5-6 into a unit, which if you recall, is accomplished as follows. First, pick a suitable name for the unit and save the file using that name. Let's save Listing 5-6 as FRENCHVB.PAS. Next, we replace the line reading

```
program Listing 5_6;
```

with the statements

```
unit FrenchVb;
interface
```

at the top of the listing. Next, we insert the statement

```
implementation
```

just before the declaration of the constructor `Verb.Init`. Finally, we delete the variable declarations and the begin/end loop at the end of the listing, leaving just the statement:

```
end.
```

to complete the file. Now save the file and compile it to generate a .TPU file (used by other programs that `use` the FrenchVb unit.

This ability to implement many forms of behavior that is nevertheless comprehensible to existing object types is called *polymorphism* (literally meaning *many forms* in Greek), and is an important characteristic in object-oriented systems.

Postscript

You might ask: If virtual methods are so all-fired powerful, why not use them all the time? Why not build virtual methods into Turbo Pascal so that all methods are virtual?

The answer to these questions is basically this: you don't want to overdo using virtual methods because they slow you down. Every time your code calls a virtual method, the CPU executes some extra code to figure out just exactly what code to execute. If you've played around with any interpreted languages, you know that interpreted code runs significantly slower than compiled code, mostly because the computer has to figure out what to do before doing it. While the use of virtual methods in Turbo Pascal isn't the same as interpreting a BASIC program, there is a similarity from the point of view of performance. When you must use virtual methods, use them; otherwise, avoid them.

In the next chapter, we'll take a look at linked lists in Turbo Pascal, in an implementation different from the one that comes with the Turbo Pascal software. We'll then use the developed code in conjunction with the Turbo Pascal environment debugging facilities and the Turbo Debugger to learn more about both linked lists and debugging in Turbo Pascal.

6

LIST: AN ALL-PURPOSE OBJECT TYPE

I sometimes think lists are as essential to our lives as is the air we breathe. We are surrounded by lists of one form or another: telephone directories, bank statements, shopping lists, "to do" lists, etc. Some lists are not so obvious. For example, sentences may be considered to be lists of words; documents, lists of sentences. Lists find extensive application in computing. There is even a language (LISP) whose central theme is the processing of lists.

In this chapter, we'll design a `List` object type of our own that doesn't use streams and is capable of finding objects that satisfy specified criteria. We'll then use the Turbo Debugger to help illustrate the behavior of our `List` type after making some general observations about debugging in Turbo Pascal.

Lists

The linked list is a well-known data structure in conventional programming practice. By subtly varying the way a list is implemented, we may arrive at a number of constructs such as trees and graphs. The list is an ideal candidate for implementation as a Turbo Pascal object type because its essentials lend themselves well to abstraction and encapsulation. A schematic diagram of a bare-bones linked list is shown in Figure 6.1.

Figure 6.1 — Schematic diagram of a linked list

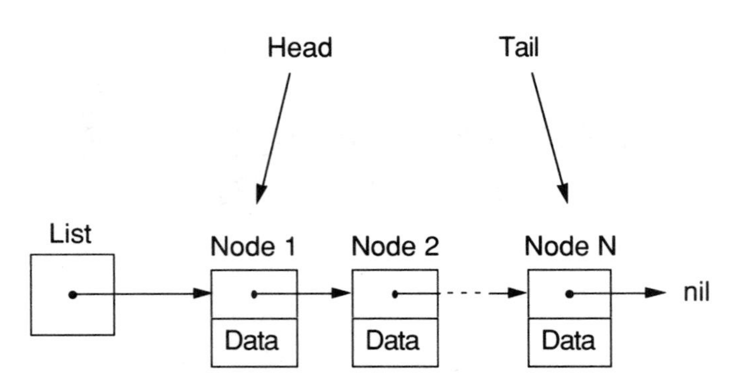

Classic Linked List

The building block of a linked list is a data structure called a node. While there are many possible ways of implementing a node, the basic structure consists of a pointer (to the node data type) and one or more fields to contain the data belonging to the node. The list itself consists simply of a pointer (also to the node data type); it is, in effect a landmark. If we can access the list, we can access all the nodes in the list. In use, the node pointer in the list variable points at the start of the linked list, commonly called the "head" of the list.

If you want to add something to the list, you trace your way along the chain of node pointers until you reach the end, or "tail," of the list, and then set the pointer of the tail to the address of the new node. Figure 6.2 illustrates the structure of a list before and after adding a node.

Figure 6.2 — List structure before and after adding a node

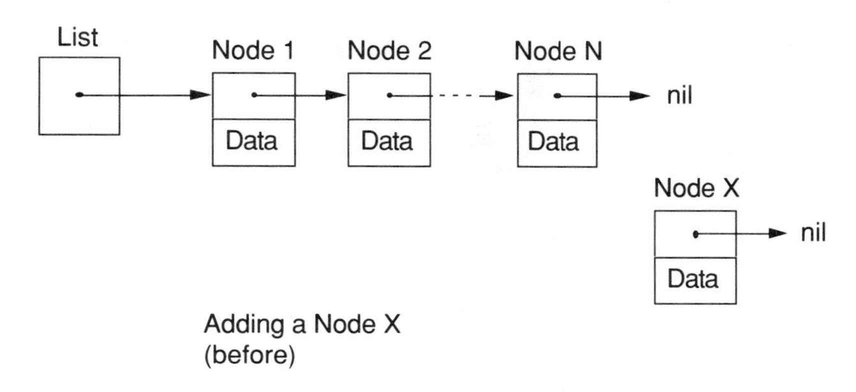

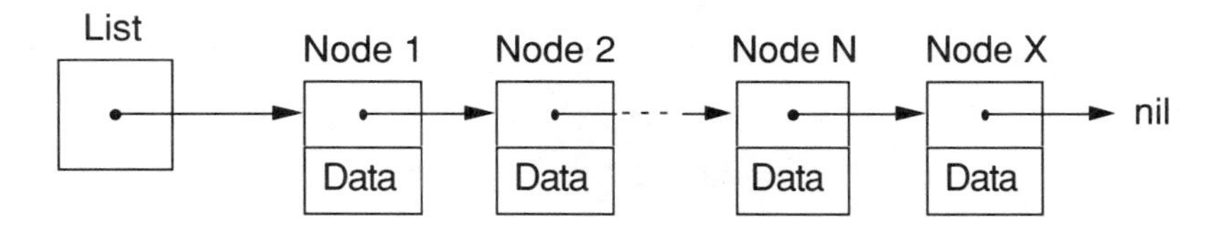

Adding a Node X
(after)

Taking a node out of a list is somewhat more complicated, but nevertheless straightforward. You again trace your way along the node pointers until you find the node you want to delete. You then copy the address of the node it points to into the corresponding pointer of the node that points to it. Figure 6.3 illustrates this procedure.

Figure 6.3 — Procedure for a taking a node out of a list

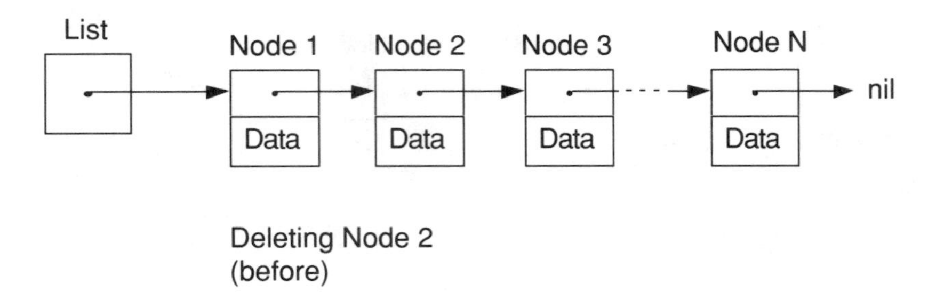

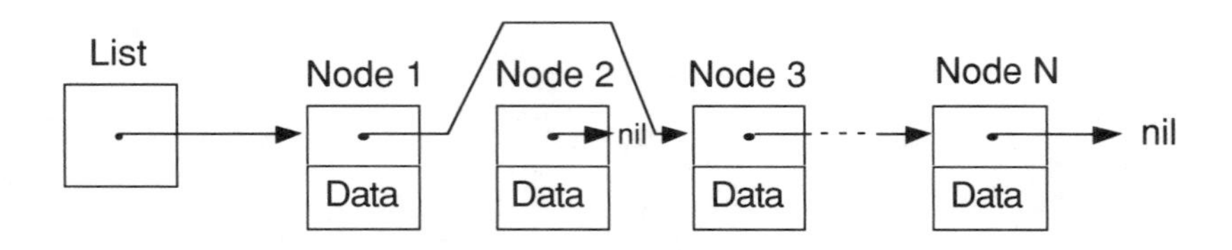

Deleting Node 2 (after)

As alluded to previously, there are hundreds of ways to implement linked lists, and an equal number of useful manipulations that can be devised for their efficient use for a particular purpose. For example, by adding items to one end of the list and removing them from the other, you can implement what is called a first-in-first-out (FIFO) queue, which might be useful in simulating the behavior of a line, say, at a bank teller's window. By adding and removing items from the same end of a list, you get a last-in-first-out (LIFO) structure, which is commonly called a stack in computer circles. A small but useful set of properties and methods has been implemented in the unit LISTOBJ.PAS, which is presented in Listing 6-1, and described in the following sections.

Listing 6-1

```
unit ListObj;
{$A+,B-,D+,E+,F-,I+,L+,N-,O-,R-,S+,V+}
{$M 16384,0,655360}

interface

type
    NodePtr = ^Node;
    ListPtr = ^List;
    ListDemonType = function( pNode : pointer ) : boolean;

    List = object
            Head   : NodePtr;
            Tail   : NodePtr;
            Cursor : NodePtr;
            NMem   : integer;
            FindObjectDemon : ListDemonType;
            constructor Init;
            destructor Done;
            procedure Append( pNode : NodePtr );
            procedure Prepend( pNode : NodePtr );
            function PopFirst       : pointer;
            function PopLast        : pointer;
            function PopCursor      : pointer;
            function GetCursor      : pointer;
            function FindObject: boolean;
            function FindNextObject : boolean;
            end;

    Node = object
         pNext : NodePtr;
         Size : integer;
          procedure Init;
         procedure AppendToList( var AList : List ) ;
         procedure PrependToList( var AList : List ) ;
         end;

function FindAll( pNode :pointer ) : boolean;

implementation

constructor List.Init;
begin
     Head := nil;
     Tail := nil;
     Cursor := nil;
     NMem := 0;
     FindObjectDemon := FindAll;
```

```
 end;
destructor List.Done;
begin
     while (NMem>0) and
          (PopFirst<> nil) do
          {nothing};
end;

 procedure List.Append( pNode : NodePtr );
 begin
      if Head = nil then
         begin
         Head := pNode;
         Tail := pNode;
         Inc(NMem);
         end
      else
         begin
         Tail^.pNext := pNode;
         Tail := pNode;
         Inc(NMem);
         end;
      pNode^.pNext := nil;
 end;

 procedure List.Prepend( pNode : NodePtr );
 begin
      if Head = nil then
         begin
         Head := pNode;
         Tail := pNode;
         pNode^.pNext := nil;
         Inc(NMem);
         end
      else
         begin
         pNode^.pNext := Head;
         Head := pNode;
         Inc(NMem);
         end;
 end;


 function List.PopFirst : pointer;
 begin
      if NMem = 1 then begin
         PopFirst := Head;
         Head := nil;
         Tail := nil;
         Cursor := nil;
         Dec(NMem);
```

```
            end
         else
            if NMem > 0 then
               begin
               PopFirst := Head;
               if Head <> Tail then
                  begin
                  if Cursor = Head then
                     Cursor := Head^.pNext;
                  Head := Head^.pNext;
                  end;
               Dec(Nmem);
               end
            else
               begin
               Writeln('ERROR: Attempt to remove element from empty list.');
               PopFirst := nil;
               end;
 end;

function List.PopLast : pointer;
 var
 pTempNode : NodePtr;
 begin
         if NMem = 1 then begin
            PopLast := Head;
            Head := nil;
            Tail := nil;
            Cursor := nil;
            Dec(NMem);
            end
         { if there are members in List }
         else
            if NMem > 0 then
               begin
               { set pNode to be the Head }
               pTempNode := Head;
               { until we find a node that points at the Tail, keep moving }
               while pTempNode^.pNext <> Tail do
                     pTempNode := pTempNode^.pNext;
               { retrieve the object }
               PopLast := Tail;
               { the next-to-last node will point at nothing }
               pTempNode^.pNext := nil;
               { if the Cursor pointed at the old Tail }
               if Cursor = Tail then
                  Cursor := pTempNode;
               Tail := pTempNode;
               Dec(Nmem);
               end
            else
```

```
            begin
            Writeln('ERROR: Attempt to remove element from empty list.');
            PopLast := nil;
            end;
end;

function List.PopCursor : pointer;
var
pTempNode : NodePtr;



begin
     if NMem = 1 then
        begin
        PopCursor := Cursor;
        Head := nil;
        Tail := nil;
        Cursor := nil;
        Dec(NMem);
        end
     else if NMem > 0 then
        begin
        PopCursor := Cursor;
        Dec(Nmem);
        if Cursor <> Head then
           begin
           pTempNode := Head;
           while pTempNode^.pNext <> Cursor do
                 pTempNode := pTempNode^.pNext;
           { pTempNode points at object in front of Cursor }
           if Cursor <> Tail then
              begin
              { if Cursor is not pointing at Tail of List }
              { make the object in front of the Cursor point }
              { to the object in back of the cursor }
              pTempNode^.pNext := Cursor^.pNext;
              end
           else
              begin
              { if the Cursor is pointing at the Tail, }
              { make the object in front of the Cursor point to nil }
              { and adjust the Tail }
              pTempNode^.pNext := nil;
              Tail := pTempNode;
              end;
           { set Cursor to point at object in front of itself }
           Cursor := pTempNode;
           end
        else
           begin { if Cursor = Head }
```

```
            Head := Head^.pNext;
            Cursor := Cursor^.pNext;
            end
         end
      else
         begin
         Writeln('ERROR: Attempt to remove element from empty list.');
         PopCursor := nil;
         end;
end;


function List.GetCursor : pointer
begin
      if NMem > 0 then
         begin
         GetCursor := Cursor;
         { if the Cursor is pointing at the tail, then point it at nil }
         { so that we know we've 'GetCursor'ed the last item in the list }
         if Cursor = Tail then
            Cursor := nil
         else
            Cursor := Cursor^.pNext;
         end
      else
         GetCursor := nil;
end;

function List.FindObject : boolean;
begin
      Cursor := Head;
      FindObject := FindNextObject;
end;

function List.FindNextObject : boolean;
var FoundStatus, AtEnd : boolean;
begin
{ initialize 'FoundStatus' and 'AtEnd' flags }
      FoundStatus := false;
      AtEnd := false;
      { If there are objects in the list and the Cursor is not nil }
      { (indicating that we did a GetCursor operation on the last object }
      {  in the list) }
      if (NMem > 0) and (Cursor <> nil) then
         begin
         while (AtEnd = false) and (FoundStatus = false) do
               begin
               if FindObjectDemon( Cursor ) = true then
                  FoundStatus := true
               else
                  if Cursor^.pNext <> nil then
```

```
                    Cursor := Cursor^.pNext
                 else
                    AtEnd := true
              end;
        end;
     FindNextObject := FoundStatus;
end;

procedure Node.Init(ASize : integer);
begin
     pNext := nil;
     Size := ASize;
end;

procedure Node.AppendToList( var AList : List ) ;
begin
     if AList.Head = nil then
        begin
        AList.Head := @Self;
        AList.Tail := @Self;
        Inc(AList.NMem)
        end
     else
        begin
        AList.Tail^.pNext := @Self;
        AList.Tail := @Self;
        Inc(AList.NMem);
        end;
     pNext := nil;

procedure Node.PrependToList( var AList : List ) ;
begin
     if AList.Head = nil then
        begin
        AList.Head := @Self;
        AList.Tail := @Self;
        pNext := nil;
        Inc(AList.NMem)
        end
     else
        begin
        pNext := AList.Head;
        AList.Head := @Self;
        Inc(AList.NMem);
        end;
end;

{$F+}
function FindAll( pNode : pointer ) : boolean;
{$F-}
begin
```

```
    FindAll := true;
end;

end.
```

The Node Object Type

The object type for the Node in our implementation of the linked list will have two properties: a pointer to an object of type Node, and an integer to hold the Size of the Node. Anything we intend to place in a list will be a descendant type of Node. We shall also give the Node object enough intelligence to understand how to attach itself to either the beginning or end of a list, so we have the methods .PrependToList and .AppendToList, respectively.

If you caught yourself raising your eyebrows at the idea of a node attaching itself to a list, it's probably because you're familiar with doing it the other way around (that is, hand the node to the list for processing). While there is nothing wrong with passing a Node as a parameter to a List object, there is equally nothing wrong with passing a List as a parameter to a Node! This is an important point, so let's review it in detail. There are basically two approaches to getting a data entered into a linked list. The first approach hands a node pointer to a List variable, resulting in a line of code that might look something like:

```
ListVariable.AddNodeToSelf( NodePointer );
```

The alternative approach hands the identity of a List object to a node, which proceeds to attach itself to the List, resulting in a line of code that looks like:

```
NodeVariable.AddSelfToList( ListVariable );.
```

I liken this situation to a new student arriving for a first day at school. On the one hand, the principal may call the teacher down to the office to escort the student up to the classroom, which is analogous to the program handing the node to the list. On the other hand, the principal may give the student a note containing directions to the classroom and instruct the student to go to the classroom, go in, and sit down at an empty desk, which is analogous to the program handing the name of a list to a node. While I'm sure many people would agree that the first scenario is preferable in a school setting, both practices are equally valid in OOP.

Ideally, you wouldn't want to have to bother with packaging data into nodes at all, and the `List` type presented in the OBJECTS.PAS unit (which is supplied with the Turbo Pascal software) goes a long way in that direction. However, that's difficult to do in light of the strict typing rules inherent in Turbo Pascal, so for the sake of clarity, we won't attempt that in our unit. For illustration, both methods of building lists will be implemented in our design.

Finding Objects

The previous discussion considers the addition and removal of nodes without regard for any particular node. FIFO lists always add items to the end and remove nodes from the front, LIFO lists always add and remove nodes from he same end, etc. However, an important list-handling technique allows the identification of particular nodes, based on particular conditions. Of course, once a node is identified, it is a relatively simple matter to manipulate the node, for example, by removing or copying it from the list. We'll get into this more as we develop the design for the `List` object type.

The List Object Type

The linked list shown in Figure 6.1 shows a bare minimum for a linked list data structure. To make life easier, however, we will have three separate pointers to help keep track of the list: a pointer to the head of the list, another to the tail, and a third to a place-marker called a cursor.

The purpose of the `Head` and `Tail` pointers is fairly obvious. If you want to know what the first or last node in the list is, look at where the `Head` and `Tail` pointers point, respectively. If you want to append a node to the list, you don't have to grope along the chain of nodes to find the tail, because the `Tail` pointer already points to the end of the chain.

The `Cursor` pointer points at a node that, for one reason or another, we want to keep track of. For example, we may want to sequentially examine each node in the list to see if it satisfies some condition. To do this, we start by pointing the `Cursor` at the head of the list and then, each time we fetch a node, we point the `Cursor` at the next node in the list. When the `Cursor` points to nil (as it will after it finishes pointing to the tail of the list), the list is exhausted.

Since it is a simple matter to increment or decrement an integer every time we add or remove a node from the list, we will keep track of the number of nodes in the list in the variable `NMem`. This will come in handy, since there are a few special cases we'll want to consider when the number of nodes in a list is exactly 1.

Most of the methods for the `List` object type deal with getting information out of the list. The methods `.PopFirst`, `.PopLast`, and `.PopCursor` remove the node at the `Head`, the `Tail`, and at the `Cursor` position in the list, respectively. When the method `.PopFirst` is called, the node that was formerly second in the list becomes the new `Head`. Analogously, the node that was formerly next to last becomes the `Tail` of the list after `.PopLast` is called. When `.PopCursor` is called, the node pointed to by the `Cursor` is removed, the `Cursor` points to the next node in the list, and the removed node's neighbors close ranks.

Similar in spirit to `.PopCursor` is `.GetCursor`, which merely returns a pointer to the node pointed to by `Cursor` (without removing it from the list).

The methods `.FindObject` and `.FindNextObject` are used to find nodes that satisfy certain conditions. The difference between the two lies in the setting of the `Cursor`. Calling `.FindObject` points the `Cursor` at the head of the list, so that the search spans all the nodes. Calling `.FindNextObject` searches only those nodes between the node pointed to by `Cursor` and the tail of the list.

You might be wondering how the `List` object, which only "sees" `Node` objects, is capable of comparing the nodes in the list against any sort of criterion. The answer lies in the use of the `FindObjectDemon`, a procedural variable property of the `List` object type. `FindObjectDemon` is a function of one parameter (a pointer) returning a boolean value. The way the `List` object type determines whether a `Node` satisfies a condition is to pass a pointer to the `Node` to the `FindObjectDemon`; if the return value is true, the `Node` satisfies the condition, if not, it doesn't. The default function attached to the `FindObjectDemon` is called `FindAll`, which as its name implies, always returns a true value. If the programmer wants to use some other function for selecting list nodes, the address of that function must be stored in `FindObjectDemon`.

Methods `.Append` and `.Prepend` add nodes to the tail and the head of the list.

Mixed Nodes

In principle, there is nothing to prevent you from adding objects of mixed type to a `List` object type. The only requisite for adding a node to a list is that such objects are descendants of type `Node`. The problem arises in retrieving the nodes from the list, and is best explained by using the Turbo Debugger. We'll take a closer look at this problem later, after we discuss the debugging facilities at the disposal of the Turbo Pascal programmer.

Debugging Objects

There was a time when the only way of debugging programs (short of spending a lot of time learning to use assembly-language level debuggers) was to edit them to include calls to the `writeln` function. These calls would inform us of the progress of the program, where it was (and where it wasn't), and provide a rudimentary logging capability if we sent the output to the printer or a disk file. Indeed, if you have the time and the situation calls for it, using calls to `writeln` is a perfectly acceptable way of catching and killing bugs. Unfortunately, nobody seems to have the time anymore, and the bugs that populate our programs get more and more subtle all the time.

Fortunately, the Turbo Pascal integrated development environment (IDE) includes some useful debugging capabilities such as the ability to set and clear breakpoints, evaluate expressions and change their value, set and clear watch variables, and single-step or trace through the code as it executes. To take advantage of these capabilities, you must have the Debug/Integrated Debugging option set to On.

If you've used the IDE's debugging capabilities and have experience with records, the way the IDE deals with objects will seem very familiar. If you're new to the IDE, let's look at how objects are represented, and take a look at several features I find particularly useful.

We start by loading Listing 6-2, which declares a couple of simple object types that are descendants of the `Node` type. An instance of each type, along with a `List` variable, go through a simple procedure where all are initialized and both `Node` descendants are added to the `List`.

Listing 6-2

```
program Listing6_2;

uses ListObj;

type

ClassA = object(Node)
         Number1 : integer;
         Number2 : integer;
         Number3 : integer;
         procedure Init( N1, N2, N3 : integer );
         end;

ClassB = object(Node)
         Real1 : real;
         procedure Init( R1 : real );
         end;

procedure ClassA.Init( N1, N2, N3 : integer );
begin
{    Node.Init(SizeOf (Self)); } {This line "missing" in first run}
     Number1 := N1;
     Number2 := N2;
     Number3 := N3;
end;

procedure ClassB.Init( R1 : real );
begin
{    Node.Init(SizeOf (Self)); } {This line "missing" in first run}
     Real1 := R1;
end;

var
   ObjectA : ClassA;
   ObjectB : ClassB;
   MixList : List;
begin
     MixList.Init;
     ObjectA.Init( 1,2,3 );
     ObjectB.Init( 3.1415 );
     ObjectA.AppendToList( MixList );
     MixList.Append( @ObjectB );
end.
```

After loading the program, we press F7 to start. The highlight bar drops down to the line that initializes the `List` object. If we are not sure what the `.Init` procedure does, we can look at it by pressing

Alt-D (for Debug) and F (for Find Procedure). Notice that the procedure name `List.Init` is already filled in for us (see Figure 6.4). If we hit Enter, the IDE will load the appropriate file (LISTOBJ.PAS) and show us the `List.Init` procedure, with the cursor at the first line of the procedure (Figure 6.5). The Find Procedure feature can sometimes be a real time-saver, especially when you have a program spread out among several source files.

Figure 6.4 — Finding the procedure List.Init

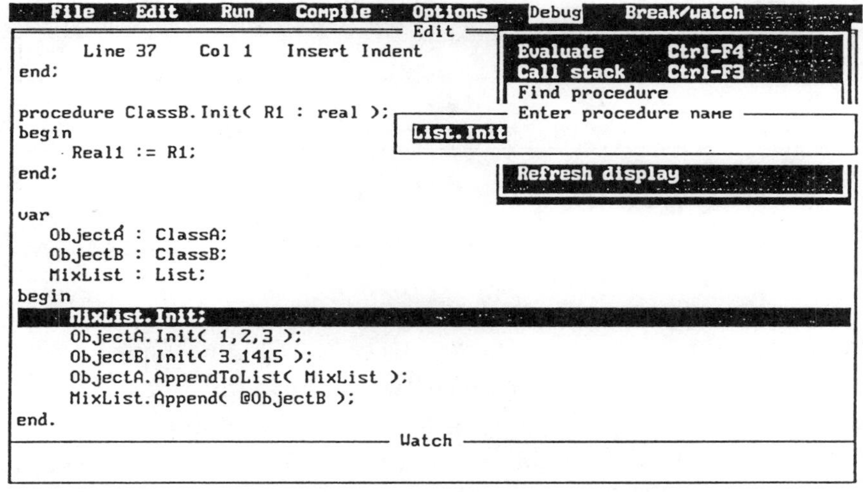

Figure 6.5 — The sought-after procedure (List.Init) is displayed

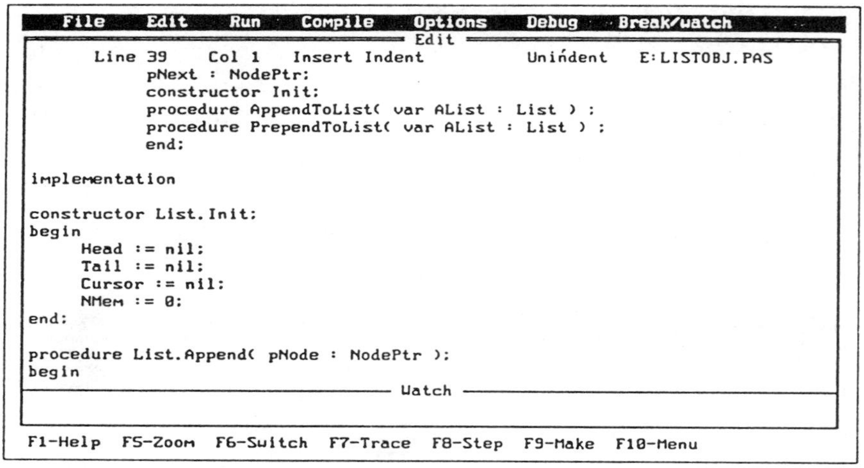

```
   File   Edit   Run   Compile   Options   Debug   Break/watch
                              Edit
      Line 39    Col 1    Insert Indent          Unindent    E:LISTOBJ.PAS
          pNext : NodePtr;
          constructor Init;
          procedure AppendToList( var AList : List ) ;
          procedure PrependToList( var AList : List ) ;
          end;

implementation

constructor List.Init;
begin
     Head := nil;
     Tail := nil;
     Cursor := nil;
     NMem := 0;
end;

procedure List.Append( pNode : NodePtr );
begin
                              Watch

F1-Help  F5-Zoom  F6-Switch  F7-Trace  F8-Step  F9-Make  F10-Menu
```

If we feel we need to step through this procedure, we can press F7. However, this is a simple procedure, so we'll bypass stepping through it and press F8 (Trace) instead.

We can now take a look at the `MixList` variable by typing Ctrl-F7 and entering MixList. Alternatively, we can place the screen cursor at the name (for example, by typing Ctrl-E and Ctrl-F) and then Ctrl-F7. If the Cursor is at a variable name, the *Add Watch* window will appear already filled in for us. Pressing Enter displays the `MixList` object in the Watch window at the bottom of the screen. Before proceeding further, we'll also display `ObjectA` and `ObjectB` in the Watch window and then press F8 twice to trace through the program lines that initialize those objects. The result is shown in Figure 6.6, and don't worry if the values shown on your screen look different.

By inspection we can see that `ObjectA` seems all right, with the right numbers in the right places and the node pointer set to NIL. However, though ObjectB contains the right real number, its node pointer is pointing off somewhere into memory. This isn't right at all. What's missing? Wait a minute! Did we forget to call the ancestor .Init procedure for both ObjectA and ObjectB? Sure enough! (It is coincidence that ObjectA's node pointer is NIL in this case.) Let's go back and add these to the code for both .Init procedures, save our work with F2, and then recompile with F9. Note that all the items in the Watch window now have "Unknown identifier" next to them. This is normal, because we haven't yet started to step through the program.

Figure 6.6 — What's with ObjectB? Why isn't its pointer NIL? Bug!

```
 File    Edit    Run    Compile    Options    Debug    Break/watch
                                  Edit
      Line 40    Col 6   Insert Indent          Unindent    E:LIST6-2.PAS
     Real1 := R1;
end;

var
   ObjectA : ClassA;
   ObjectB : ClassB;
   MixList : List;
begin
     MixList.Init;
     ObjectA.Init( 1,2,3 );
     ObjectB.Init( 3.1415 );
     ObjectA.AppendToList( MixList );
     MixList.Append( @ObjectB );
end.

                                  Watch
•ObjectB: (PTR($52FB,$0),3.1415)
 ObjectA: (NIL,1,2,3)
 MixList: (NIL,NIL,NIL,0,PTR($2,$32))
F1-Help  F5-Zoom  F6-Switch  F7-Trace  F8-Step  F9-Make  F10-Menu
```

We can retrace our steps by pressing F8 until all three objects are initialized. Notice in Figure 6.7 that both ObjectA and ObjectB seem healthy (Both ObjectA's and ObjectB's node pointer now point to NIL, as they're supposed to). Again, don't worry if the values on your screen are different from those illustrated. The relationships we're about to point out, however, should hold.

After pressing F8 one more time to append ObjectA to list MixList; notice a change in the contents of MixList. The first two pointers of MixList now have the same value (because the head and tail of the list are the same node) and the number of items in the list is 1. We can verify that the `Head` and `Tail` pointers point to `ObjectA` by entering *ObjectA* into the AddWatch window, which results in the display of `ObjectA`'s address appearing in the Watch window, as shown in Figure 6.8. We'll display the address of `ObjectB` in similar fashion, and then press F8 to execute the last line of the program. Figure 6.9 shows the status of all the objects at the end of the program. As we can see, the `MixList` object's `Head` pointer points at `ObjectA`, its `Tail` pointer points at `ObjectB`, and the count of nodes stands at 2. Also note that, as it should, `ObjectA`'s pointer contains the address of `ObjectB`.

Figure 6.7 — Bug is fixed! (from Listing 6-2)

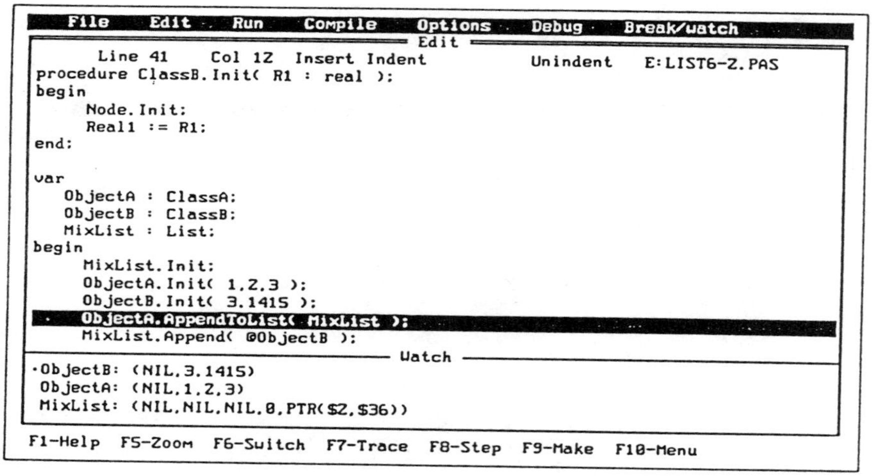

```
 File   Edit   Run   Compile   Options   Debug   Break/watch
                               Edit
      Line 41     Col 12   Insert Indent          Unindent     E:LIST6-2.PAS
procedure ClassB.Init( R1 : real );
begin
     Node.Init;
     Real1 := R1;
end;

var
   ObjectA : ClassA;
   ObjectB : ClassB;
   MixList : List;
begin
     MixList.Init;
     ObjectA.Init( 1,2,3 );
     ObjectB.Init( 3.1415 );
     ObjectA.AppendToList( MixList );
     MixList.Append( @ObjectB );
                               Watch
·ObjectB: (NIL,3.1415)
 ObjectA: (NIL,1,2,3)
 MixList: (NIL,NIL,NIL,0,PTR($2,$36))

F1-Help  F5-Zoom  F6-Switch  F7-Trace  F8-Step  F9-Make  F10-Menu
```

Figure 6.8 — ObjectA is in the List (from Listing 6-2)

```
  File   Edit   Run   Compile   Options   Debug   Break/watch
                              Edit
     Line 41    Col 12   Insert Indent          Unindent    E:LIST6-2.PAS
begin
     Node.Init;
     Real1 := R1;
end;

var
   ObjectA : ClassA;
   ObjectB : ClassB;
   MixList : List;
begin
     MixList.Init;
     ObjectA.Init( 1,2,3 );
     ObjectB.Init( 3.1415 );
     ObjectA.AppendToList( MixList );
     MixList.Append( @ObjectB );
                              Watch
·@ObjectA: PTR(DSEG,$42)
 ObjectB: (NIL,3.1415)
 ObjectA: (NIL,1,2,3)
 MixList: (PTR(DSEG,$42),PTR(DSEG,$42),NIL,1,PTR($2,$36))
F1-Help  F5-Zoom  F6-Switch  F7-Trace  F8-Step  F9-Make  F10-Menu
```

Figure 6.9 — At the end of Listing 6-2

```
  File   Edit   Run   Compile   Options   Debug   Break/watch
                              Edit
     Line 43    Col 12   Insert Indent          Unindent    E:LIST6-2.PAS
end;

var
   ObjectA : ClassA;
   ObjectB : ClassB;
   MixList : List;
begin
     MixList.Init;
     ObjectA.Init( 1,2,3 );
     ObjectB.Init( 3.1415 );
     ObjectA.AppendToList( MixList );
     MixList.Append( @ObjectB );
end.

                              Watch
·@ObjectB: PTR(DSEG,$4E)
 @ObjectA: PTR(DSEG,$42)
 ObjectB: (NIL,3.1415)
 ObjectA: (PTR(DSEG,$4E),1,2,3)
 MixList: (PTR(DSEG,$42),PTR(DSEG,$4E),NIL,2,PTR($2,$36))
F1-Help  F5-Zoom  F6-Switch  F7-Trace  F8-Step  F9-Make  F10-Menu
```

Now let's make a small modification to the program. Add two variables, `TypeA` and `TypeB`, which are pointers to `ClassA` and `ClassB`, respectively. The modified program is shown in Listing 6-3. We then call the function `FindObject` to set the `Cursor` to point at the head of the list, and then call `GetCursor` twice to get pointers to `ObjectA` and `ObjectB`. The trick here is that we will assign `ObjectA`'s pointer to the pointer variable `ClassB`, and vice versa. Let's see what happens.

Listing 6-3

```
program Listing6_3;

uses ListObj;

type

ClassA = object(Node)
         Number1 : integer;
         Number2 : integer;
         Number3 : integer;
         procedure Init( N1, N2, N3 : integer );
         end;

ClassB = object(Node)
         Real1 : real;
         procedure Init( R1 : real );
         end;

procedure ClassA.Init( N1, N2, N3 : integer );
begin
     Node.Init;
     Number1 := N1;
     Number2 := N2;
     Number3 := N3;
end;

procedure ClassB.Init( R1 : real );
begin
     Node.Init;
     Real1 := R1;
end;

var
   ObjectA : ClassA;
   ObjectB : ClassB;
   MixList : List;
   TypeA : ^ClassA;
   TypeB : ^ClassB;
begin
     MixList.Init;
     ObjectA.Init( 1,2,3 );
```

```
      ObjectB.Init( 3.1415 );
      ObjectA.AppendToList( MixList );
      MixList.Append( @ObjectB );
      if MixList.FindObject = true then
         begin
         TypeB := MixList.GetCursor; {TypeB points to ObjectA}
         TypeA := MixList.GetCursor; {TypeA points to ObjectB}
         end;
end.
```

Set up the watch window as shown in Figure 6.10, with entries for `ObjectA`, `ObjectB`, `TypeA^` and `TypeB^` (don't forget the caret). Now type Ctrl-F9 to run the program to completion, and the result will resemble Figure 6.11. Where did those numbers for TypeA and TypeB come from? To better explain that, let's get familiar with the Turbo Debugger.

Figure 6.10 — Before starting execution of Listing 6-3

```
   File    Edit    Run    Compile    Options    Debug    Break/watch
                                 Edit
     Line 39    Col 9   Insert Indent          Unindent     E:DBG.PAS
   ObjectB : ClassB;
   MixList : List;
   TypeA : ^ClassA;
   TypeB : ^ClassB;
begin
     MixList.Init;
     ObjectA.Init( 1,2,3 );
     ObjectB.Init( 3.1415 );
     ObjectA.AppendToList( MixList );
     MixList.Append( @ObjectB );
     if MixList.FindObject = true then
        begin
        TypeB := MixList.GetCursor;
        TypeA := MixList.GetCursor;
        end;
                                 Watch
·TypeA^: (PTR($75C,$26AB),22,4467,1884)
 TypeB^: (PTR($26AB,$390B),8.6694490946E-6)
 ObjectB: (PTR($52FB,$0),2.4267060764E24)
 ObjectA: (NIL,0,0,0)
F1-Help  F5-Zoom  F6-Switch  F7-Trace  F8-Step  F9-Make  F10-Menu
```

Figure 6.11 — After Listing 6-3 finishes executing

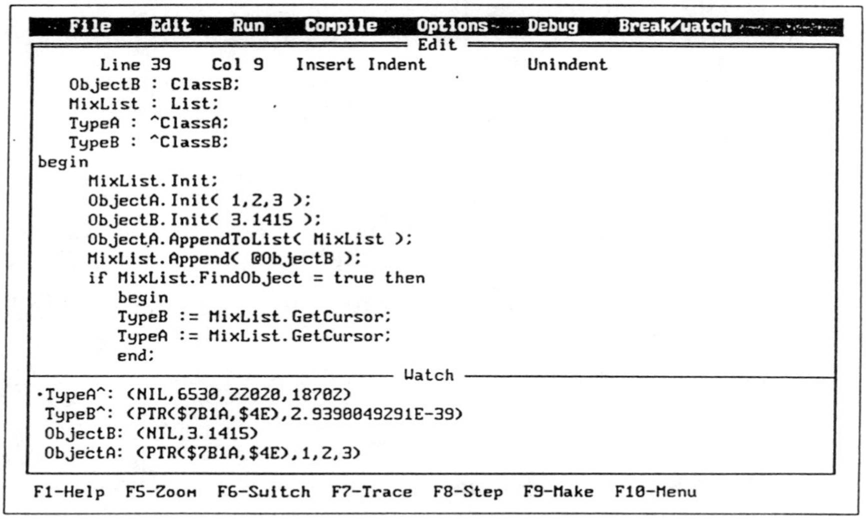

```
  File   Edit   Run   Compile   Options   Debug   Break/watch
═══════════════════════════════ Edit ══════════════════════════════
      Line 39    Col 9    Insert Indent          Unindent
   ObjectB : ClassB;
   MixList : List;
   TypeA : ^ClassA;
   TypeB : ^ClassB;
begin
     MixList.Init;
     ObjectA.Init( 1,2,3 );
     ObjectB.Init( 3.1415 );
     ObjectA.AppendToList( MixList );
     MixList.Append( @ObjectB );
     if MixList.FindObject = true then
        begin
        TypeB := MixList.GetCursor;
        TypeA := MixList.GetCursor;
        end;
─────────────────────────────── Watch ─────────────────────────────
•TypeA^: (NIL,6530,22020,18702)
 TypeB^: (PTR($7B1A,$4E),2.9390049291E-39)
 ObjectB: (NIL,3.1415)
 ObjectA: (PTR($7B1A,$4E),1,2,3)
 F1-Help  F5-Zoom  F6-Switch  F7-Trace  F8-Step  F9-Make  F10-Menu
```

Using Turbo Debugger

Though the debugging capabilities of the IDE are quite powerful by themselves, these capabilities are limited, particularly when it comes to examining the contents of complex structures in memory, or tracing where exactly pointers are pointing to. To the rescue here is the Borland Turbo Debugger, which is a source-level debugger that provides an interactive user interface with advanced debugging features. Versions 1.5 and later of the Turbo Debugger support the object-oriented extensions of Turbo Pascal 5.5. Before discussing the Debugger, let's take a look at what preparations must be made in the Turbo Pascal IDE before we call the Debugger.

In order to take full advantage of the Turbo Debugger from Turbo Pascal, you must have the Debug switch turned on. If it isn't already, you can set it on by calling up Options/Compiler/Debug Information. Alternatively, you can turn the switch on by placing the directive {$D+} at the start of your code. You should also place the directive {$L+} at the start of your code to include local symbol debugging information. You then must make sure that when you compile, the resulting executable file is saved to disk (or else you won't be able to load it into the Turbo Debugger which is a separate program!). To do this, set the Compile/Destination to Disk. Finally, set Debug/Standalone Debugging to On, and save the configuration to disk so that you keep these changes for future use.

The net effects of these changes are a somewhat slower compilation time while in the IDE (because you're compiling to disk, not to memory), and some extra debugging information appended to the .EXE file. This information, by the way, will not slow down execution at all if you run the program as-is; the only risk here is running out of memory when executing large programs. With these changes in place, you're all set to use the debugger.

Let's recompile the program in Listing 6-3 after making the above changes to the IDE environment. Then, exit Turbo Pascal and load the Turbo Debugger, providing the path and name of the program in Listing 6-3 as a command line argument.

The opening screen of the Turbo Debugger (version 2.0) is shown in Figure 6.12 and resembles the layout of the IDE. There are several options in the menu bar across the top, a main window labeled *Module: LISTING6_3* followed by disk, path and file name, and a window labeled *Watches* across the status line on the bottom above a row of function key definitions. If you press the Ctrl and Alt buttons, you'll see the bottom row change according to what key's pressed. A small arrowhead points to the `begin` at the start of the program.

Figure 6.12 — Opening screen of Turbo Debugger with program LIST6-3

```
≡ File View Run Breakpoints Data Options Window Help                READY
[■]=Module: LISTING6_3  File: C:\TP\LIST6-3.PAS 39================1=[↑][↓]
    ObjectB : ClassB;
    MixList : List;
    TypeA : ^ClassA;
    TypeB : ^ClassB;
► begin
     MixList.Init;
     ObjectA.Init( 1,2,3 );
     ObjectB.Init( 3.1415 );
     ObjectA.AppendToList( MixList );
     MixList.Append( @ObjectB );
     if MixList.FindObject = true then
        begin
        TypeB := MixList.GetCursor;
        TypeA := MixList.GetCursor;
        end;
  end.

 Watches--------------------------------------------------------2--

F1-Help F2-Bkpt F3-Mod F4-Here F5-Zoom F6-Next F7-Trace F8-Step F9-Run F10-Menu
```

Upon startup, the main window is also the active window, which is indicated by the double border and the scroll bars across the bottom and right-hand sides. The marker in the right-hand scroll bar shows that we are looking at code about two-thirds of the way through the file. At the lower right-hand corner (where the scroll bars almost meet) is a mouse-sensitive region that allows you to resize the window by pressing the left mouse button, keeping it depressed and moving the mouse (this is called "dragging"). The window can also be moved around the screen by dragging the window by its top border, called the "title bar."

The indicator at the top left of the title bar, which looks like a small square enclosed in square brackets, is the "close box." Clicking the mouse on this box will close the window, as will pressing the Alt-F3 key. Mousing on the up-arrow (called the "zoom box") at the right side of the window will zoom it to full-screen size (as will pressing F5), while mousing on the down-arrow next to it will iconize, or shrink it. In addition to mouse actions and function keystrokes, all of these actions are available through the Window option from the main menu bar.

We can post a variable to the watch list here by pressing Alt-D (for Data) and then W (for Watch), or we can type Ctrl-F7 and enter a name into a dialog box. We can also open an Inspection window by entering a name into a dialog box after typing Alt-D and I, or we can bypass the menus by placing the screen cursor on the name and pressing Ctrl-I.

Before doing anything, let's place the `MixList` object in the watch list and open an Inspection window. We'll use the mouse (or the Ctrl-F5 key) to resize and move the Inspection window, to arrive at a screen that looks like Figure 6.13.

Figure 6.13 — MixList in Watch and Inspector window

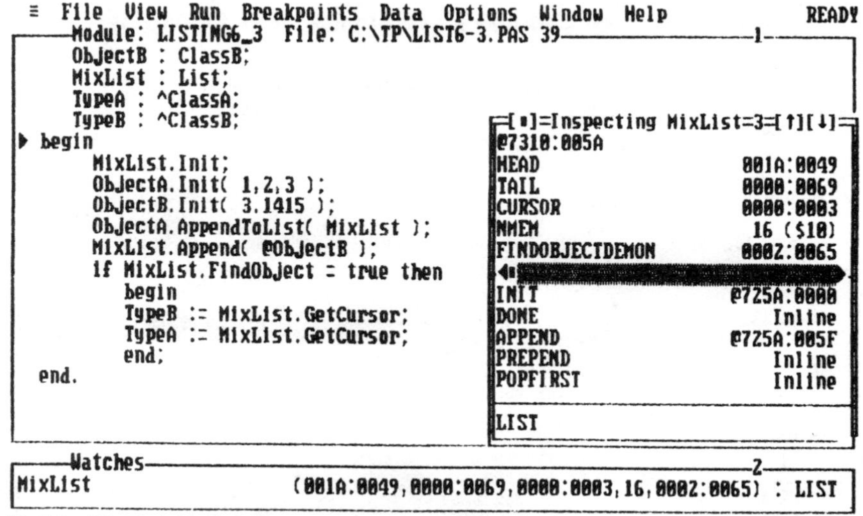

Before starting the program, the pointers in MixList were, predictably, pointing to random locations in memory (so again, your screen may reflect different values). After pressing F8 (Step) twice, all the pointers become NIL and the property `NMem` is zeroed out. Notice that the properties of `MixList` are displayed in the watch window pretty much as they were in the IDE.

If the Inspection window does not have a double line around it, press a mouse button while inside it or press Alt and the number in the upper right hand corner of the window (for example, Alt-3) to select the window. If you now press F5, you see a zoomed view of the Inspection window, as depicted in Figure 6.14. Notice that the address of `FindObjectDemon` is identified both in hexadecimal and with the label [LISTOBJ.FINDALL] identifying the address as the start of `FindAll` in the file LISTOBJ.PAS. Notice also that the addresses for methods such as `.PopFirst` are all "inline," which means they were not linked into the final program (a result of Turbo Pascal's "smart linking" feature). Press F5 again to unzoom the window, or mouse on the zoom box, which shows a double-headed arrow.

Figure 6.14 — Zoomed inspection window for MixList

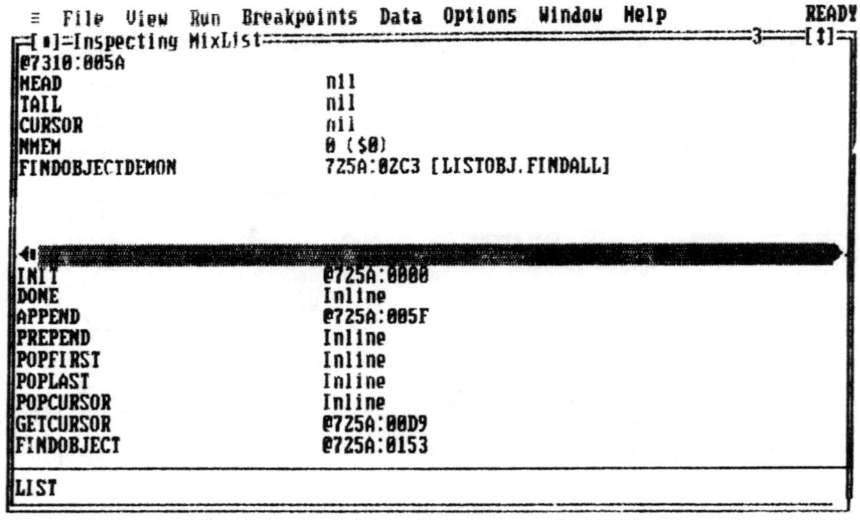

We press F8 three more times so that the arrow in the Module window points at the line

```
MixList.Append( @ObjectB);
```

If we zoom the `MixList` Inspection window now, we see that both the `Head` and `Tail` point at [LISTING6_3.OBJECTA]. Without changing the screen, if we press F8 again, we see the `Tail` now points to [LISTING6_3.OBJECTB], as shown in Figure 6.15.

Figure 6.15 — Mixlist inspection window after adding ObjectA and ObjectB

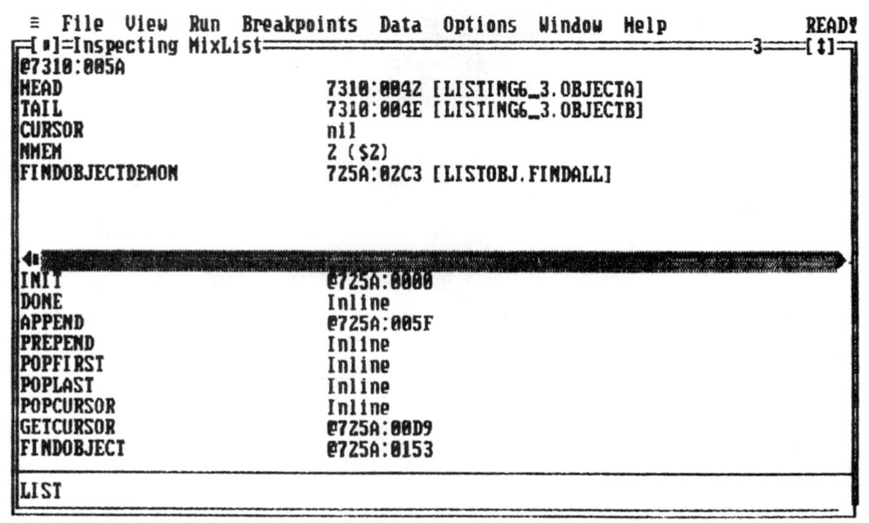

If we tap the down arrow, we highlight the line starting with HEAD. Type Ctrl-I to open another Inspection window, or put the mouse on the HEAD line, press the right button, and then select Inspect from the menu that pops up the `Head` pointer. Press F5 to zoom this window and notice that the only information about [LISTING6_3.OBJECTA] that is available to HEAD is that the

PNEXT pointer points at [LISTING6_3.OBJECTB]. This is because HEAD can only point at a Node object.

We can use our favorite method to open an Inspection window for ObjectA, then resize and move the new window to arrive at a display that looks like Figure 6.16. Notice that the PNEXT for both `ObjectA` and the `Node` pointed to by HEAD are identical (as we'd expect).

Figure 6.16 — Comparing HEAD of MixList to ObjectA

```
≡ File View Run Breakpoints Data Options Window Help              READY
 ---Inspecting HEAD---5---            =[■]=Inspecting ObjectA=======3=[↑][↓]=
@7310:005A : 7310:0042 [LISTING6_3  @7310:0042
PNEXT 7310:004E [LISTING6_3.OBJECT  NODE.PNEXT 7310:004E [LISTING6_3.OBJECTB]
SIZE                      12 ($C)   NODE.SIZE                    12 ($C)
                                    NUMBER1                       1 ($1)
                                    NUMBER2                       2 ($2)
                                    NUMBER3                       3 ($3)

INIT                  @725A:021C    NODE.APPENDTOLIST            @725A:0241
APPENDTOLIST          @725A:0241    NODE.PREPENDTOLIST           Inline
PREPENDTOLIST             Inline    INIT                         @7249:0000

NODEPTR                             CLASSA

LIST
F1-Help F2-Bkpt F3-Mod F4-Here F5-Zoom F6-Next F7-Trace F8-Step F9-Run F10-Menu
```

Press Escape until you're back at the main Module window. Now press Ctrl-F9 to run the program to completion. Mouse on "OK' or press Enter to acknowledge an exit code of 0. Now open Inspection windows for TypeA (don't include the caret) and `ObjectB` using one of the methods described above. After appropriate resizing, we get a screen that resembles Figure 6.17.

Figure 6.17 — Inspecting Type A and ObjectB

```
≡ File View Run Breakpoints Data Options Window Help                  READY
┌──Inspecting TypeA─────────3──┐╔[■]=Inspecting ObjectB══════════4=[↑][↓]╗
@7310:006E : 7310:004E          @7310:004E
NODE.PNEXT                nil   NODE.PNEXT                    nil
NODE.SIZE             12 ($C)   NODE.SIZE                     12 ($C)
NUMBER1          6530 ($1982)   REAL1                         3.1415
NUMBER2         22020 ($5604)
NUMBER3         18702 ($490E)

NODE.APPENDTOLIST  @725A:0241   NODE.APPENDTOLIST             @725A:0241
NODE.PREPENDTOLIST     Inline   NODE.PREPENDTOLIST            Inline
INIT               @7249:0000   INIT                          @7249:0038

^CLASSA                         CLASSB

──Watches─────────────────────────────────────────────────2──

F1-Help F2-Bkpt F3-Mod F4-Here F5-Zoom F6-Next F7-Trace F8-Step F9-Run F10-Menu
```

As we can see from the figure, the address of the pointer `TypeA` is @7310:006E, and it contains the address of `ObjectB` (@7310:004E). If you're familiar with the way real numbers and integers are laid out in memory, you know that the six bytes occupied by a real number take up the same space as three contiguous integer numbers, and 3.1415 is stored in six bytes as the integers 6530 ($1982), 22020 ($5604), and 18702 ($490E). To show this with the Turbo Debugger, select one of the two new Inspection windows, make sure the highlight is on the address (for example, @7310:004C of `ObjectB`) and type Alt-V (for View) and D (for Dump). A window will appear with a "dump" of memory locations starting at the specified address, as in Figure 6.18. Note that after four blank bytes (the memory for storing PNEXT), and two bytes $0C and $00 (containing the SIZE property), we have a sequence of numbers starting $82, $19 (which is $1982 in low-byte-high-byte order) that match the integer values shown in `TypeA`.

Figure 6.18 — Viewing contents of memory using a Dump window

```
≡ File View Run Breakpoints Data Options Window Help                  READY
 ——Inspecting TypeA———3———————————  ——Inspecting ObjectB———————4——
@7310:006E : 7310:004E              @7310:004E
NODE.PNEXT                     nil  NODE.PNEXT             nil
NODE.SIZE                 12 ($C)   NODE.SIZE              12 ($C)
NUMBER1              6530 ($1982)   REAL1                  3.1415
NUMBER2             22020 ($5604)
NUMBER3             18702 ($490E)

NODE.APPENDTOLIST       @725A:0241  NODE.APPENDTOLIST      @725A:0241
NODE.PREPENDTOLIST          Inline  NODE.PREPENDTOLIST     Inline
INIT                    @7249:0000  INIT                   @7249:0038

                      [■]=Dump—————————————————————————5=[↑][↓]=
                      7310:004E 00 00 00 00 0C 00 82 19
                      7310:0056 04 56 0E 49 42 00 10 73
^CLASSA               7310:005E 4E 00 10 73 00 00 00 00
                      7310:0066 02 00 C4 02 5A 72 02 00
 ——Watches——————————  7310:006E 4E 00 10 73 42 00 10 73
                      7310:0076 00 00 B0 D7 80 00 00 00
F1-Help F2-Bkpt F3-Mod F4-Here F5-Zoom F6-Next F7-Trace F8-Step F9-Run F10-Menu
```

There is not enough room here to go into much detail about how the Debugger works, or to describe the many features that make a programmer's life easier. One of the best ways toward mastery of the program is to investigate just one new feature every time you fire it up. As your experience builds, you'll be able to uncover and fix bugs faster than ever before. It sure beats peppering your code with `writeln` calls, believe me.

Up to here, the main emphasis of the material has been to explain how the object-oriented extensions in Turbo Pascal 5.5 work. In the following chapters, we'll emphasize applications of OOP, presenting a range of applications of limited scope. In the next chapter, for example, we'll take a look at the design of a windowing system in the graphics mode with mouse support.

7

WINDOWS

Applications with a strongly visual element are generally good subjects for object-oriented design. This is understandable in light of everyday experience, where our understanding of objects is grounded heavily on seeing them and how they behave. In this chapter, we'll use the `list` object type developed in the previous chapter to help build a set of objects to implement a window system on a graphics screen using a mouse. We'll also take a stab at mouse programming, including the integration of an assembly language routine into our program.

Windowing systems are a stock in trade when talking about OOP because such windows can so easily be thought of as objects. Each window is a region of the computer screen with its own boundaries and behavior. What we are going to do in this chapter is create a Turbo Pascal unit that will work with the interrupt-driven capabilities of the mouse to create an environment with the following behaviors:

1. When we press and release (or "click") the right mouse button while the mouse is not inside the boundaries of a window, the mouse cursor will "freeze" on the screen. Then, pressing the left mouse button and pulling the mouse (still with the left button depressed, which is called "dragging") will show a flickering outline of a window. When we have an outline of the desired size, releasing the left button will create a window.

2. When we click the right mouse button with the mouse cursor inside the most recently created window, the window closes and restores the screen underneath.

3. If we click the right mouse button with the mouse inside some window other than the most recently created window, the computer beeps and does nothing.

4. If we depress the left button over the screen background, nothing happens.

5. If we depress the left button inside a window, change the color of the pixel at the mouse's "hot spot" changes to white. If the mouse is dragged, inside a window, a trail of pixels is turned white. Do not draw outside the boundary of the window.

To implement this windowing system, we're going to have to put together some code for the mouse (including a special routine to take advantage of the mouse's interrupt capability), as well as some object type descriptions for both the screen and each individual window.

The Mouse

Before we get into the details of how the mouse was implemented in the above example, let's discuss the utility of encapsulating the mouse as an object.

You can manipulate the mouse's behavior both physically (you move it when you move the physical mouse with your hand) and with software (as you tell it to appear, disappear, report its button status, etc.). The only characteristic that limits the applicability of a mouse as a object in OOP is the fact that there is only one of them. You would be hard pressed to have multiple instances of a mouse on the screen. Now, just because you can't have multiple "mice" doesn't mean you couldn't encapsulate mouse behavior inside of an object type, because another reason for encapsulating behavior inside an object is to allow a descendant type to inherit its behavior. However, for the sake of simplicity, we'll treat code dealing with the mouse as ordinary Turbo Pascal code. Aside from keeping things simple, it also helps to remind us that there is no obligation to encapsulate everything inside of objects in Turbo Pascal 5.5.

A lot of people love the convenience of using a mouse when they use a computer, but turn pale at the thought of programming the mouse to do what they want. In actuality, programming the mouse is not terribly difficult. Sure, you've got to know a little something about the guts of the machine, since most mouse programming has to do with loading certain CPU registers with a set of parameters (depending on what you want to do) and then calling interrupt 51 ($33 hex). If assembly language is not your forte, you can use Turbo Pascal's `Registers` type in combination with the `Intr` procedure to program the mouse. A selection of mouse functions have been coded for this chapter and are presented in Listing 7-1.

Listing 7-1

```
unit Mouse; {Listing 7-1}

interface

uses Dos;
type
procedure MouseCoords( var x,y : integer );
function MouseLPressed : boolean;
function MouseRPressed : boolean;
function MouseLReleased : boolean;
function MouseRReleased : boolean;
function MouseInit : Boolean;
procedure MouseShow;
procedure MouseHide;
procedure MouseSetPosition( x,y : integer );
procedure MouseGetBPressInfo( var Status, Count : integer;
                                       Button : integer );
procedure MouseGetBRelInfo( var Status, Count : integer;
                                       Button : integer );
procedure MouseSetHMinMax( Min, Max : integer );
procedure MouseSetVMinMax( Min, Max : integer );
procedure MouseReset;
```

```
implementation
var
   i : integer;

procedure MouseCursor.Mouse;
var R : Registers;
begin
     R.AX := 9;
     R.BX := HotX;
     R.CX := HotY;
     R.DX := Ofs(Cursor);
     R.ES := Seg(Cursor);
     Intr( $33, R );
end;

procedure MouseReset;
var R : Registers;
begin
     R.AX := $21;
     R.BX := 0;
     R.CX := 0;
     R.DX := 0;
     R.SI := 0;
     R.DI := 0;
     R.DS := 0;
     R.ES := 0;
     Intr( $33, R );
end;

function MouseLPressed : boolean ;
var Status,Count : integer;
begin
     MouseGetBPressInfo( Status, Count, 0 );
     if (Status AND $1)=$1 then
        MouseLPressed := true
     else
        MouseLPressed := false;
end;

function MouseLReleased : boolean ;
var Status,Count : integer;
begin
     MouseGetBRelInfo( Status, Count, 0 );
     if (((Status AND $1) = 0) AND (Count > 0)) then
        MouseLReleased := true
     else
        MouseLReleased := false;
end;
```

```
function MouseRPressed : boolean ;
var Status,Count : integer;
begin
     MouseGetBPressInfo( Status, Count, 1 );
     if (Status AND $2) = 2 then
        MouseRPressed := true
     else
        MouseRPressed := false;
end;

function MouseRReleased : boolean ;
var Status,Count : integer;
begin
     MouseGetBRelInfo( Status, Count, 1 );
     if (((Status AND $2) = 0) AND (Count > 0)) then
        MouseRReleased := true
     else
        MouseRReleased := false;
end;

function MouseInit : Boolean;
var R : Registers;
begin
     R.AX := 0;
     R.BX := 0;
     R.CX := 0;
     R.DX := 0;
     R.SI := 0;
     R.DI := 0;
     R.DS := 0;
     R.ES := 0;
     Intr( $33, R );
     if R.AX <> 0 then MouseInit := true else MouseInit := false;
end;

procedure MouseShow;
var R : Registers;
begin
     R.AX := 1;
     R.BX := 0;
     R.CX := 0;
     R.DX := 0;
     R.SI := 0;
     R.DI := 0;
     R.DS := 0;
     R.ES := 0;
     Intr( $33, R );
end;

procedure MouseHide;
var R : Registers;
```

```
begin
     R.AX := 2;
     R.BX := 0;
     R.CX := 0;
     R.DX := 0;
     R.SI := 0;
     R.DI := 0;
     R.DS := 0;
     R.ES := 0;
     Intr( $33, R );
end;

procedure MouseCoords( var x,y : integer );
var R : Registers;
begin
     R.AX := 3;
     R.BX := 0;
     R.CX := 0;
     R.DX := 0;
     R.SI := 0;
     R.DI := 0;
     R.DS := 0;
     R.ES := 0;
     Intr( $33, R );
     x := R.CX;
     y := R.DX;
end;

procedure MouseSetPosition( x,y : integer );
var R : Registers;
begin
     R.AX := 4;
     R.BX := 0;
     R.CX := x;
     R.DX := y;
     R.SI := 0;
     R.DI := 0;
     R.DS := 0;
     R.ES := 0;
     Intr( $33, R );
end;

procedure MouseGetBPressInfo( var Status, Count : integer;
                                          Button : integer );
var R : Registers;
begin
     R.AX := 5;
     R.BX := Button;
     R.CX := 0;
     R.DX := 0;
     R.SI := 0;
```

```
     R.DI := 0;
     R.DS := 0;
     R.ES := 0;
     Intr( $33, R );
     Status := R.AX;
     Count := R.BX;
end;

procedure MouseGetBRelInfo( var Status, Count : integer;
                                               Button : integer );
var R : Registers;
begin
     R.AX := 6;
     R.BX := Button;
     R.CX := 0;
     R.DX := 0;
     R.SI := 0;
     R.DI := 0;
     R.DS := 0;
     R.ES := 0;
     Intr( $33, R );
     Status := R.AX;
     Count := R.BX;
end;

procedure MouseSetHMinMax( Min, Max : integer );
var R : Registers;
begin
     R.AX := 7;
     R.BX := 0;
     R.CX := Min;
     R.DX := Max;
     R.SI := 0;
     R.DI := 0;
     R.DS := 0;
     R.ES := 0;
     Intr( $33, R );
end;

procedure MouseSetVMinMax( Min, Max : integer );
var R : Registers;
begin
     R.AX := 8;
     R.BX := 0;
     R.CX := Min;
     R.DX := Max;
     R.SI := 0;
     R.DI := 0;
     R.DS := 0;
     R.ES := 0;
     Intr( $33, R );
```

```
end;
end.
```

Recall that the Turbo Pascal Registers type looks like:

```
type
Registers = record
       case integer of
       0: (AX,BX,CX,DX,BP,SI,DI,DS,ES,Flags : word);
       1: (AL,AH,BL,BH,CL,CH,DL,DH : byte );
       end;
```

This is an example of a variant record, which basically lets you access the same data in different ways. For example, if we declare `R` to be a `Register` variable, then `R.BL` references a byte quantity, while `R.BX` references a word at the same point in the record, as shown in Fig. 7.01. Let's see how this structure works for the mouse function `MouseShow`.

```
procedure MouseShow;
var R : Registers;
begin
R.AX := 1;
R.BX := 0;
R.CX := 0;
R.DX := 0;
R.SI := 0;
R.DI := 0;
R.DS := 0;
R.ES := 0;
Intr( $33, R );
end;
```

Figure 7.1 — Structure of the Registers variant record type

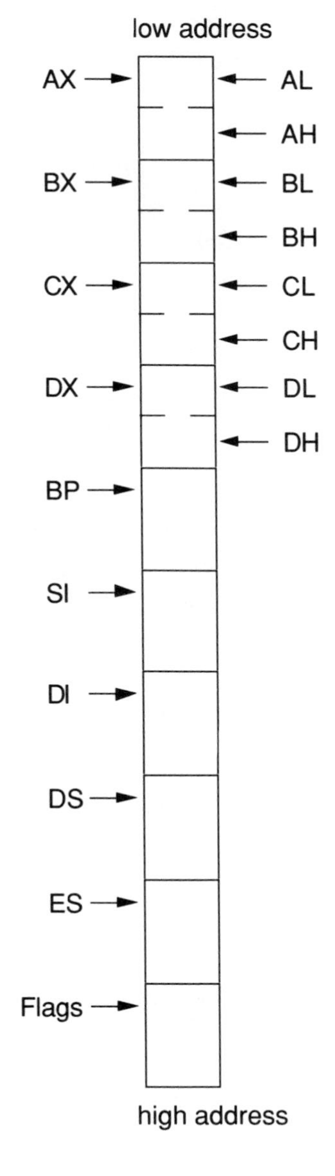

As you can see from the code, there is only one requirement to satisfy before calling the interrupt in `MouseShow`: load a 1 into the AX register. All the other registers are zero and there is no return value to worry about. `Intr` is called with the interrupt number ($33 or decimal 51, the mouse interrupt) and `R`, which is the `Register` variable we just finished loading for the call.

Other mouse functions are a bit more complex, and some, like the procedure `MouseGetBPressInfo`, actually return information to us stored in the CPU registers. We will be using only a subset of the mouse functions available. If you want to pursue programming the mouse, probably the most complete source is the *Microsoft Mouse Programmer's Reference*, although a number of other books on DOS programming also cover mouse programming.

Of the mouse functions we'll be using, probably the most powerful is function 12, which is formally known as *Set Interrupt Subroutine Call Mask and Address*. By supplying what is termed a "call mask" and a subroutine address to this function, we can cause the mouse to interrupt the execution of our program and call the specified subroutine any time one or more of the conditions defined by the call mask occur. When the subroutine finishes executing, control returns to the main program. For our purposes, the main control program, which is shown in Listing 7-2, consists of an infinite loop waiting for a key to be pressed on the keyboard, followed by a call to the SetMouseHandler function that sets the call mask to zero (so that mouse activity after the program terminates won't play havoc with your system), and a call to `RestoreCRTMode`.

Listing 7-2

```
program Listing7_2;
uses Mywindow, graph, mouse, crt;

begin
repeat until Keypressed;
SetMouseHandler(0); { so mouse actions don't persist }
RestoreCRTMode;
end.
```

Using function 12 will help us avoid writing a convoluted program that constantly polls the mouse to determine its position, the status of its buttons, etc. To activate this function we pass the action mask in the CX register, and the segment and offset of the subroutine to execute in the DX and ES registers, respectively.

The call mask is an integer value that defines which conditions cause an interrupt. Each bit in the call mask corresponds to a specific condition, as shown in the following table:

Mask bit	Condition
0	Cursor position changes
1	Left mouse button pressed
2	Left mouse button released
3	Right mouse button pressed
4	Right mouse button released
5–15	Not used

If you want the subroutine to execute for a particular condition, you set the corresponding bit to 1. For example, if you want the subroutine to be called every time the cursor position changes, you pass a call mask value of 1 (or 0000000000000001 in binary). If you want the subroutine to execute every time anything happens with a button (left or right, press or release) you'd pass a call mask value of 30 (0000000000011110 in binary). In fact, what we do in the program is set the mask to 30 (that is, react to all buttons) when we're not creating windows, and to 0 (ignore everything) when we are.

When an action corresponding to a set bit in the call mask occurs, the mouse software makes a call to the subroutine. When the subroutine starts executing, a variety of information is stored in the CPU registers. For example, the horizontal and vertical cursor coordinates are stored in the CX and DX registers, respectively. The subroutine we're going to write for function 12 is not going to be very sophisticated. It will do the following things: (a) it will store the horizontal and vertical cursor coordinates in a pair of variables that can be accessed from the rest of the Turbo Pascal code, and (b) it will call a procedure that will, in turn, figure out what to do. Although it would be grand to write a subroutine that directly calls the object method we need to call, the additional code would be hard to follow unless you were pretty proficient with assembly language. The commented code for our subroutine is presented in Listing 7-3, written in Turbo Assembler.

Listing 7-3

```
;       MTEST5.ASM
;       Listing 7-3
;       a.lane 10/27/89
;
DATA    SEGMENT WORD PUBLIC     ; data segment is word aligned
        ASSUME DS:DATA          ; DS is set to this segment
        EXTRN XPOS:WORD         ; XPOS, YPOS are external,
        EXTRN YPOS:WORD         ; word-sized variables
DATA    ENDS                    ; end of data segment
CODE    SEGMENT BYTE PUBLIC     ; code segment is byte-aligned
        ASSUME CS:CODE          ; CS is set to this segment
        EXTRN EntryPoint : FAR  ; EntryPoint is external
                                ; and a FAR (8-byte) call

mstart  PROC  FAR               ; mstart is a FAR procedure
        PUBLIC mstart           ; ...and is public.
        push ds                 ; save mouse DS
        mov ax, SEG DATA        ; get address of TP global DS
        mov ds, ax              ; copy TP global into DS
        mov ds:XPOS,cx          ; store x coordinate in XPOS
        mov ds:YPOS,dx          ; store y coordinate in YPOS
        CALL EntryPoint         ; call EntryPoint in program
        pop ds                  ; restore mouse DS
        RET                     ; outta here!
        ENDP                    ; procedure is finished.

CODE    ENDS                    ; end of code segment
        END
```

If you don't have TASM, or if you didn't buy the disk edition of this book, you can run the Turbo Pascal program in Appendix 1 to create an object file that is identical to the file output by TASM for Listing 7-3.

Listing 7-4 presents the code for the windowing system. It contains the code for the `Screen` object type, the graphic window (`GWindow`) object type, and a few auxiliary routines that help glue it all together.

Listing 7-4

```
unit Mywindow; { Listing7_4}
{$A+,B-,D+,E+,F+,I+,L+,N-,O-,R-,S+,V+}
{$M 16384,0,655360}

interface

uses Graph, ListObj, Crt, Mouse, Dos;
const
     PathToDriver : string = 'C:\TP'; { your path may differ }

type

ScreenPtr = ^Screen;
GWindowPtr = ^GWindow;


Proc = procedure;
ProcPtr = ^Proc;

VPort = object
        Value : ViewPortType;
        procedure Init( Left, Top, Right, Bottom : integer;
                            ClipQ, SetQ : boolean );
        procedure SetValue;
        procedure GetValue( var AValue : ViewPortType );
        end;

Screen = object(List)
         SViewPort : VPort;
         SColor    : integer;
         SFill     : integer;
         SLine     : integer;
         MouseToken : GWindowPtr;
         MouseX     : integer;
         MouseY     : integer;
         CloseHead  : boolean;
         procedure Init( L,T,R,B,Color,Fill,Line : integer;
                                           Clip : boolean );
         procedure RestoreVP;
         procedure UpdateMouse;
         procedure DefaultMouseAction;
         end;
```

```
GWindow = object(Node)
          GWViewPort  : VPort;
          WindName    : string;
          BelowGWArea : pointer;
          BelowGWSize : word;
          GWFillS     : integer;
          GWFillC     : integer;
          GWColor1    : integer;
          ParentScr   : ScreenPtr;
          constructor Init( FillStyle, FillColor,
                            BColor1 : integer;
                            PScreen : ScreenPtr; WLabel : string );
          destructor Done;
          procedure PrependToList( var AList : List );
          function InboundMouse : boolean;
          procedure MouseAction;
          procedure LocalMouseCoords( var  x, y : integer );
          end;

procedure mstart;
procedure EntryPoint;
procedure SetMouseHandler( mask : integer );

var
   S,T : Screen;
   GraphDriver, Graphmode : integer;

implementation
var
   xpos, ypos : integer;
   ConMask : integer;
   index : integer;

function FindAll( pNode : pointer ) : boolean;
begin
     FindAll := true;
end;

function FindMouse( ANode : pointer ) : boolean;
var pGW : GWindowPtr;
begin
     pGW := ANode;
     if pGW^.InBoundMouse = true then
        begin
        pGW^.ParentScr^.MouseToken := pGW;
        FindMouse := true;
        end
     else
        FindMouse := false;
end;
```

```
{$L MTEST5.OBJ}
{$F-}

procedure mstart; external;
{$F+}
procedure SetMouseHandler( mask : integer );
var R : registers;
begin
     R.AX := $C;
     R.BX := $0;
     R.CX := mask;
     R.DX := Ofs(mstart);
     R.ES := Seg(mstart);
     Intr( $33, R );
end;

procedure Screen.Init( L,T,R,B,Color,Fill,Line : integer;
                                              Clip : boolean );
var
   UMP : array[0..3] of byte;
   a,c : word;
   UMPDest : pointer;
   i : integer;
begin
     List.Init;  {Initialize the list part of the Screen object }
{ Initialize the mouse and set the mouse handler with all bits in }
     { the condition mask set for button activity}
     FindObjectDemon := FindMouse;
     SViewPort.Init( L, T, R, B, Clip, true );
     if MouseInit = true then  SetMouseHandler( 30 );
 { should be 30 if you don't want to track movement; 31 if you do }
     SColor := Color;
     SFill  := Fill;
     SLine  := Line;
     CloseHead := false;
     SetFillStyle( Fill, Color );
     SetLineStyle( Line, 0, white );
     bar( L, T, R, B );
     MouseToken := nil;
     MouseShow;
end;

procedure Screen.DefaultMouseAction;
var
   pNewWindow : GWindowPtr;
begin
   SetMouseHandler(0);
   if MouseRPressed = true then
      begin
      sound(300);delay(40);nosound;
      New(pNewWindow,
```

```
          Init( solidfill, blue, white, @S, 'Window #'));
      end;
   SetMouseHandler(30);
end;

procedure Screen.RestoreVP;  {restores the screen's viewport }
begin
     SViewPort.SetValue;
end;

{ The handler set in Screen.Init calls this function.   Anytime the
  buttons are pushed, this routine gets called. }
procedure Screen.UpdateMouse;
var
   VP :ViewPortType;
begin
if FindObject = true then
   begin
   GetViewSettings(VP);
   MouseToken := GetCursor;
   MouseToken^.GWViewPort.SetValue;
   MouseToken^.MouseAction;
   with VP do
        SetViewPort( x1, y1, x2, y2, true );
   if CloseHead = true then  { if top window requests closing }
      begin
      MouseToken := PopFirst;
      Dispose(MouseToken,Done);             { Close the window }
      CloseHead := false;     { reset request flag }
      end;
   end
else
   DefaultMouseAction;
end;

procedure GetGWCoords( var x1, y1, x2, y2 : integer);
var
t, a1, a2, b1, b2 : integer;
    color : word;
    P : array[0..4] of pointer;
    LS : LineSettingsType;

    function Max( x, y : integer ): integer;
    begin
         if x > y then Max := x else Max := y;
    end;

    function Min( x, y : integer) : integer;
    begin
         if x < y then Min := x else Min := y;
    end;
```

```
    procedure Shadow( x1, y1, x2, y2 : integer );
    begin
         Mark(P[0]);
         GetMem( P[1], ImageSize( x1, y1, x2, y1) );
         GetImage( x1, y1, x2, y1, P[1]^ ); { top }
         GetMem( P[2], ImageSize( x2, y2, x2, y1) );
         GetImage( x2, y2, x2, y1, P[2]^ ); {right}
         GetMem( P[3], ImageSize( x1, y1, x1, y2) );
         GetImage( x1, y1, x1, y2, P[3]^ ); { left }
         GetMem( P[4], ImageSize( x1, y2, x2, y2) );
         GetImage( x1, y2, x2, y2, P[4]^ ); {bottom }
         Rectangle( x1, y1, x2, y2 );
         PutImage( Min(x1, x2), y1, P[1]^, NormalPut );
         PutImage( x2, Min( y1, y2 ), P[2]^, NormalPut );
         PutImage( x1, Min( y1, y2), P[3]^, NormalPut );
         PutImage( Min(x1,x2), y2, P[4]^, NormalPut );
         Release(P[0]);
    end;

begin
     MouseCoords( x1, y1);  {grab the x,y coordinates!}
     repeat
     until MouseLPressed = true;
     MouseHide;
     repeat
           MouseCoords(x2,y2);
           Shadow(x1, y1, x2, y2);
     until MouseLReleased = true;
     if x1 > x2 then begin
        t := x1;
        x1 := x2;
        x2 := t;
        end;
     if y1 > y2 then begin
        t := y1;
        y1 := y2;
        y2 := t;
        end;
end;

constructor GWindow.Init( FillStyle, FillColor,
                          BColor1 : integer;
                          PScreen : ScreenPtr; WLabel : string );
var
    OldVPort : VPort;
    OldColor : integer;
    OldFill  : FillSettingsType;
    L, T, R, B : integer;
    srg : string;
```

```
function SaveArea( L, T, R, B : integer ) : boolean;
begin
     BelowGWSize := ImageSize( L, T, R, B);
     GetMem( BelowGWArea, BelowGWSize );
     if (BelowGWArea = nil) or (BelowGWSize < 255) then
        SaveArea := false
     else begin
        GetImage( L, T, R, B, BelowGWArea^ );
        SaveArea := true;
        end;
end;

procedure AdrToHexStr( Adr : pointer; var s : string );
var
   r : array[1..9] of byte;
   tmp : word;
   i   : integer;
begin
     tmp := Seg( Adr^ );
     r[4] := (tmp and $F);
     r[3] := (tmp and $F0) shr 4;
     r[2] := (tmp and $F00) shr 8;
     r[1] := (tmp and $F000) shr 12;
     tmp := Ofs( Adr^ );
     r[9] := (tmp and $F);
     r[8] := (tmp and $F0) shr 4;
     r[7] := (tmp and $F00) shr 8;
     r[6] := (tmp and $F000) shr 12;
     r[5] := 0;
     for i := 1 to 9 do
         if r[i] < 10 then
            s[i] := Chr($30 + r[i])
         else
            s[i] := Chr($37 + r[i]);
     s[5] := ':';
     s[0] := Chr(9);
end;


begin
     Node.Init; (SizeOF( Self));
     GetFillSettings( OldFill );

     GWFillS  := FillStyle;      { Save fill style }
     GWFillC  := FillColor;
     GWColor1 := BColor1;        { Save primary fill color }
     Str( index, srg );
     Windname := WLabel+srg;
     Inc(index);
     OldColor := GetColor;
```

```
     ParentScr := PScreen;        { Save pointer to parent screen }
     GetViewSettings(OldVPort.Value);
     ParentScr^.RestoreVP;        { Restore parent screen viewport }
     GetGWCoords( L, T, R, B );
     if not SaveArea( L, T, R, B ) then
        begin
        sound(600);delay(100);nosound;
        OldVPort.SetValue;
        MoveTo( 0,0 );
        GWindow.Done;
        MouseShow;
        fail;
        end
     else
        begin
        SetColor(GWColor1);                 { set window's color }
        SetFillStyle(GWFillS,GWFillC);      { set fill data }
        SetLineStyle(Solidln,0,NormWidth); { set line style }
        Bar3D( L, T, R, B, 0, false );  { draw window }
        Line( L, T+(2*TextHeight(WindName)), R,
                   T+(2*TextHeight(WindName)) );
        GWViewPort.Init( L, T, R, B, true, true );  {store & set }
        SetTextJustify( CenterText, CenterText );
        OutTextXY( Round((R-L)/2), TextHeight(WindName),
                              WindName);
        AdrToHexStr(HeapPtr, srg);
        OutTextXY( Round((R-L)/2), Round((B-T)/2), srg );
        Str(BelowGWSize, srg);
        OutTextXY( 40, 40, srg );
        PrependToList( ParentScr^ ); { add this window to screen }
        SetColor( OldColor );          {  restore old color... }
        SetFillStyle( OldFill.Pattern, OldFill.Color ); { ...fill}
        end;
      MouseShow;
end;

destructor GWindow.Done;
begin
     GWViewPort.SetValue;
     MouseHide;
     if BelowGWArea <> nil then
        begin
        PutImage(0,0,BelowGWArea^,CopyPut);
        FreeMem( BelowGWArea, BelowGWSize );
        end;
     MouseShow;
end;

function GWindow.InboundMouse : boolean;
begin
     if (GWViewPort.Value.x1 <= ParentScr^.MouseX) and
```

```
        (GWViewPort.Value.x2 >= ParentScr^.MouseX) and
        (GWViewPort.Value.y1 <= ParentScr^.MouseY) and
        (GWViewPort.Value.y2 >= ParentScr^.MouseY) then
             InboundMouse := true
        else
             InboundMouse := false;
end;

procedure GWindow.PrependToList( var AList : List );
begin
     Node.PrependToList( AList );
     MouseShow;
end;

procedure GWindow.LocalMouseCoords( var x, y : integer );
var
   VP :ViewPortType;
begin
     GWViewPort.GetValue(VP);
     MouseCoords( x, y );
     ParentScr^.MouseX := x;
     ParentScr^.MouseY := y;
     with VP do
          begin
          x := x - x1;
          y := y - y1;
          end;
end;

procedure GWindow.MouseAction;
var
   x,y :integer;
   str : string;
begin
     while MouseLPressed = true do
         begin
         LocalMouseCoords(x,y);
         MouseHide;
         if (ParentScr^.FindObject = true) then
            begin
            if @Self = ParentScr^.MouseToken then
               begin
               PutPixel(x,y,white);
               end;
            end;
         MouseShow;
         end;
     while MouseRPressed = true do
          begin
          sound(400);delay(100); nosound;
          if @Self = ParentScr^.Head then
```

```
            ParentScr^.CloseHead := true;
         end;
end;

procedure VPort.Init( Left, Top, Right, Bottom : integer;
                      ClipQ, SetQ : boolean );
begin
     Value.x1 := Left;
     Value.y1 := Top;
     Value.x2 := Right;
     Value.y2 := Bottom;
     Value.Clip := ClipQ;
     if SetQ = true then
        SetValue;
end;

procedure VPort.SetValue;
begin
     SetViewPort( Value.x1, Value.y1, Value.x2, Value.y2, Value.Clip );
end;

procedure VPort.GetValue( var AValue : ViewPortType );
begin
     GetViewSettings( AValue );
end;

{$F+}
procedure EntryPoint;
{$F-}
begin
     S.MouseX := xpos;
     S.MouseY := ypos;
     S.UpdateMouse;
end;

{$F+}
function HeapFunc( size : word ) : integer;
{$F-}
begin
     HeapFunc := 1;
end;

begin
     HeapError := @HeapFunc;
     index := 1;
     GraphDriver := Detect;  { Detect the graphics driver }
     InitGraph( GraphDriver, GraphMode, PathToDriver );
                                { Initialize graphics }
     S.Init( 0, 0, GetMaxX, GetMaxY, cyan, solidfill, solidln,
                                        true );
end.
```

The Screen

Think of the screen as an object. It has boundaries. It has a color, a fill style, a line style. These may be the Turbo Pascal defaults, or they may be specifically chosen values. The screen may contain some number of windows. In our design, the screen is a descendant of the `List` object type, which gives it a convenient way of keeping track of an arbitrary number of windows (subject, of course to memory limitations). The declaration of the `Screen` object type looks like:

```
Screen = object(List)
    SViewPort : VPort;
    SColor    : integer;
    SFill     : integer;
    SLine     : integer;
    MouseToken : GWindowPtr;
    MouseX     : integer;
    MouseY     : integer;
    CloseHead  : boolean;
    procedure Init( L,T,R,B,Color,Fill,Line :
                                        integer;
                                 Clip : boolean );
    procedure RestoreVP;
    procedure UpdateMouse;
    procedure DefaultMouseAction;
    end;
```

The `Screen` object type has a `VPort` object type as a property. The `VPort` type was created simply to permit a shorthand way of restoring a viewport's parameters (using the `.SetValue` method), retrieving them (using `.GetValue`), and initializing them (with `.Init`). Most people think there's only one screen — physically, *is* only one. However, if you defined two viewports (each taking up half the screen), you could in theory have two screen objects coexisting at the same time. Once you do that, though, you introduce a lot of needless complication, so for our system, the viewport parameters for the screen will take up the entire screen.

Most of the remaining properties are "bookkeeping" properties, there to hold some piece of information about the screen such as the background color, fillstyle, etc. A noteworthy property is `MouseToken`, which is a pointer to the graphics window inside of whose boundaries the mouse is found. This is determined by setting the `List` object type's `FindObjectDemon` to a function called `FindMouse`. Anytime the mouse moves, or when buttons are pushed, a value is found for MouseToken, which causes the appropriate window viewport to be set, and some action to be performed.

Another property that deserves mention is `CloseHead`, which is set true any time there is a need to close and dispose of the window pointed to by the `Screen`'s `Head` pointer.

The `Screen` object type's methods include:

.Init: This old friend instantiates the `Screen` object type with initialization values. If the `FindActionDemon` does not find the mouse inside of any window, then the `.DefaultMouseAction` method is executed. In our design, the only action that takes place in the `.DefaultMouseAction` method occurs when the right mouse button is pressed and released to signal the creation of a new window.

.RestoreVP: This simply calls the `.SetValue` method of the `VPort` object that is the `SViewPort` property of `Screen`.

.UpdateMouse: This method ends up being called every time the mouse interrupt executes the subroutine whose address is supplied in the call to mouse function 12. If `FindObject` is true (that is, if the mouse is inside the boundaries of a window), then the program saves the current viewport settings, establishes the viewport of the identified window, performs a specified action, and then restores the originally saved viewport settings. If the requested mouse action is to close the most recently created window, then pop the first window from the Screen list and deallocate the memory associated with this window.

.DefaultMouseAction: This method defines what to do when the mouse interrupt occurs and the mouse is not inside of any window.

The Graphics Window

The windows in our system (called GWindows, for Graphics Window) are all Node descendants. This allows the windows to be placed the list maintained by the Screen object type. Each GWindow, like the larger screen, has its own boundaries, as stored in a VPort object, as well as its own fillstyle (GWFillS), fillcolor (GWFillC), as well as primary and secondary drawing colors (GWColor1 and GWColor2). Each GWindow has a title, which is stored in the WindName property. The GWindow object type has the following declaration:

```
GWindow = object(Node)
     GWViewPort  : VPort;
     WindName    : string;
     BelowGWArea : pointer;
     BelowGWSize : word;
     GWFillS     : integer;
     GWFillC     : integer;
     GWColor1    : integer;
     ParentScr   : ScreenPtr;
     constructor Init( FillStyle, FillColor, BColor1 : integer;
                       PScreen : ScreenPtr; WLabel : string );
     destructor Done;
     procedure PrependToList( var AList : List );
     function InboundMouse : boolean;
     procedure MouseAction;
     procedure LocalMouseCoords(var x, y : integer );
     end;
```

Other GWindow properties include the ParentScr pointer, which points to the Screen object the GWindow is a member of (very useful for setting the screen's viewport from inside a window), and the related properties BelowGWArea and BelowGWSize, which we'll discuss more when we look at the GWindow methods, of which there are only a handful, as follows:

.Init: This constructor basically initializes the properties, generates a unique name, and then calls the GetGWCoords procedure. The first set of x,y coordinates are grabbed upon entry to the procedure. Then, when the left mouse button is depressed, the procedure calls an internal procedure that very rapidly draws and redraws a box from the initial x,y coordinates to wherever the mouse is located, saving the background so that it is not obliterated by the lines of the box. When the mouse button is released, a second x,y coordinate is identified and then both pairs of coordinates are rearranged as necessary so that the values returned by the procedure identify the left, top, right, and bottom coordinates, respectively.

A crucial decision to create or not create a window is then made in the function `SaveArea`, which is part of the `GWindow.Init` constructor. The function is defined as follows:

```
function SaveArea( L, T, R, B : integer ) : boolean;
begin
BelowGWSize := ImageSize( L, T, R, B);
GetMem( BelowGWArea, BelowGWSize );
if (BelowGWArea = nil) or (BelowGWSize < 255) then
   SaveArea := false
else
   begin
   GetImage( L, T, R, B, BelowGWArea^ );
   SaveArea := true;
   end;
end;
```

`BelowGWArea` is a pointer that contains the starting address of a block of memory that is reserved to save a copy of what is underneath the window before we plaster it onto the screen. The act of reserving blocks of memory is called allocation, and the memory is allocated from a region called the heap. Loosely defined, the *heap* is the part of your computer's memory that isn't occupied by a program just after it is loaded.

Saving the image underneath a new window is a common windowing feature, and allows the screen to be restored when the window is removed; you just paste the image back into place. The property `BelowGWSize` holds the size of the area pointed to by `BelowGWArea`, and comes in particularly useful when the time comes to dispose of the window.

Note that the function returns a false value if either the pointer is nil (which basically means there is no memory left on the heap), or if the size of the area under the window is less than 255 bytes. The latter condition will occur if you mark out an area that's too small to manage as a window, or (even more important) for the case where you mark out an area that exceeds 64K (in which case `BelowGWSize` will be 0).

If `SaveArea` returns a false value, then the `.Init` method restores the old viewport settings, calls the `.Done` method, causes the mouse to reappear on the screen, and then calls the Turbo Pascal standard procedure `fail`. In our code, the call to `fail` stops the creation of a dynamic window dead in its tracks, but gracefully. Any memory already allocated for the window is deallocated, and the program recovers from the error. As an additional note about error recovery, we also install a simple heap error function that gets called whenever the heap manager cannot complete an allocation request.

Since the `GWindow` object type has a constructor `.Init` (and a destructor `.Done`), we can illustrate the use of these methods with the Turbo Pascal functions `New` (which allocates memory for dynamic variables) and `Dispose` (which deallocates that memory). One thing you'll notice about the code in Listing 7-4 is the almost complete reliance on pointers and dynamic variables, so issues related to the allocation and deallocation of memory become very important.

.Done: Just as we use `.Init` as a default name for an object type's instantiation routine (whether it is a procedure or a constructor), the method name `.Done` is used as a default to "uninstantiate" an instance. We've not had to use this type of method up to now because virtually all the object types in the sample programs thus far have been static — that is, declared as variables at the start of the program.

While static variables and objects have their place, they are also quite limiting. Take for example this windowing system. If you had to identify and name every window that could pop up, you'd obviously have a limited number of windows that could be open at a time, since you'd have to have a separate variable name for each one. Not a very flexible system, and fraught with its own problems (managing boundaries, for example).

`.Done` is a *destructor* method, which as you might imagine, is the opposite of a constructor. In our particular case, the primary task of .Done is to set the viewport of the settings of the window that is in the process of expiring and then "paste" the image stored in `BelowGWArea` over itself. Once that is finished and the mouse is redisplayed, Turbo Pascal finishes the job of closing the window by deallocating the memory occupied by the dynamic `GWindow` instance.

.PrependToList: This method simply calls the ancestor `Node.PrependToList` method and then issues a function call to show the mouse.

.InboundMouse: This is a function that returns true if the mouse cursor is inside the GWindow instance that calls this method, and false otherwise.

.MouseAction: This method explains what to do when the left or right mouse buttons are depressed. While the left button is depressed, the "local" mouse coordinates (coordinates that use the window's viewport as a frame of reference) are determined, we verify that the mouse is still inside the window, and then color the pixel at the mouse coordinates. While the right button is depressed, the method sounds a beep, delays for 100 milliseconds, and then, if it turns out that the mouse cursor is inside the most recently created window (the window pointed to by `Screen.Head`), the `CloseHead` flag is set true in the `Screen` object variable.

.LocalMouseCoords: This method calls the `MouseCoords` function (the mouse function that returns the x,y coordinates of the mouse), stores them in the ParentScr's `MouseX` and `MouseY` properties, respectively, and then subtracts the respective x,y coordinates of the current window's upper left corner. This gives a set of coordinates with respect to the window's (not the screen's) 0,0 point.

The Interplay

Basically, the operation of the entire program occurs inside the code for the screen and window object types; the main begin/end block just keeps looping, doing nothing, until a key is pressed to signal the end of the program.

Just so there's something to see in the window after we bring it up, print the address pointed to by the Turbo Pascal `HeapPtr` (heap pointer) variable in the center of the screen. The memory address stored in the heap pointer increases as memory is allocated to window objects, and decreases as memory is freed when the windows are closed. A more complete description of the heap pointer may be found in the Turbo Pascal documentation. A sample output screen is presented in Fig. 7.02. We use the procedure `AdrToHexStr` to convert whatever address the heap pointer points to into a segment:offset format in hexadecimal. I had introduced this code into the `.Init` method because I had experienced difficulty in disposing of windows, resulting in an exhaustion of memory.

Figure 7.2 — Sample output screen for window program

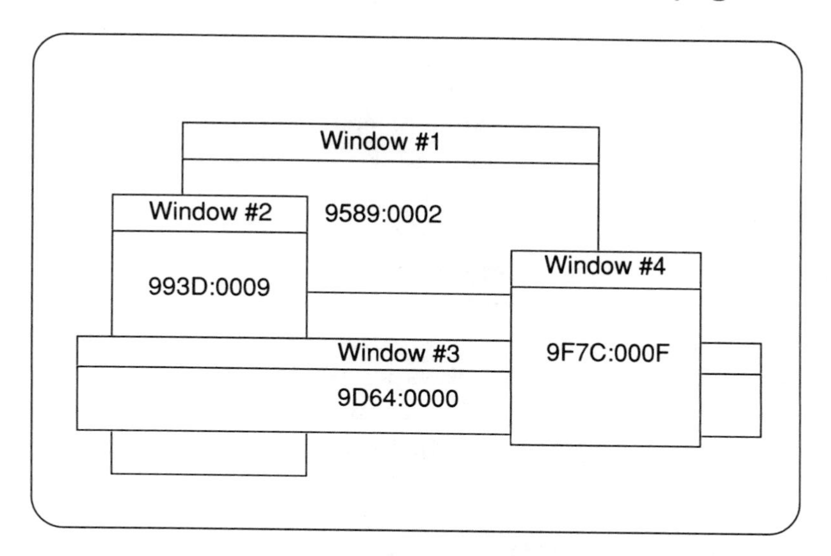

In the `GWindow.Done` method, the call to `FreeMem` had originally read:

```
FreeMem( BelowGWArea, SizeOf(BelowGWArea) )
```

which sounds very nice, but actually deallocates only 4 bytes of memory (since that's the size of the pointer) instead of the much larger quantity you'd expect. The result was that the memory allocated to old, closed windows, never was freed completely and put back in the heap, so that after a dozen windows or so, I was suddenly out of memory.

You can prove this to yourself by replacing the correct line with the one above. Notice when you run the program, no matter how many windows you close, new windows show an ever-increasing heap pointer address. Eventually, no matter what you do, you'll run out of heap and have no choice but to press a key and stop the program.

Postscript

The windowing system presented in this chapter is far from complete, as you can plainly see. However the point of this exercise was to show how behavior can be so completely encapsulated inside of an object that there is literally nothing for a user program to do but keep running!

Ideas for enhancement? Well, if you wanted to close any window (instead of just the top one) you'd have to figure out which window to close, then temporarily remove all overlapping windows, close the window, and replace the windows temporarily removed. Much the same procedure would occur if you wanted to bring a window to the top of the screen. Another idea that extends the concept of windows is menus (for what is a menu if not a small collection of windows?)

In the next chapter, we'll discuss the uses of object-oriented programming in artificial intelligence and present an example of an object type that implements a simple AI algorithm to solve a puzzle.

8

OOP IN ARTIFICIAL INTELLIGENCE

For a number of reasons, people who are casually acquainted with OOP sometimes mistakenly think of it as some variant of Artificial Intelligence (AI). Indeed, I've met people who think the two are synonymous. In fact, although OOP works well in tandem with AI techniques, the two are nevertheless distinct: AI is not OOP, and OOP is not AI. In this chapter we shall implement a classic AI search algorithm using objects in Turbo Pascal 5.5, and then we'll improve the basic algorithm using a heuristic to reduce the workload on the way to a solution.

Artificial Intelligence

Broadly speaking, AI is a branch of computer science that studies how computers can be made to be intelligent. AI researchers, in attempting to understand the principles that make intelligence possible, have uncovered a number of computational techniques that make computers more useful. Leaving aside the question of whether computers will ever be able to actually think, software designers can exploit these AI techniques to let computers simulate intelligent, problem-solving behavior.

For example, one of the classic areas of study in AI is the *search* problem, which places the problem solver in a situation where one choice leads to another until a goal is reached. Applications as diverse as sentence analysis, obstacle avoidance, route finding, and game playing all depend on the ability to search for a solution in some logical fashion. We will use a technique called *depth-first search* to solve a game called the triangle puzzle.

The Triangle Puzzle

My first acquaintance with this game took place in a roadside diner somewhere in Georgia, though I'm sure you can find this mind-twister all over the country. The game board for the puzzle is a triangular piece of wood with 15 holes arranged in the pattern of an equilateral triangle, as shown in Figure 8.1. Supplied are 14 pegs, which are inserted into holes on the board at the start of the game, leaving one hole empty. The game is played by jumping pegs in "checker" style (that is, moving a peg from its position, over another peg into an empty position) and then removing the jumped peg. Play continues until no more moves are possible. If only one peg remains on the board, you've won; otherwise, you lose.

Figure 8.1 — The triangle puzzle

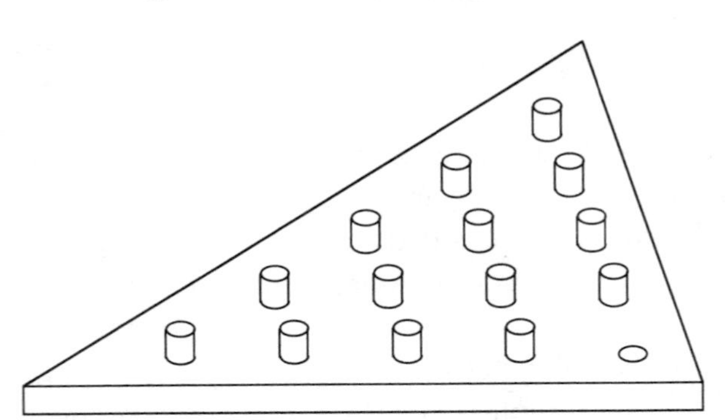

Most people go about solving the puzzle using trial and error, resulting in a number of false starts and dead ends before a win is found. At the start, there are only a couple of ways to make a legal jump. However, at about the fifth move, it's not unusual to have a half dozen alternatives to choose from. The player is faced with a situation where one game position leads to another, and so on, until a goal is achieved, which as we noted before is the classic characteristic of a search problem.

To introduce some helpful terminology, a game position (or just *position*) obtained by making a legal move in an earlier position will be called a *child*, and the earlier position will be called the *parent*. All the children of a position will be collectively called its *offspring*, and the children are *siblings* to each other. Finally, all offspring positions reflecting the same number of moves will be called a *generation*. These relationships are illustrated in Figure 8.2.

Figure 8.2 — Relationships among positions (nodes) in triangle puzzle

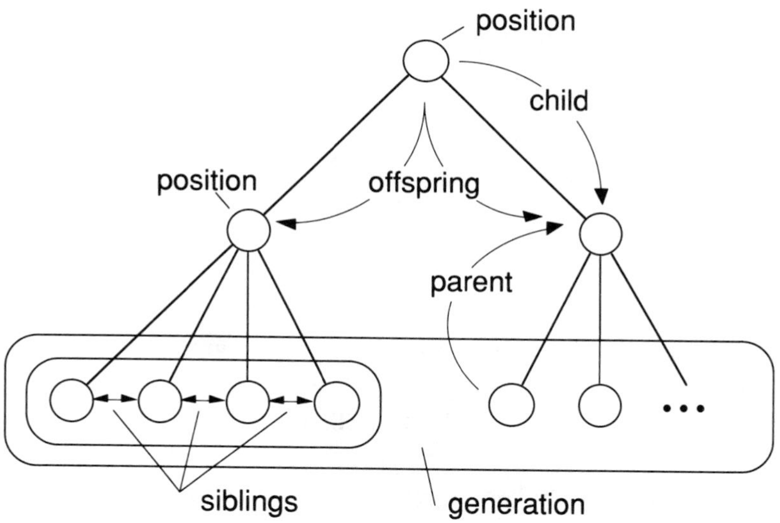

There are two basic methods of searching for a solution: breadth-first search and depth-first search. The breadth-first method involves first generating the offspring of a position, and then evaluating each child to see if there's a winner among them. If not, we then repeat the procedure for each child until we do find a winner. This procedure is illustrated in Figure 8.3. Notice how the resulting structure of generated positions resembles an upside-down tree, and how the search method proceeds side-to-side, resulting in the apt name: breadth-first.

Figure 8.3 — Breadth-first search among nodes

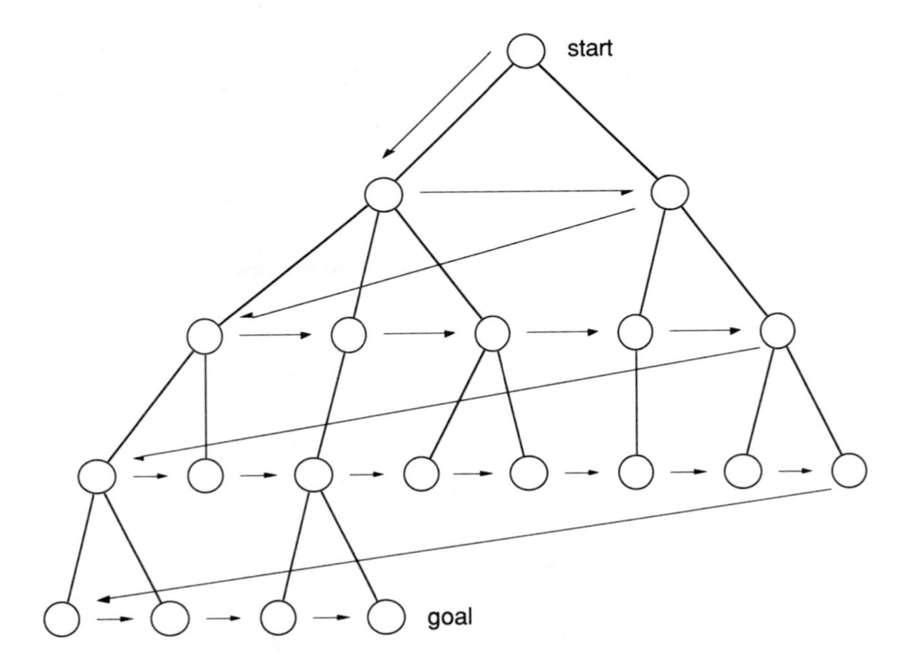

If we were trying to figure out the best way to get from New York to Los Angeles through a number of intermediate cities, the breadth-first search (or some variant) would be a likely candidate for solving the problem. The triangle puzzle, on the other hand, is a depth-first search problem, mainly because the solution is guaranteed not to occur before we've made 13 moves.

The classic depth-first search also involves the creation of offspring, except that instead of evaluating all the offspring of a position before going on to the next generation, we look at only the first child. If the child is a winner, the problem is solved. If it is not, the depth-first method generates all the offspring of the child and repeats the process of examining the first child of the next generation. As long as a child has offspring, we follow this method. If a child is not a winner and has no offspring, it is dropped from consideration and we repeat this method with the child's next sibling. Similarly, if a child is not a winner and none of its offspring are winners, it is also dropped from consideration, and attention passes to the next sibling in line. This procedure is illustrated in Figure 8.4.

Figure 8.4

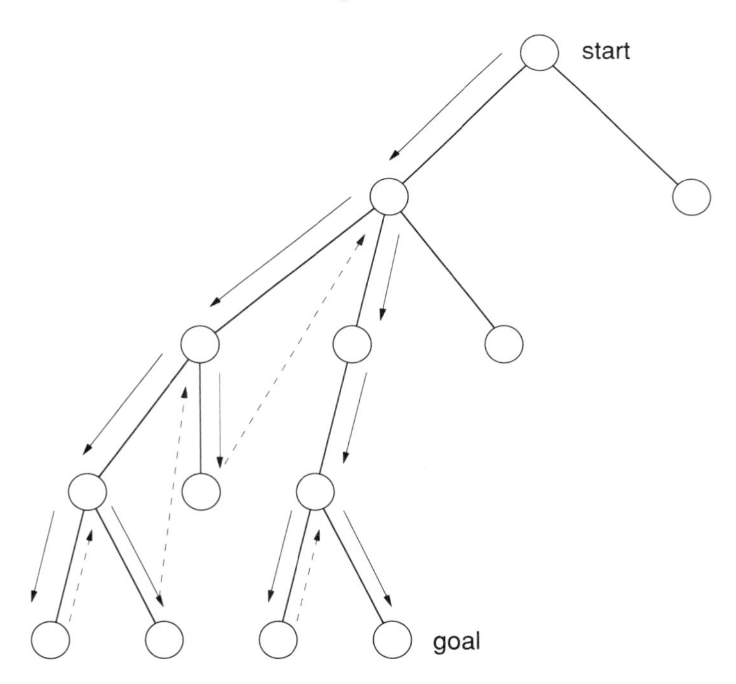

In the classic depth-first algorithm, winners are sought at every generation. For the triangle problem, we'll save some time by not looking for a win until we arrive at a position that has no children. The logic here is: if we can still move, there can't possibly be only one peg left on the board!

In Figure 8.3 or Figure 8.4, you'll notice a position and its offspring form a sort of structure that repeats itself at each generation. This leads to a very natural representation of an object containing (1) a position, and (2) a list of all its offspring. From the description of the depth-first methodology, we can also see that the solution of the problem will rely heavily on the abstraction of basic functions into an object type that will allow the solution to be found by calling the same function from different object instances.

For example, the solution of the triangle puzzle will require each position to know how to generate its own offspring positions. Each individual child will, in turn, have to know how to generate its offspring. Similarly, every position must be able to figure out whether it is a win or not. Knowing how to do these two things will allow the triangle puzzle to be solved with a single call to a top-level object that holds a starting position.

With these considerations in mind, we can design an object type that can represent a position, hold a list of all its offspring, and is capable of finding a win and of letting us know about it. We can also include a few more goodies, explained below. This object type, called `Triangle`, is presented in Listing 8-1 (TRIGL.PAS) and looks like this:

```
Triangle = object( Node )
             Position : String15;
             Offspring : List;
             Generation : integer;
             constructor Init( APosition : String15;
                               Gen : integer );
             destructor Done;
             procedure ShowPosition;
             procedure ShowWin;
             procedure ShowStats;
             function Heuristic : boolean; virtual;
             function FindWin : boolean;
             function FindChildren : boolean;
             function ValidMove( AMove : integer ); MoveDirection;
```

```
procedure MovePeg( MoveNumber : integer;
Direction : MoveDirection;
var NewPosition : String15);
procedure GenChild( NewPosition  String15 ); virtual;
function CheckForWin : boolean;
end;
```

Listing 8-1

```
unit Trigl;
interface

uses ListObj,CRT;

const
MaxGen = 13;

var
   PosStats : array[0..MaxGen] of longint;

type
String15 = string[15];
MoveArray = array[1..3] of integer;
MoveDirection = (no_move, down, up);
MoveFunc = function( i : integer) : MoveDirection;
MoveFuncPtr = ^MoveFunc;

const
MaxNumMove = 18;
LegalMoves : array[1..18] of MoveArray =
             ( (1,2,4),    (1,3,6),    (2,4,7),   (2,5,9),
               (3,5,8),    (3,6,10),   (4,5,6),   (4,7,11),
               (4,8,13),   (5,8,12),   (5,9,14),  (6,9,13),
               (6,10,15),  (7,8,9),    (8,9,10),  (11,12,13),
               (12,13,14), (13,14,15) );

type

Triangle = object( Node )
           position : String15;
           Offspring : List;
           Generation : integer;
           constructor Init( APosition : String15; Gen : integer );
           destructor Done;
```

```
          procedure ShowPosition;
          procedure ShowWin;
          procedure ShowStats;
          function Heuristic : boolean; virtual;
          function FindWin : boolean;
          function FindChildren : boolean;
          function ValidMove( AMove : integer ) : MoveDirection;
          procedure MovePeg( MoveNumber : integer;
                             Direction : MoveDirection;
                             var NewPosition : String15 );
          procedure GenChild( NewPosition : string15 ); virtual;
          function CheckForWin : boolean;
          end;

type
TrianglePtr = ^Triangle;

procedure Step;
procedure InitStats;
procedure DisplayPosition( Position : String15; x, y : integer);

implementation

procedure Step;
var
   Dummy : char;
begin
          Dummy := ReadKey;
end;

destructor Triangle.Done;
begin
     FreeMem( @Offspring, sizeof(Offspring) );
end;

procedure Triangle.ShowWin;
var
   pTriangle : TrianglePtr;
   i : integer;
begin
     if Generation = 0 then
        begin
        ShowPosition;
        Step;
        end;
     if Offspring.Head <> nil then
        begin
        Offspring.Cursor := Offspring.Head;
        pTriangle := Offspring.GetCursor;;
        pTriangle^.ShowPosition;
        Step;
```

```
        pTriangle^.ShowWin;
        end;
end;

procedure Triangle.ShowStats;
var
   i : integer;
   t : longint;
begin
     ClrScr;
     t := 0;
     for i := 0 to MaxGen do
         begin
         writeln('Number of generation ', i:2, ' positions: ',
                                                    PosStats[i]);
         t := t + PosStats[i];
         end;
     writeln;
     writeln('Total number of positions examined: ', t );
     Step;
end;

function Triangle.FindWin : boolean;
var
   pTriangle : TrianglePtr;
   WinFlag   : boolean;
begin
     if FindChildren = true then
        begin
        WinFlag := false;
        OffSpring.Cursor := OffSpring.Head; { point at head }
        while (Offspring.FindNextObject = true) and
                                    (WinFlag = false) do
              begin
              pTriangle := OffSpring.GetCursor; { copy head }
              WinFlag := pTriangle^.FindWin;
              { find if it leads to win }
              if WinFlag = false then  { if it doesn't }
                 begin
                 pTriangle := Offspring.PopFirst;
                 Dispose( pTriangle, Done );
                 end;
              end;
        FindWin := WinFlag;
        end
     else
        begin
        if CheckForWin = true then
           { This means that the Self triangle is
                                         a winner! }
           begin
```

```
            writeln( 'I found a win!');
            ShowPosition;
            FindWin := true;
            end
         else
            begin
            FindWin := false;
            end;
         end;
end;

{ A triangle node has the ability to find its own children.
  If it successfully finds its children, the function returns true.
  If a triangle has no children, then we check to see if a winning
  position has been found. }
function Triangle.FindChildren : boolean;
var
   i : integer;
   vflag : MoveDirection;
   NewPosition : String15;
begin
     FindChildren := false;
     if Heuristic = true then
        for i := 1 to MaxNumMove do
             begin
             vflag := ValidMove(i);
             if vflag <> no_move then
                begin
                Inc(PosStats[Generation+1]);
                MovePeg( i, vflag, NewPosition );
                GenChild(NewPosition);
                FindChildren := true;
                end
             end;
end;

function Triangle.Heuristic : boolean;
begin
        Heuristic := true  {this simple function always returns true}
end;

{ a triangle knows whether a particular type of move is valid for
  its position.  the function returns NO_MOVE if no move is
  possible, UP if a peg can jump from the 3 position to the 1
  position (as described in the move array), or DOWN if a peg can
  jump from the 1 to the 3 position. }
function Triangle.ValidMove( AMove : integer ) : MoveDirection;
begin
         if (Position[ LegalMoves[AMove,1] ] = 'X') and
            (Position[ LegalMoves[AMove,2] ] = 'X') and
            (Position[ LegalMoves[AMove,3] ] = 'O') then
```

```
            ValidMove := down
         else
            if (Position[ LegalMoves[AMove,1] ] = 'O') and
               (Position[ LegalMoves[AMove,2] ] = 'X') and
               (Position[ LegalMoves[AMove,3] ] = 'X') then
               ValidMove := up
            else
               ValidMove := no_move;
end;

{ given a type of move and a direction (UP or DOWN), a triangle
  knows how to reflect the move in the Position array, and how to
  create a new Triangle object whose position is the new position,
  and to attach the new Triangle object as a member of Offspring
  list }
procedure Triangle.MovePeg( MoveNumber : integer;
Direction : MoveDirection;
                           var NewPosition : String15 );
var
   pNewTriangle : TrianglePtr;
   c : char;
begin
     NewPosition := Position;
     NewPosition[ LegalMoves[MoveNumber, 2] ] := 'O';
     if Direction = down then
        begin
        NewPosition[ LegalMoves[MoveNumber, 1] ] := 'O';
        NewPosition[ LegalMoves[MoveNumber, 3] ] := 'X';
        end
     else
        begin
        NewPosition[ LegalMoves[MoveNumber, 3] ] := 'O';
        NewPosition[ LegalMoves[MoveNumber, 1] ] := 'X';
        end;
end;

procedure Triangle.GenChild( NewPosition : string15 );
var
   pNewTriangle : TrianglePtr;
begin
     New( pNewTriangle, Init( NewPosition, Succ(Generation) ) );
     { if you want to speed things up, comment out the next line }
     pNewTriangle^.ShowPosition;
     Offspring.Prepend( pNewTriangle );
     Offspring.Cursor := OffSpring.Head;
end;

constructor Triangle.Init( APosition : String15; Gen : integer );
begin
     Position := APosition;
     Offspring.Init;
```

```
     Node.Init; (SizeOf( Self );
     Generation := Gen;
end;

procedure DisplayPosition( Position : String15; x, y : integer);
begin
     gotoXY(x,y);
     writeln( '          ', Position[1]);
     gotoXY(x,y+2);
     writeln( '        ', Position[2], '    ', Position[3] );
     gotoXY(x,y+4);
     writeln( '      ', Position[4], '    ', Position[5],
              '   ', Position[6]);
     gotoXY(x,y+6);
     writeln( '    ', Position[7], '    ', Position[8],
              '   ',  Position[9], '    ', Position[10] );
     gotoXY(x,y+8);
     writeln( '  ', Position[11], '    ', Position[12], '    ',
              Position[13], '    ', Position[14], '    ',
Position[15] );
end;

procedure Triangle.ShowPosition;
begin
     gotoXY(16,10);
     writeln( 'Generation: ' , Generation:2 );
     DisplayPosition( Position, 16, 12 );
end;

function Triangle.CheckForWin;
var
   FirstX : integer;
   SubS   : string;
begin
     FirstX := Pos( 'X', Position );
     SubS := Copy( Position, (FirstX+1), 255 );
     if Pos( 'X', SubS ) = 0 then
        CheckForWin := true
     else
        CheckForWin := false;
end;

procedure InitStats;
var
   i : integer;
begin

      PosStats[0] := 1;
      for i := 1 to MaxGen do
          PosStats[i] := 0;
end;
```

```
begin
InitStats;
end.
```

The property requirements for the `Triangle` object type are simple. First, a 15-character string represents the position associated with the object (called the "current position"). The first character represents the peg or hole at the top apex of the triangle, and the last five characters represent the five pegs/holes at the base of the puzzle. The next property, `offspring`, is a list consisting of all positions that can be legally generated from the current position. The third property, `generation`, is an integer that shows how many moves have been made on the board thus far, which corresponds to the "generation" of the position. For example, the starting position has a generation number of 0; the final position, 13. This number will come in handy as we study the triangle puzzle.

Let's take a detailed look at the methods associated with the `Triangle` object type:

.ShowPosition. This method takes the string representation of the position, which is hard to interpret visually even after much familiarity with the program, and represents it as a triangle, with X's denoting pegs and O's denoting holes. The `.ShowPosition` method calls the procedure `DisplayPosition`, which actually does most of the work of displaying the board. `DisplayPosition` has other uses, as we'll see when it comes to writing a program to exercise the `Triangle` object type.

.ShowWin. Once a solution has been found, this method permits the user to step through it by repeatedly pressing a key on the keyboard.

.ShowStats. An array called `PosStats` is declared globally in the unit with the Triangle object type. The `.FindChildren` method increments an element of this array every time a new child object is generated. The element incremented corresponds to the generation of the child being created. Thus, `PosStats` keeps track of how many children are created for each generation. This method clears the screen, presents the information in `PosStats`, and finally publishes the overall number of child positions generated.

.Heuristic. It would be nice (not to mention more efficient) to be able to tell in advance if we are embarking down a dead-end road when we start to evaluate a position. This method returns true if further investigation of the position is worth pursuing. The specific method implemented for the `Triangle` object type always returns true, resulting in an exhaustive search of a solution among all children.

.FindWin. This method is the problem-solving workhorse. First, it determines whether any offspring can be generated from the current position (that is, the position stored in the `Position` property of the object calling the method). If no children can be found, the position is tested to see if it is a win by calling the `.CheckForWin` method. If the position is a win, `.FindWin` returns true; if not, `.FindWin` returns false.

If, on the other hand, the position does have offspring, the `.FindWin` method of each offspring (starting with the child pointed to by `Offspring.Head`) is called. What in effect happens is that execution of the parents' `.FindWin` method pauses while the `.FindWin` method is executed for its offspring. This technique of having a routine call itself repeatedly (each time with slightly different position to work with) is called *recursion,* and it continues until a win is found. If no win is found for any given offspring, it is removed from its parents' list of offspring (and the memory they occupied is deallocated). If no offspring lead to a win, `.FindWin` returns false.

.FindChildren. This method uses the current position and the `LegalMoves` array to figure out whether any children can be generated from the current position. The method `.Heuristic` is used to determine whether any children should be generated. If a child can be generated, a new position string is formed by calling the `.MovePeg` method, after which a call to the `.GenChild` method actually allocates the memory for the new object and instantiates it.

The array `LegalMoves` identifies 18 combinations of holes that can participate in a jump, as shown in Figure 8.5. For example, you can jump a peg in 1 over a peg in 2 into 4. You can also jump a peg in 4 over the peg in 2 into 1. In all, there are 36 possible moves on the puzzle board.

.ValidMove. This method is called by .FindChildren to determine (a) whether a move involving a particular set of three holes is legal and (b) if it is, in what direction the move may be made. One direction is arbitrarily called *up* and the other, *down*.

.MovePeg. Using the string representing the current position and the result of the `.ValidMove` method, this method creates a new string that represents the position after the legal move returned by `.ValidMove` has been made.

.GenChild. Given a string that represents a position, this method allocates memory for the new object and instantiates it. The method then displays the position on the screen and adds the object to the head of the `Offspring` list.

Figure 8.5 — Legal moves in the triangle puzzle

1 2 3 4 5 6 7 8 9 10 11 12 13 14 15	1 2 3 4 5 6 7 8 9 10 11 12 13 14 15	1 2 3 4 5 6 7 8 9 10 11 12 13 14 15
1 2 3 4 5 6 7 8 9 10 11 12 13 14 15	1 2 3 4 5 6 7 8 9 10 11 12 13 14 15	1 2 3 4 5 6 7 8 9 10 11 12 13 14 15
1 2 3 4 5 6 7 8 9 10 11 12 13 14 15	1 2 3 4 5 6 7 8 9 10 11 12 13 14 15	1 2 3 4 5 6 7 8 9 10 11 12 13 14 15
1 2 3 4 5 6 7 8 9 10 11 12 13 14 15	1 2 3 4 5 6 7 8 9 10 11 12 13 14 15	1 2 3 4 5 6 7 8 9 10 11 12 13 14 15
1 2 3 4 5 6 7 8 9 10 11 12 13 14 15	1 2 3 4 5 6 7 8 9 10 11 12 13 14 15	1 2 3 4 5 6 7 8 9 10 11 12 13 14 15
1 2 3 4 5 6 7 8 9 10 11 12 13 14 15	1 2 3 4 5 6 7 8 9 10 11 12 13 14 15	1 2 3 4 5 6 7 8 9 10 11 12 13 14 15

Improving the Triangle

If you play with the triangle puzzle enough, you start to notice some telltale signs that seem indicative of whether you are on the right track or not. For example, at some point you might notice (as I did after many hours of playing with the puzzle) that if the center three positions are vacant, it becomes very difficult to successfully solve the puzzle. Trust me. In fact, you could devise a rule of thumb that says: at generation 9, if the central three holes are empty, don't go any further. Assume that all offspring will fail to win. Go back now. Although you may somehow happen to miss a win using this rule, you will, as we will show, save heaps of time in the long run.

What we have just formulated is known as a *heuristic*, a word with Greek roots meaning to invent or to discover (Archimedes used a variant when he cried "Eureka!). Since what in effect happens is the cutting off (or "pruning") of portions of the search tree, this heuristic is called a "pruning heuristic." Let's see how we can implement it in a descendant object type we'll call `BetterTrigl`, presented in the declaration of Listing 8-2 (TRIANGLE.PAS).

Listing 8-2

```
program Triangle_Puzzle;

uses Trigl,ListObj,Crt,Dos;

const

BasicSetups : array[1..4] of String15 =
              ( 'XXXXXXXXXXXXXXO',
              'XXXXOXXXXXXXXXX',
              'XXXXXXXXXOXXXXX',
              'XXXOXXXXXXXXXXX' );

type

Pair = array[1..2] of word;

BetterTrigl = object(Triangle)
              procedure GenChild( NewPosition : String15 ); virtual;
```

```
              function Heuristic : boolean; virtual;
              end;

function BetterTrigl.Heuristic : boolean;
begin
     if ((Generation = 9) and (Position[5] = '0') and
                              (Position[8] = '0') and
                              (Position[9] = '0')) then
        Heuristic := false
     else
        Heuristic := true;
end;

procedure BetterTrigl.GenChild( NewPosition : String15 );
var
   pNewTriangle : ^BetterTrigl;
begin
     New( pNewTriangle, Init( NewPosition, Succ(Generation) ) );
     { comment out next line for speedup }
     pNewTriangle^.ShowPosition;

     Offspring.Prepend( pNewTriangle );
     Offspring.Cursor := OffSpring.Head;
end;

{publish the difference in time between two times}
procedure TimeDiff( H, M, S, HS : Pair);
var
   MS, SS : string[2];
begin
        if S[2] < S[1] then
           begin
           S[2] := S[2] + 60;
           Dec(M[2]);
           end;
        if M[2] < M[1] then
           begin
           M[2] := M[2] + 60;
           Dec(H[2]);
           end;
        if H[2] < H[1] then
           H[2] := H[2] + 24;
        gotoXY(1,1);
        Str( M[2]-M[1], MS );
        Str( S[2]-S[1], SS );
        if Length(MS) = 1 then MS := Concat( '0', MS );
        if Length(SS) = 1 then SS := Concat( '0', SS );
        GoToXY( 1,3 );
        writeln('Elapsed time = ', H[2]-H[1], ':', MS,
                          ':', SS );
end;
```

```
var
   T : Triangle;
   B : BetterTrigl;
   H,M,S,HS : Pair;
   Choice : integer;
begin
     ClrScr;
     GoToXY(1,1);
     write( '1:' );
     DisplayPosition( BasicSetups[1], 3, 1 );
     GoToXY(40,1);
     write( '2:' );
     DisplayPosition( BasicSetups[2], 42,1 );
     GoToXY(1,12);
     write( '3:' );
     DisplayPosition( BasicSetups[3], 3, 12 );
     GoToXY(40,12);
     write( '4:' );
     DisplayPosition( BasicSetups[4], 42, 12 );
     repeat
     GoToXY( 5, 23 );
     write( 'Select a starting position (1-4):    ');
     GoToXY( 39,23);
     readln( Choice );
     until (Choice >0) and (Choice<5);

     ClrScr;
     writeln('STANDARD TRIANGLE:');
     T.Init( BasicSetups[Choice],0);
     GetTime( H[1], M[1], S[1], HS[1] );
     if T.FindWin = true then
        begin
        GetTime( H[2], M[2], S[2], HS[2] );
        TimeDiff( H,M,S,HS);
        T.ShowWin;
        T.ShowStats;
        end;

     ClrScr;
     writeln( 'BETTER TRIANGLE:' );
     InitStats;  { must be done explicitly after the first time }
     B.Init( BasicSetups[Choice],0 );    { Shortest solution time }
     GetTime( H[1], M[1], S[1], HS[1] );
     if B.FindWin = true then
        begin
        GetTime( H[2], M[2], S[2], HS[2] );
        TimeDiff( H,M,S,HS);
        B.ShowWin;
        B.ShowStats;
        end;
end.
```

BetterTrigl adds no new properties to the base Triangle object type. In fact, it only overrides two methods of the base Triangle object type: .Heuristic and .GenChild. Since both methods interact strongly with other ancestor object type methods, both of these methods are declared to be virtual.

As noted before, the .Heuristic method determines whether further investigation of the current position is worth pursuing. The pruning heuristic stated above may be expressed compactly as:

```
function BetterTrigl.Heuristic : boolean;
begin
     if ((Generation = 9) and (Position[5] = '0') and
                              (Position[8] = '0') and
                              (Position[9] = '0')) then
        Heuristic := false
     else
        Heuristic := true;
end;
```

The tradeoff here is that although it takes longer to evaluate this function than the simple one supplied with the Triangle object type, this more complex version will reduce the number of positions evaluated.

To make sure that offspring of the BetterTrigl object type are generated throughout the solution, the BetterTrigl object type must supply its own .GenChild method. Note that the .GenChild is virtually identical to the ancestor method, with the sole exception of instantiating a BetterTrigl object.

Playing the Game

A program to test both object types is presented at the end of Listing 8-2 (TRIANGLE.PAS).

At first glance, it's pretty obvious that there are 15 starting positions for the triangle puzzle. However, if you think about all the rotations and reflections that can occur, there are really only four unique starting positions (see Figure 8.6).

Figure 8.6 — Reducing the 15 possible starting positions to 4 for the triangle puzzle

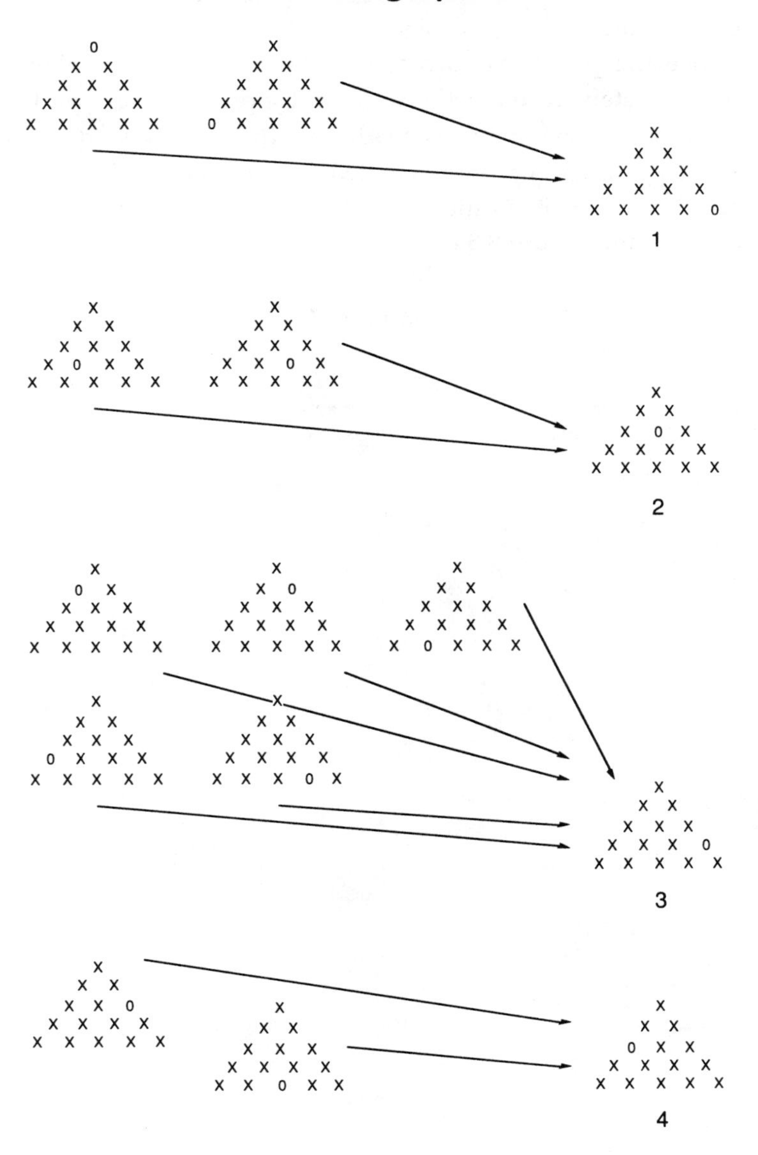

The beginning part of the program thus displays four representatives starting positions and asks the user to select one. Note how the code for DisplayPosition comes in handy here.

Once the starting position has been selected, the program solves the puzzle using the `Triangle` object type (that is, the "standard" triangle). Once the puzzle is solved, the elapsed time is displayed and the user can "step" through the solution by pressing keys on the keyboard. After the last move is made, another keypress displays the number of positions that were created for each generation, as well as the overall number of positions created. This sequence is reflected in Figure 8.7a-n and Figure 8.8.

Figure 8.7

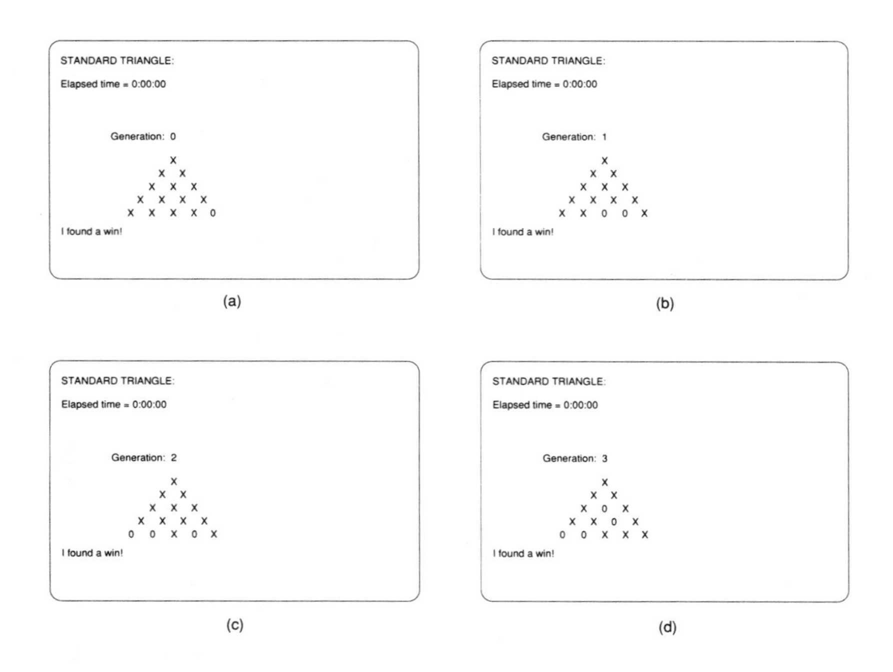

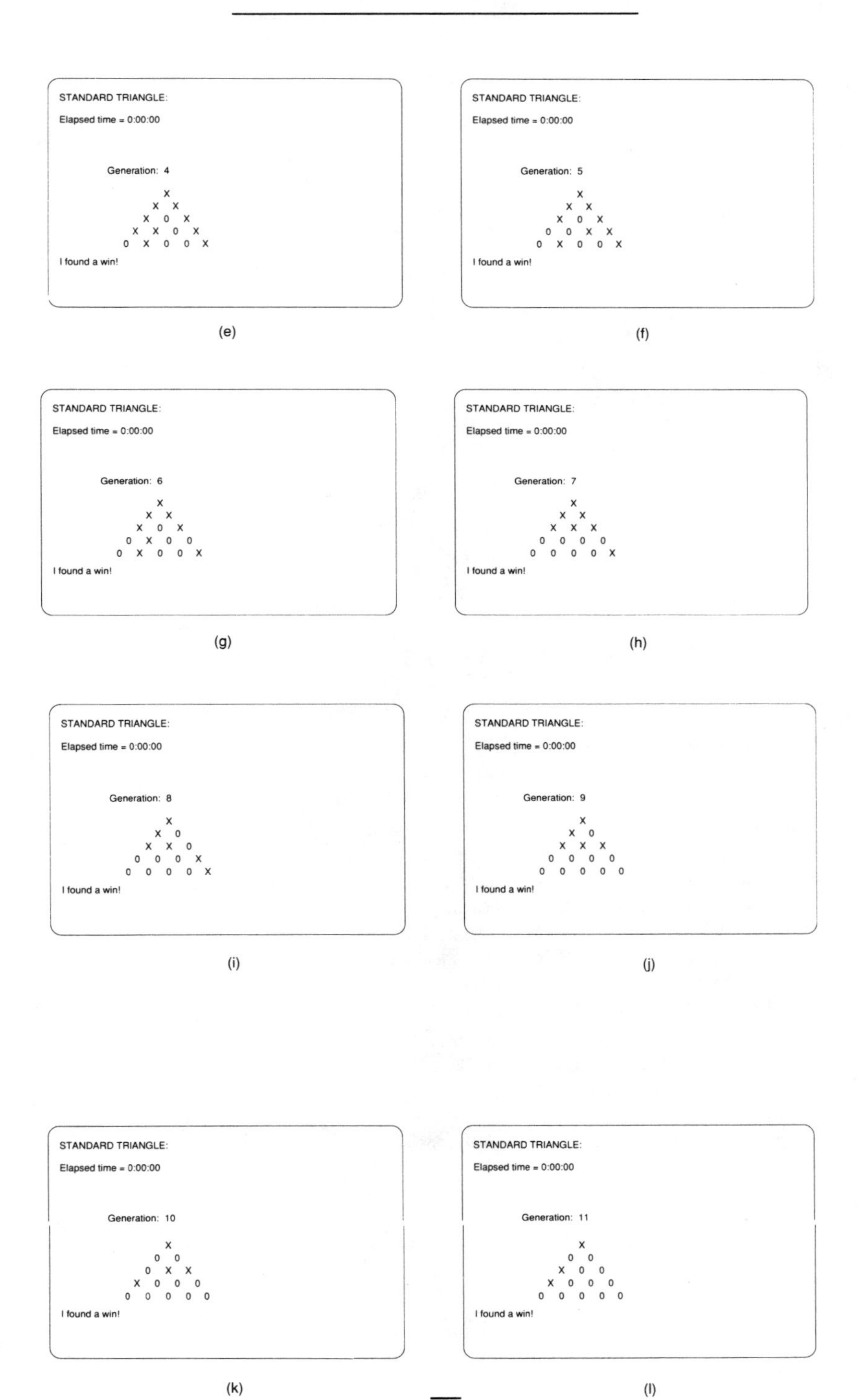
STANDARD TRIANGLE:
Elapsed time = 0:00:00
Generation: 4
X
X X
X 0 X
X X 0 X
0 X 0 0 X
I found a win!
(e)
STANDARD TRIANGLE:
Elapsed time = 0:00:00
Generation: 5
X
X X
X 0 X
0 0 X X
0 X 0 0 X
I found a win!
(f)
STANDARD TRIANGLE:
Elapsed time = 0:00:00
Generation: 6
X
X X
X 0 X
0 X 0 0
0 X 0 0 X
I found a win!
(g)
STANDARD TRIANGLE:
Elapsed time = 0:00:00
Generation: 7
X
X X
X X X
0 0 0 0
0 0 0 0 X
I found a win!
(h)
STANDARD TRIANGLE:
Elapsed time = 0:00:00
Generation: 8
X
X 0
X X 0
0 0 0 X
0 0 0 0 X
I found a win!
(i)
STANDARD TRIANGLE:
Elapsed time = 0:00:00
Generation: 9
X
X 0
X X X
0 0 0 0
0 0 0 0 0
I found a win!
(j)
STANDARD TRIANGLE:
Elapsed time = 0:00:00
Generation: 10
X
0 0
0 X X
X 0 0 0
0 0 0 0 0
I found a win!
(k)
STANDARD TRIANGLE:
Elapsed time = 0:00:00
Generation: 11
X
0 0
X 0 0
X 0 0 0
0 0 0 0 0
I found a win!
(l)

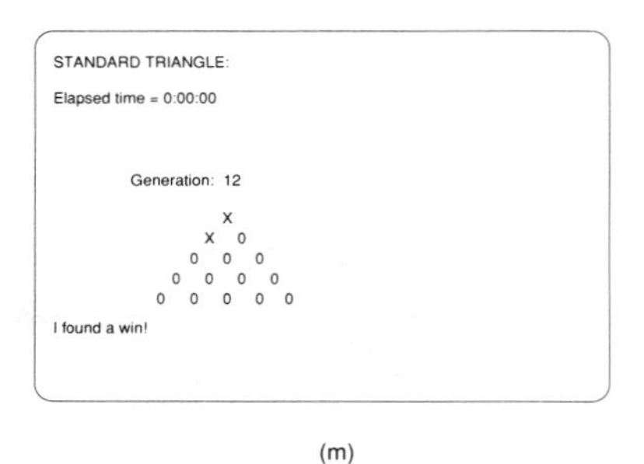

(m)

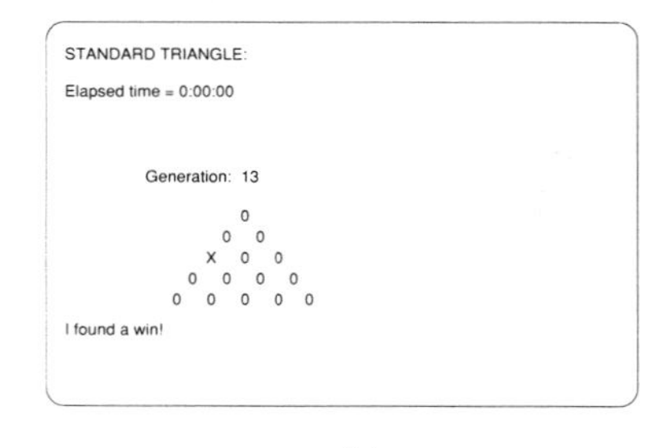

(n)

Figure 8.8

```
Number of generation  0 positions: 1
Number of generation  1 positions: 2
Number of generation  2 positions: 4
Number of generation  3 positions: 3
Number of generation  4 positions: 3
Number of generation  5 positions: 4
Number of generation  6 positions: 3
Number of generation  7 positions: 4
Number of generation  8 positions: 4
Number of generation  9 positions: 4
Number of generation 10 positions: 2
Number of generation 11 positions: 2
Number of generation 12 positions: 2
Number of generation 13 positions: 1

Total number of positions examined: 39
```

The program then repeats the process using the `BetterTrigl` object type (that is, the "better" triangle). Let's take a look at some results I obtained on a 16-MHz 80386-based microcomputer:

Starting	Standard Triangle		Better Triangle	
Position	Time	# pos.	Time	# pos.
1	0:00	39	0:00	39
2	0:47	8898	0:30	5844
3	2:58	34111	1:45	20578
4	0:01	103	0:01	90

Notice that for starting position 1, the solution is found so quickly that the heuristic is of no help at all, while in starting position 4, although about 10% of the positions are pruned, there is similarly no savings in time. For starting positions 2 and 3, there is a significant improvement in time for solving the "better" triangle, resulting from pruning approximately 40% of the children that were generated for the "standard" triangle.

Postscript

If you play with this simple puzzle long enough, you'll find several other heuristics for cutting down the search tree. I call one of them "togetherness," which is based on the observation that positions where X's were grouped together stood a better chance of being winners than otherwise. Another heuristic was "four-holes-in-a-row," which is based on the observation that winning is difficult if a row of four holes (for example, positions 7, 8, 9, and 10) are all empty early on in the solution. There is a lot to work with here.

AI applications of OOP are not restricted to the example shown in this chapter. Object-oriented techniques are being used profitably in a number of areas of AI, notably expert systems development, but that is the subject of another book. In the next chapter, we'll take a look at an example of another topical application of OOP: object-oriented databases.

9

OBJECT-ORIENTED DATABASES

In pre-OOP days, the conventional view of databases saw three basic data models: relational, network, and hierarchical. Scratch any commercial database management system (DBMS), and you'd undoubtedly find one of these models, with the most common model being the relational one. Today, in parallel with the move towards OOP in general, the rush is on to implement object-oriented databases. The idea here is to be able to create data objects that have built-in behavior that allows for much more intelligent, efficient, and in general better manipulation of data.

In this chapter, we're going to take a brief look at the popular relational database model (using as little jargon and math as possible), briefly discuss the salient points of how an object-oriented approach might differ from the relational model, and present an example of a small object-oriented database application written in Turbo Pascal.

The Relational Database Model

It is very difficult to talk about databases (relational or otherwise) without getting mired in mathematical and notational detail, so we'll take a different approach than you might find in a standard computer science text. Purists will find references to "real" database textbooks in the Postscript. Having said that, let's get down to the basics: What's so relational about a relational database?

Let's say you have a pair of properties, like DayOfWeek and Weather. Each property has a specified set of permitted values. We can express this using Turbo Pascal's enumerated types as follows:

```
type

DayOfWeek = (Sun,Mon,Tue,Wed,Thu,Fri,Sat)
Weather   = (Sunny, PartlyCloudy, Cloudy, Overcast, Rain);
```

The fact that Turbo Pascal "maps" the days of the week and the weather types into integers between 0 and 255 is immaterial here. What is important is that we can now define a record type that combines the two properties, like this:

```
Report = record
         Day : DayOfWeek;
         Sky : Weather;
         end;
```

If you think about it, there are only 35 different types of Report record that can exist (the field Day can take on seven values for each of Sky's five permitted values).

The point of this little exercise is this: Any subset of this "universe" of 35 types of Report record is called a "relation."

Said a little differently: If you take some set of properties (or fields) and imagine a set consisting of every possible combination of these properties, then a *relation* is any subset of this set.

Said even a little more differently: Given any Turbo Pascal record or object, any combination of values in their fields or properties, respectively, is a relation. So is any collection of similar records or objects.

What can we do with these relations? Well, imagine we keep track of the weather for one week. The most obvious thing we can do is look at every entry and see what the weather was that day. This corresponds to the query: "For every day of the week, show me the weather."

However, we can also be selective and, for example, look at only those days that had sunny weather by querying: "For every day whose weather is sunny, show me the day of the week."

Objects and Databases

From an intuitive point of view, an object-oriented database in Turbo Pascal differs from a "conventional" database in much the same way an object differs from a Turbo Pascal record: the object-oriented approach takes advantage of inheritance and methods.

We ran across an example of this earlier in Chapter 2 in the example of a database of persons at a university. Quite obviously, everybody at the university — students, faculty, administrators, maintenance people, etc. — shares a "core" of properties that can be represented in an object. These properties might include name, campus address, social security number, date of birth, and so on. Everybody at the university shares these properties. Students, on the other hand, would have the additional properties of number of credits earned, major, and grade point average. Faculty, administrators, and maintenance people might have the properties of salary, title, and date of employment. Faculty would have added properties of department, tenure status, and class schedule. A schematic of how these properties are inherited is shown in Figure 9.1. To many people, this hierarchical structure forms the essence of an object-oriented database.

Figure 9.1 — Inherited properties for University example

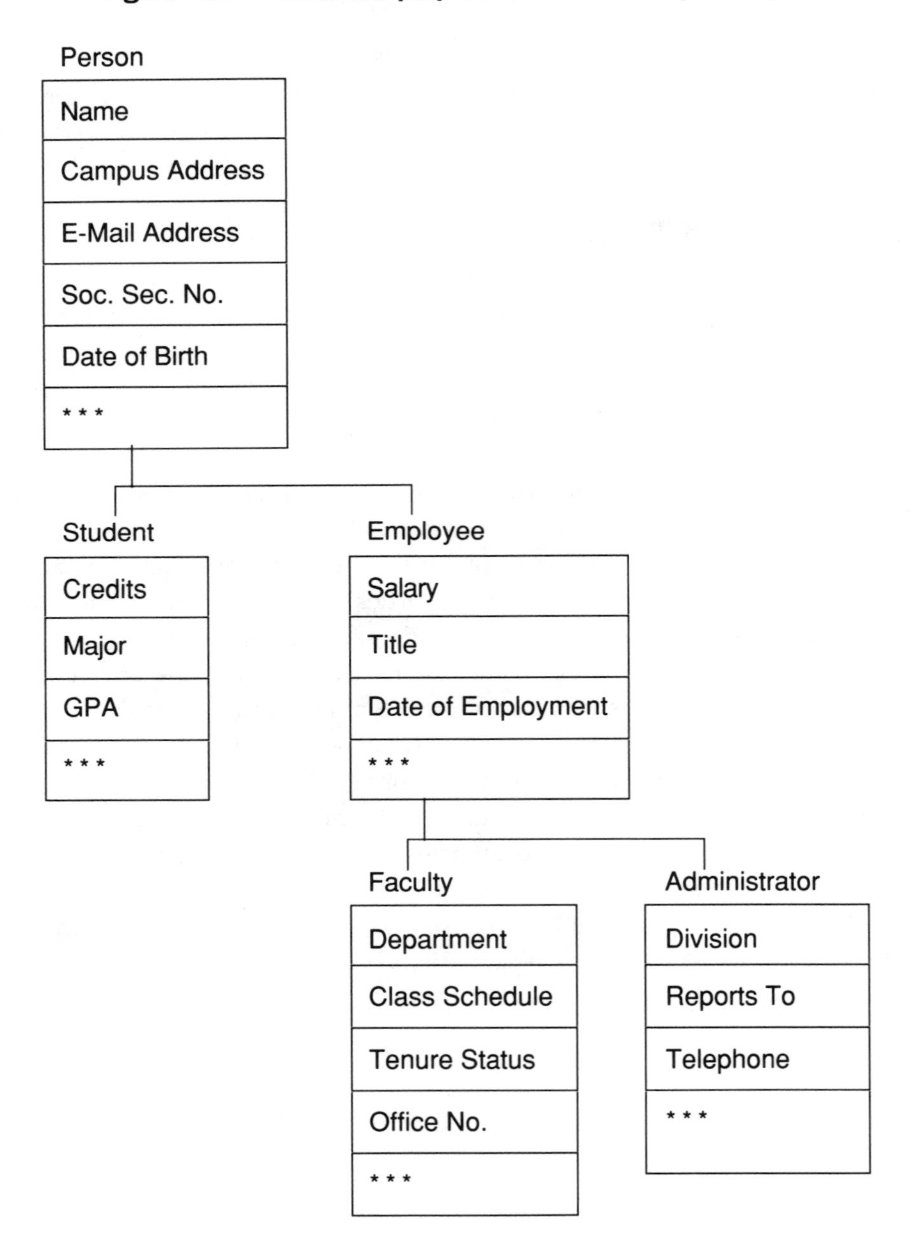

However, if representing this hierarchical structure was all there was to implementing object-oriented databases, there really wouldn't be much to it, since it's a relatively standard exercise to represent this hierarchical structure using ordinary (that is, non-object-oriented) relations in conjunction with the "join" operation, which in essence permits data from two or more relations to be connected and manipulated.

Going back to the DayOfWeek and Weather example, we could define another record that represents a relation comprised of the days of the week and a boolean that indicates whether the stock market has risen or fallen that day, like so:

```
StockReport = record
              Day : DayOfWeek;
              MarketUpQ : Boolean;
              end;
```

Using both the Report and the StockReport record types, we could answer queries like: "For each day the market rises, show the weather for that day."

We could implement these two records as two object types, like so (ignoring methods):

```
Report = object
         Day : DayOfWeek;
         Sky : Weather;
         end;

StockReport = object(Report)
              MarketUpQ : Boolean;
              end;
```

and achieve essentially the same result.

Since it's so easy to "fake" a hierarchical structure using ordinary relations, what is essential to an object-oriented database is for the relation (which is represented as an object) to take advantage of the object's ability to execute methods.

To examine this more closely, let's design a simple application that will allow us to represent a relation as a Turbo Pascal object type, and implement a suitable set of methods for this type.

Looking at Your Budget

The basics of keeping a budget is to figure out a reasonable amount of money you intend to spend for some purpose, say, entertainment or credit payments, and then to manage your actual outlay of money for that purpose so as not to exceed the budgeted amount. In principle, this looks easy, but in practice, when there may be dozens of budget categories and hundreds of expenditures to keep track of, it's nice to have a computer and a database program close at hand.

However, even with a DBMS, you generally have to write procedures that will display the information in the database in some sort of intelligible fashion. In many ways, "programming" a DBMS system parallels the types of effort that are needed to write a program in a language like Turbo Pascal. Along the same lines, using the OOP technique of abstracting the database functions we need inside of object types will streamline the application-building process, just as it does in non-database applications.

There are three fundamental types in our object-oriented budget helper, which is presented in Listing 9-1 as the file BUDGET.PAS.

Listing 9-1

```
program Budget;
uses ListObj, Crt;

type

String15 = string[15];
String24 = string[24];
var
   ParentName : String15;
   Root           : ListPtr;

type
```

```
BudgetPtr = ^BaseBudget;
BudItemPtr = ^BudItem;
BudCatPtr = ^BudCat;

BaseBudget = object( List ) { "Trunk" of tree }
             procedure Init;
             procedure Report;
             end;

BudCat = object( Node )  { This object is a "Branch" }
         Category : String15;
         Budgeted : real;
         Actual   : real;
         Items    : List;
         Parent   : ListPtr;
         constructor Init( CatName : String15;
                           HowMuchBudgeted : real );
         function GetActual : real;
         function GetVariance : real;
         procedure Report;
         end;

BudItem = object( Node )  { Objects of this type are "Leaves" }
          Category : String15;  { Name of the parent category }
          ToWhom   : String24;
          ForWhat  : String24;
          HowMuch  : real;
          procedure Init( CatName : String15;
                          Who, What : String24;
                          Amount : real );
          procedure Show;
          end;

{$F+}
function FindBudCat( pNode : pointer ) : boolean;
{$F-}
var
   pBudCat : ^BudCat;
begin
     pBudCat := pNode;
     if pBudCat^.Category = ParentName then
        FindBudCat := true
     else
        FindBudCat := false;
end;

procedure BaseBudget.Init;
begin
```

```
     List.Init;
     Root := @Self;
end;

procedure BaseBudget.Report;
var
   pBudCat : BudCatPtr;
   Spent : real;
   Budgeted : real;
begin
     Spent := 0;
     Budgeted := 0;
     writeln;
     writeln( 'BUDGET REPORT':40 );
     if FindObject = true then {if there are members of BaseBudget}
        repeat
        pBudCat := GetCursor;
        pBudCat^.Report;
        Spent := Spent + pBudCat^.Actual;
        Budgeted := Budgeted + pBudCat^.Budgeted;
        until FindnextObject = false;
     write( 'ALL CATEGORIES: Budgeted: $', Budgeted:4:2,
            ' Spent: $', Spent:4:2 );
     if Budgeted >= Spent then
        write( ' UNDER budget by $', (Budgeted - Spent):4:2 )
     else
        write( ' OVER budget by $', (Spent - Budgeted ):4:2 );
end;

procedure BudCat.Report;
var
   pBudItem : BudItemPtr;
   Header : string;
begin
     Header := Category {plus 79 hyphens}
               + '----------------------------------------'
               + '----------------------------------------';
     writeln( Copy( Header, 1, 79 ));

     if Items.FindObject = true then
        repeat
        pBudItem := Items.GetCursor;
        pBudItem^.Show;
        until Items.FindNextObject = false;
     writeln( 'Total spent in ', Category, ' budget category: $',
              GetActual:4:2 );
     if GetVariance > 0 then { over budget! }
        writeln( 'You spent MORE than the budgeted $',
                 Budgeted:4:2,
                 ' by $', GetVariance:4:2 )
     else
```

```
        if GetVariance < 0 then { under budget !}
           writeln( 'Hooray! You spent $', -GetVariance:4:2,
                  ' LESS than the $', Budgeted:4:2,
                  ' budgeted for this category.')
        else
           writeln(
           'You''ve spent exactly the amount budgeted for the ',
           Category, ' category.' );
     writeln;
end;


constructor BudCat.Init( CatName : String15;
                         HowMuchBudgeted : real );
var
   code : integer;
   SAns : string;
begin
     Node.Init; (Node.Init(SizeOf(Self));
     Items.Init;
     Category := CatName;
     if HowMuchBudgeted > 0 then
        Budgeted := HowMuchBudgeted
     else
        repeat
              write( ' How much to budget for the new category ''',
                     CatName, '''? :' );
              readln( SAns );
              Val( SAns, Budgeted, code );
        until code = 0;
     Actual := -99.99;
     Parent := Root;
     AppendToList( Parent^ );
end;

function BudCat.GetActual : real;
var
   pBudItem : BuditemPtr;
begin
     if Items.FindObject = true then
        begin
        Actual := 0.0;
        repeat
        pBudItem := Items.GetCursor;
        Actual := Actual + pBudItem^.HowMuch;
        until Items.FindNextObject = false;
        end
     else
        Actual := -99.99;
     GetActual := Actual;
end;
```

```
function BudCat.GetVariance : real;
begin
     GetVariance := GetActual - Budgeted;
end;

procedure BudItem.Show;
begin
     writeln( ToWhom:32, '| ', ForWhat:32, '| $', HowMuch:4:2 );
end;

procedure BudItem.Init( CatName : String15;
                          Who, What : String24;
                          Amount : real );
var
   pToParent : BudCatPtr;
   Tmp : ListDemonType;
begin
     Node.Init; Node.Init(SizeOf(Self));
     ToWhom := Who;
     ForWhat := What;
     Category := CatName;
     HowMuch := Amount;
     Tmp := Root^.FindObjectDemon;
     Root^.FindObjectDemon := FindBudCat;
     ParentName := Category;
     if Root^.FindObject = true then
        begin
        pToParent := Root^.GetCursor;
        AppendToList( pToParent^.Items );
        end
     else
        begin
        New( pToParent, Init( Category, -99.99 ) );
        AppendToList( pToParent^.Items );
        end;

     Root^.FindObjectDemon := Tmp;

end;

var
   MyBudget : BaseBudget;
   Utilities, Entertainment, CreditPayment : BudCat;
   Expense : array[0..10] of BudItem;
begin
     ClrScr;
     MyBudget.Init;
     Utilities.Init( 'Utilities', 150.00 );
     Entertainment.Init( 'Entertainment', 100.00 );
     CreditPayment.Init( 'CreditPayment', 1000.00 );
```

```
    { all of these individual items could just as easily be
      obtained from a file!  }
    Expense[0].Init( 'Utilities', 'Electric Co.',
                     'Electricity', 45.47 );
    Expense[1].Init( 'Entertainment', 'Cinema 99',
                     'Movie', 12.50 );
    Expense[2].Init( 'Utilities', 'Telco 2',
                     'Long distance', 56.12 );
    Expense[3].Init( 'CreditPayment', 'AmEx',
                     'Travel expenses', 591.20 );
    Expense[4].Init( 'CreditPayment', 'FirstBank',
                     'Car loan', 212.34 );
    Expense[5].Init( 'Utilities', 'Telco 1',
                     'Phone service', 18.07 );
    Expense[6].Init( 'Entertainment', 'Walton''s',
                     'SF books', 32.07 );
    Expense[7].Init( 'Entertainment', 'Fish shop',
                     'Rental & Bait', 47.00 );
    Expense[8].Init( 'CreditPayment', 'NextBank',
                     'Line of credit', 100.00 );
    Expense[9].Init( 'Utilities', 'AAA Oil',
                     'Heating Oil', 37.09 );
    Expense[10].Init( 'CreditPayment', 'LastBank',
                     'Computer', 96.46 );

    { Here's is the line that does all the work }
    MyBudget.Report;

    repeat until KeyPressed;
end.
```

The object type `BaseBudget` acts as an anchor point for the rest of the system. It is a `List` object with no properties of its own, and has only two methods: `.Init` and `.Report`. As you might expect from the name, `BaseBudget.Init` simply initializes itself using `List.Init` and sets the `Root` property to point at the `BaseBudget` object calling the `.Init` methods. The `.Report` method displays a complete budget report on the screen. A sample report from the program is shown in Figure 9.2.

Figure 9.2 — Output of BUDGET.PAS

```
          BUDGET REPORT
Utilities-------------------------------------------------------------------------------------
                                                          Electricity     $45.47
                                                        Long distance     $56.12
                                                        Phone Service     $18.07
                                                          Heating Oil     $37.09
 Total spent in Utilities budget category:  $156.75
 You spent MORE than the budgeted $128.00 by $36.75

Entertainment---------------------------------------------------------------------------------
                    Cinema 99 I                           Electricity     $12.50
                     Walton's I                              SF Books     $32.07
                    Fish shop I                         Rental & Bait     $47.00
 Total spent in Entertainment budget category:  $91.57
 Hooray!  You spent $8.43 LESS than the $100.00 budgeted for this category.

Credit Payment--------------------------------------------------------------------------------
                         AmEx I                       Travel expenses    $591.20
                    FirstBank                                Car loan    $212.34
                     NextBank I                        Line of credit    $100.00
                     LastBank I                              Computer     $96.46
 Total spent in CreditPayment budget category:  $1000.00
 You spent exactly the amount budgeted for the CreditPayment category.

 ALL CATEGORIES:  Budgeted:  $1228.00 Spent:  $1248.32 OVER budget by $28.32.
```

BaseBudget keeps track of BudCat objects, each of which is (necessarily) a descendant of the Node object type and corresponds to a budget category. The BudCat object type has five properties:

Category. A string that describes the budget category, for example, *Utilities*.

Budgeted. A real number that represents a budgeted amount, in dollars and cents.

Actual. A real number that represents the sum of all items associated with the BudCat object.

Items. A List that contains all budget items (individual expenditures) associated with the budget category.

Parent. A pointer to the List object that the `BudCat` object belongs to. To tell the truth, this property doesn't play a really key role in this program, because all the `BudCat` objects have the same `Parent`, whose address is already stored in the global variable `Root`. However, this property was included with an eye to future enhancement, where different budget categories might belong to different parent objects.

In addition to inheriting all the `Node` methods, the `BudCat` object type has four methods of its own:

.Init. The initialization routine is declared to be a constructor so that we can more easily create and initialize `BudCat` objects dynamically (using the `New` procedure) when the need arises. An interesting wrinkle that comes into play later is the need to supply a positive number for a budgeted amount, or else the user is prompted to supply a figure.

.GetActual. This method "walks" the list in the `Items` property and adds all the individual expenditures. The result is stored in Actual and returned by this method, which is a Turbo Pascal function. The way `.GetActual` was implemented, by the way, is only one of many valid ways to do the job. An alternative method, which involves updating the `Actual` property every time an item is added (or removed) from the Items property comes to mind, but is more complicated.

.GetVariance. This method is also a Turbo Pascal function; this one returns the difference between the amount stored in the `Budgeted` property, and the sum returned by the `.GetActual` method.

.Report. Just like the `BaseBudget` method of the same name, this method prints a report, but for the budget category only. The report consists of a line-by-line display of each member of the `Items` list, followed by a two-line summary of the overall expenditure for the category and its relation to the budgeted amount (making heavy use of the Budgeted property and the .GetActual and .GetVariance methods). By the way, don't be lulled into thinking that this method overrides the method in the BaseBudget object type. Even though the names are the same, a look at the code will show that the two object types are completely independent.

The discussion finally brings us to the basic object type in our system, the budget item object type BudItem. The BudItem type is independent of the other two types and has four properties:

Category. This string describes the category the expenditure belongs to. This is one of the categories that belongs to the BaseBudget list.

ToWhom. Here, we supply a string describing "to whom" the money was paid.

ForWhat. Analogously, we supply a string describing "for what" the money was paid.

HowMuch. Finally, we supply a dollars and cents figure that represents "how much" was paid.

In our simple application, there's really not much for a BudItem object instance to do. One thing it can do is display itself on a single line, which is taken care of in the one-line .Show method. The other behavior exhibited by the BudItem object type is its .Init method, and it can be described as follows.

During instantiation, the BudItem object sets the BaseBudget object to search for the member in its list whose Category corresponds to the BudItem's Category. Rather than attempt to use the standard FindAll function that is normally stored as the FindObjectDemon, the technique implemented here temporarily changes the

FindObjectDemon of the BaseBudget object to be the function FindBudCat, which looks like this:

```
{$F+}
function FindBudCat( pNode : pointer ) : boolean;
{$F-}
var
   pBudCat : ^BudCat;
begin
     pBudCat := pNode;
     if pBudCat^.Category = ParentName then
        FindBudCat := true
     else
        FindBudCat := false;
end;
```

By setting the global variable ParentName to the value of its Category, a BudItem can retrieve the address of the appropriate BudCat object and then attach itself to it. An important item to note about this technique is the dual dynamic nature in the use of the FindObjectDemon: first, we dynamically changed the function used as the demon; second, we changed the value of a global variable used by the demon function. A schematic of how this is done is presented in Figure 9.3.

Figure 9.3 — Dynamic modification of FindObjectDemon by BudItem object

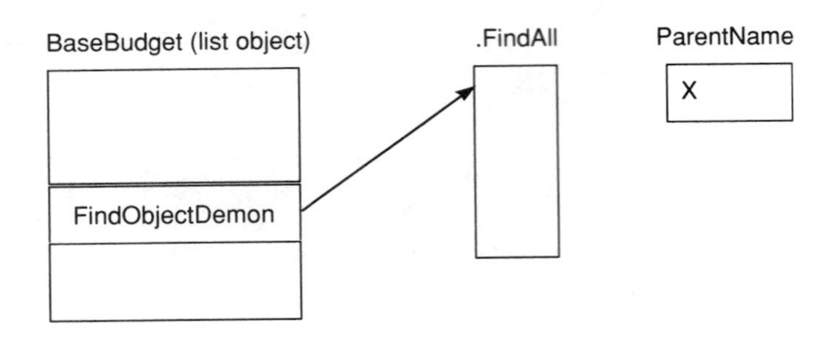

Before BudItem changes demon function

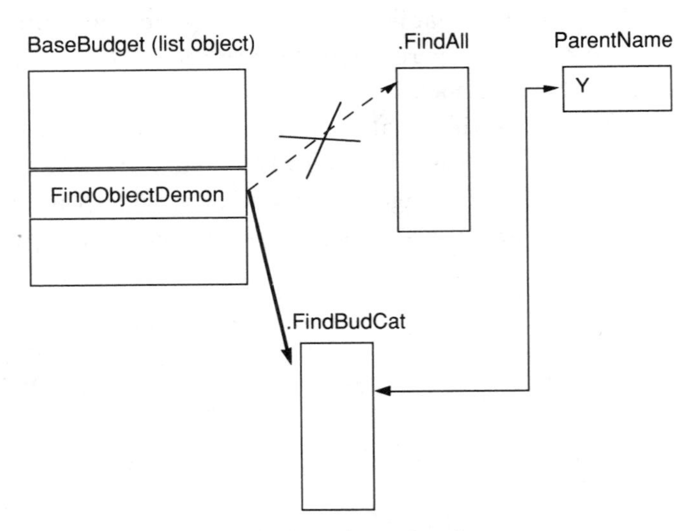

After BudItem changes demon function

This all works fine if a BudCat item with the appropriate Category has been created up front, but what if it hasn't? The BudItem has this base covered, also. If, for some reason, a BudItem's Category has no match among the BudCat items in the BaseBudget list, the program assumes that the category is valid, and instantiates a new BudCat object and causes the user to be prompted for a budget. To see how this feature works, comment out one or more of the three lines of

BUDGET.PAS that instantiate the Utilities, Entertainment, and `CreditPayment` objects of type `BudCat`. To give you an idea of the relationships among these three object types, Figure 9.4 shows an abbreviated schematic view.

Figure 9.4 — Schematic of object relationships

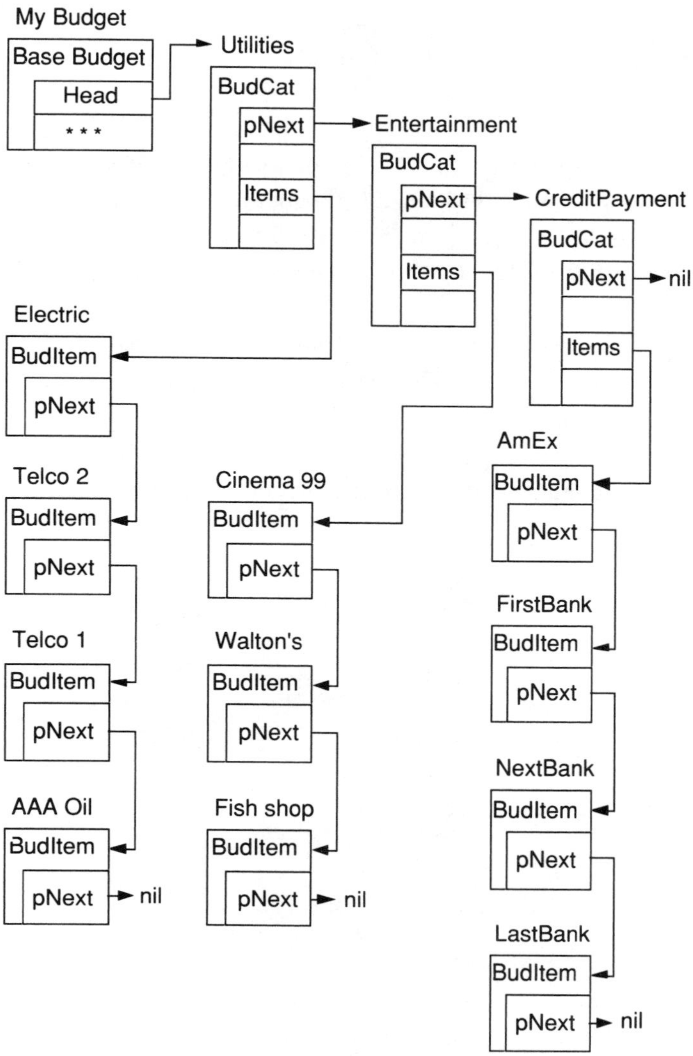

My Budget
Base Budget
Head
* * *
Utilities
BudCat
pNext
Items
Entertainment
BudCat
pNext
Items
CreditPayment
BudCat
pNext
nil
Items
Electric
BudItem
pNext
Telco 2
BudItem
pNext
Telco 1
BudItem
pNext
AAA Oil
BudItem
pNext
nil
Cinema 99
BudItem
pNext
Walton's
BudItem
pNext
Fish shop
BudItem
pNext
nil
AmEx
BudItem
pNext
FirstBank
BudItem
pNext
NextBank
BudItem
pNext
LastBank
BudItem
pNext
nil

Postscript

The example presented barely scratches the surface of what is becoming a very complex and wide-open field. Object-oriented databases, as well as object-oriented knowledge bases for AI applications, are being developed at near-fever pitch with varying degrees of object-orientedness. Ideas for future experimentation with the program in BUDGET.PAS might include keeping track of time, say on a monthly basis, or the introduction of monthly budgets that vary throughout the year.

Another idea is to devise behaviors for budget categories that are excessively over or under budget. For those interested in a more rigorous, computer- science approach to the study of object-oriented databases, I suggest reading *Object-Oriented Database Programming,* by Suad Alagic´ (Springer-Verlag, 1989), or, for a broader view of the possibilities of object-oriented database applications, take a look at *Object-Oriented Concepts, Databases, and Applications,* by Kim and Lochovsky (ACM Press, 1989). In the next chapter, we'll take a look at graphics animation using Turbo Pascal and simulate a pair of two-dimensional robot arms on our console screens.

10

ANIMATED GRAPHICS: ROBOT ARMS

You may not realize it, but your computer's monitor represents an infinitely erasable graphics tablet; an eternally renewable piece of paper. It is the ideal medium not just for pretty, static graphics, but also for graphics that appear to move. The art of arranging images so that they appear to move is called animation.

The ideas behind animation is to present an image for a split-second (long enough for the image to form on the retina of the eye, or about 1/25th of a second), erase the image and then re-display a modified image a split-second later. Done artfully, the brain can be "tricked" into seeing a moving image. What type of modifications can the image undergo? The scope is limited only by imagination. The modified image may, for example, move, rotate, change shape, or it may perform some combination of these actions. In the example presented in this chapter, we'll concentrate on the motion and rotation of a pair of robot arms.

Intuitively, it may make sense to erase the entire screen between images, which we'll call "frames." However, there are two reasons why this approach is not the best for computer graphics animation. First, it often turns out that much of the image remains static while only some key element is animated. In this case, erasing the entire screen means wasting time redrawing objects that haven't moved. Second, even with very fast machines, it simply takes too long to erase a screen. (If you played with the windowing system in Chapter 7, you'll recall how long it took for the area underneath the window to be "repainted" using the `.PutImage` procedure after a window was closed.)

A key technique to animation, then, is to erase only animated objects on the screen before redrawing them for the next frame. This is best accomplished by setting the drawing color to the background color and then "drawing" the object in this color. We'll see this technique in action as we "show" and "hide" robot arms on the screen.

Why Robot Arms?

Part of the reason for using a pair of robot arms as an example for animation, aside from whatever inherent appeal there might be in seeing a robot "find" a target on the screen, is that the development process will allow me to point out some of the pitfalls involved in real software development, and to discuss how some of the tradeoffs that must be made when modifying software can be softened by using object-oriented techniques. One of the issues we plan to tackle is modification of software, which raises the delicate question of just how many revisions the reader is willing to wade through to get to the end. As a compromise between presenting numerous intermediate versions of listings and presenting only one final version, we will present only the initial prototype listings and the final versions.

Robot A: Specification

You have been given the task of developing a two-dimensional animated figure of a robot arm that will eventually become part of a trade show demonstration. In this first cut of the software, you are expected to implement an arm consisting of a single segment that can either rotate around a fixed anchor point or move axially (that is, in such a way that the gripping end of the arm moves directly toward or away from the anchor point). The design of the arm and its permissible movements are illustrated in Figure 10.1.

Figure 10.1 — Movements available to Robot A

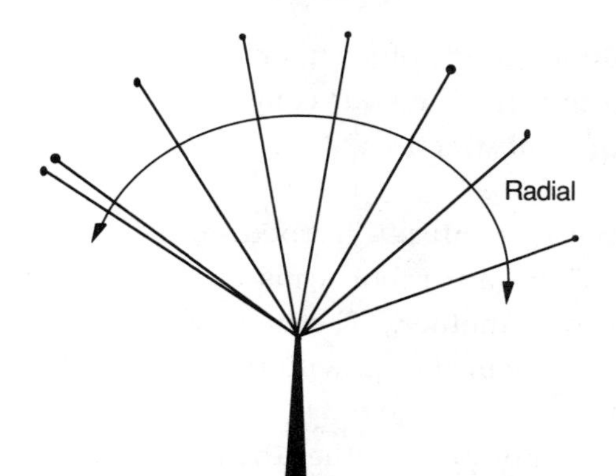

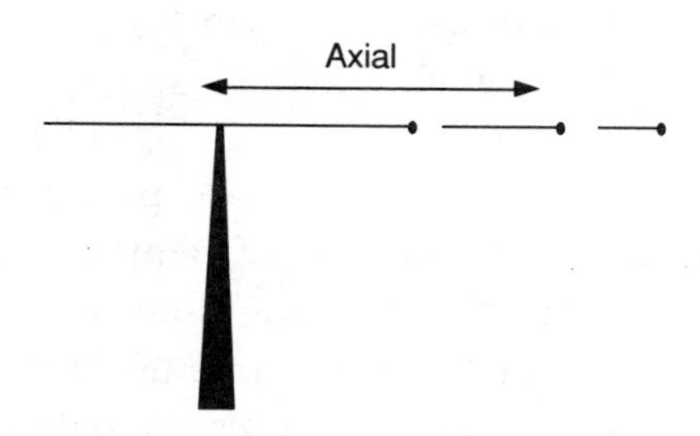

The robot arm is to be implemented as an object type with a method called .MoveTo, which will take as a parameter an object of type Point, declared as follows:

```
Point = object
   X, Y : integer;
   procedure Init( NewX, NewY : integer );
   procedure Show;
   procedure Hide;
   end;
```

An object of type Point shall be depicted as a 16x16 pixel rectangle on the screen. When the .MoveTo method is called, the arm will behave in such a way as to place the gripping end inside the rectangle.

Robot A: Design

The correct response upon receipt of such a challenging assignment is, as everyone will tell you: turn OFF your computer. Grab a pencil and a pad and start thinking "abstraction."

We must not, for example, confuse the robot arm with the segment that does the work. There are robot arms out there with multiple segments connected to one another. The more we think about it, the more it makes sense to start our design with the concept of a `Segment`.

Each `Segment` has an anchor point, either the end of another segment or the base of the robot arm. Each `Segment` also has a "busy end" that could hold either another segment or some sort of gripper (we'll make a note to depict this busy end graphically by drawing a small circle at the end of the `Segment`). Each `Segment` has a fixed length and, in our two-dimensional world, an angular orientation with respect to the horizontal.

The behaviors of a `Segment` are pretty rudimentary. First of all, it can show itself and hide itself, which will allow us to animate the `Segment`. It can also rotate around its fixed anchor point and move axially in and out from that point. That pretty much takes care of the immediate needs of the `Segment` object type.

There is a school of thought that says you should build in as much flexibility as possible into the software despite what it says in the specifications. Another philosophy says: "If it ain't in the spec, it ain't in the software." Reality, of course, steers a happy medium between the two. On the one hand, you can't build "as much flexibility as possible" into the software, simply because you don't have an unlimited amount of time or money. Then too, software that's twice as flexible is at least twice as complex, which mitigates against frivolous flexibility. On the other hand, it is nice to be able to anticipate future changes in the design so as not to have to repeatedly retrofit features into existing designs. This is particularly important in object-oriented design, since reusability is a big reason for adopting OOP methodology in the first place. Fortunately, as you do more design, you get better at intelligently guessing where there's room for building in some flexibility, even in poorly specified jobs as this one. Likely areas for "preemptive" design are the ability to restrict rotation of the arm (thus making it an axial-movement only segment), and the ability of a `Segment` to be "attached" to another segment. For the sake of clarity, we will deliberately not make allowances for this functionality in the prototype code.

We now have enough information to implement a prototype set of declarations for the `Point` and `Segment` object types, which are presented as a unit listing PROROBOT.PAS in Listing 10-1.

Listing 10-1

```
unit ProRobot;  { Listing 10-1 }
interface
uses Graph, Mouse, Crt;
const
     PI : real = 3.14159;
type
Degrees = 0..359;
Point = object
      X,Y : Integer;
      procedure Init(NewX,NewY : Integer);
      procedure Show;
      procedure Hide;
      end;

Segment = object
        Anchor      : Point;
        BusyEnd     : Point;
        Length      : integer;
        Orientation : Real;
        procedure Init( AnchorX, AnchorY, SegLen : Integer;
                        Position : Degrees );
        procedure MoveAxial( i : integer );
        procedure Rotate( i : integer );
        procedure Show;
        procedure Hide;
        end;

function Distance( P1, P2 : Point ) : real;
```

```
implementation
function Distance( P1, P2 : Point ) : real;
begin
     Distance :=
       Sqrt( Sqr( P1.X - P2.X + 0.01) + Sqr( P1.Y - P2.Y + 0.01) );
end;

procedure Point.Init( NewX, NewY : integer );
begin
     X := NewX;
     Y := NewY;
end;

procedure Point.Show;
begin
     Graph.Rectangle( X-8, Y-8, X+8, Y+8);
end;

procedure Point.Hide;
var TmpClr : integer;
begin
     TmpClr := Graph.GetColor;
     Graph.SetColor(GetBkColor);
     Show;
     Graph.SetColor(TmpClr);
end;

procedure Segment.Init( AnchorX, AnchorY, SegLen : Integer;
                        Position : Degrees );
var BX, BY : integer;
begin
     Anchor.Init( AnchorX, AnchorY );
     Orientation :=  Position * PI / 180.0;
     Length := SegLen;
     BX := Round(Anchor.X + cos(Orientation)*SegLen);
     BY := Round(Anchor.Y - sin(Orientation)*SegLen);
     BusyEnd.Init( BX, BY );
end;

procedure Segment.MoveAxial( i : integer );
var D : real;
begin
     Hide;
     D := Distance( Anchor, BusyEnd );
     if D-i >= Length then
        D := Length+i;
     BusyEnd.X := Round(Anchor.X + cos(Orientation)*(D-i));
     BusyEnd.Y := Round(Anchor.Y - sin(Orientation)*(D-i));
     Show;
end;
```

```
procedure Segment.Rotate( i : integer );
begin
     Hide;
     Orientation := Orientation + ( i * ( PI / 90.0 ) );
     Show;
end;

procedure Segment.Show;
var
    D : real;
    FX, FY : integer;
begin
     D := Distance( Anchor, BusyEnd );
     BusyEnd.X := Round(Anchor.X + cos(Orientation)*D);
     BusyEnd.Y := Round(Anchor.Y - sin(Orientation)*D);
     FX := Round(BusyEnd.X - cos(Orientation)*Length);
     FY := Round(BusyEnd.Y + sin(Orientation)*Length);
     Graph.Line( FX, FY, BusyEnd.X, BusyEnd.Y );
     Graph.Circle( BusyEnd.X, BusyEnd.Y, 2);
end;

procedure Segment.Hide;
var
   TmpClr : integer;
   LST : LineSettingsType;
begin
     TmpClr := Graph.GetColor;
     Graph.SetColor(GetBkColor);
     Show;
     Graph.SetColor(TmpClr);

end;

end.
```

In the specified task, the robot arm has only one segment, so we may formulate a `RobotArm` object type that inherits the properties of the `Segment` and adds the specified `.MoveTo` method. For the sake of display, we also include a method that will display a narrow "pie slice" of a circle to resemble the robot arm's base, and a method that outlines the outer limits of the robot arm's travel. The prototype code for the RobotArm object type is presented in Listing 10-2.

Listing 10-2

```
unit List10_2; { Listing 10-2 }

interface

uses Graph, Mouse, Crt, ProRobot;

type

RobotArm = object( Segment )
           procedure Init( AnchorX, AnchorY, ArmLen : Integer;
                           Position : Degrees;
                           DispQ : Boolean );
           procedure MoveTo( APoint : Point );
           procedure ShowBase;
           procedure ShowLimit;
           end;

implementation

procedure RobotArm.Init( AnchorX, AnchorY, ArmLen : Integer;
                         Position : Degrees;
                         DispQ : Boolean );
begin
     Segment.Init( AnchorX, AnchorY, ArmLen, Position );
     if DispQ = true then
        begin
        Show;
        ShowBase;
        end;
end;

procedure RobotArm.MoveTo( APoint : Point );
var D : real;
    RotDelta : integer;
    AxDelta  : integer;
begin
      { Phase 1 }
           RotDelta := 1; {rotate 1 degree each rotation}
           D := Distance( APoint, BusyEnd );  { find distance }
           Rotate( RotDelta );                  { rotate }
           if D < Distance( APoint, BusyEnd ) then begin
              { if new distance is greater than old distance }
              D := Distance( APoint, BusyEnd ); { set distance }
              RotDelta := -RotDelta;
              { reverse direction of rotation }
              Rotate( RotDelta ); { rotate in opposite direction }
              end;
           while D > Distance( APoint, BusyEnd ) do begin
```

```
                { new distance should be less than old }
                D :=  Distance( APoint, BusyEnd );
                Rotate( RotDelta );
                end;
                { stops when Distance starts to get big again }
          RotDelta := -RotDelta;
          Rotate( RotDelta ); { go back one }
          { End of Phase 1 }
     { Phase 2 }
     AxDelta := 4; {move 4 units Axially each time}
     { set distance }
     D := Distance( APoint, BusyEnd );
     MoveAxial( AxDelta );  { move axially }
     if D < Distance( APoint, BusyEnd ) then begin
        D := Distance( APoint, BusyEnd );
        AxDelta := -AxDelta;
        MoveAxial( AxDelta );
        end;
     while D > Distance( APoint, BusyEnd ) do begin
        D :=  Distance( APoint, BusyEnd );
        MoveAxial( AxDelta );
        end;
     AxDelta := -AxDelta div 2;
     MoveAxial( AxDelta );  { should be here }
     ShowLimit;
     ShowBase;
     { End of Phase 2 }
end;

procedure RobotArm.ShowBase;
begin
     with Anchor do
          Graph.PieSlice(X, Y, 268, 272, Round(GetMaxY/2.2));
end;

procedure RobotArm.ShowLimit;
begin
     SetColor( red );
     with Anchor do
          Circle( X, Y, Length );
     SetColor( white );
end;
end.
```

Actually moving the arm to a specified point is a challenge. In our case, since this is a first cut at the design, we will take a direct approach and divide the motion into two phases. In the first phase, we will rotate the arm until the `Anchor`, the `BusyEnd`, and the target are in a line, and then, in the second phase, we'll move the arm axially until the BusyEnd is in the target. This is illustrated in Figure 10.2.

Figure 10.2 — Moving the robot's arm to a specified point

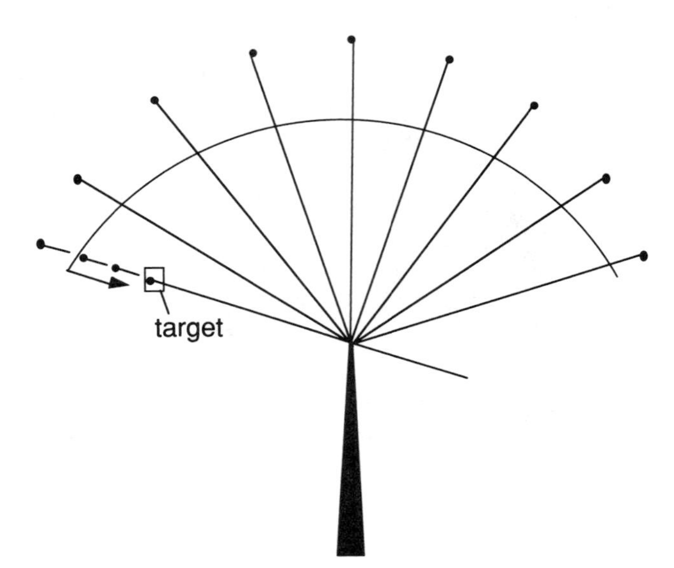

In the first phase of .MoveTo, we figure the distance between the target and the BusyEnd, rotate 1 degree counterclockwise, and remeasure the distance. If the distance has increased, we reverse the direction of rotation; otherwise, the direction remains the same. We continue to rotate (1 degree at a time) and measure distance until we pass the minimum distance and start to move "away" from the target. After rotating back one step, phase one is complete.

The .MoveTo method uses analogous steps in phase two. We again start by measuring the distance between the target and the BusyEnd, and now move the BusyEnd 4 pixels in toward the Anchor. If the distance increases, we reverse the direction of motion; otherwise, we don't. We continue to move axially until we pass the target, and then again take one step back. Phase two is now complete, and the BusyEnd should be inside the target area.

By the way, the Distance function return a real value instead of an integer to avoid problems with rounding errors. Distance uses the traditional "square-root of the sum of the squares" algorithm, which would often result in the BusyEnd stopping well short of its goal if the answer were rounded to an integer value.

Robot A: Implementation

A program to put our one-armed bandit though its paces is presented in Listing 10-3. It takes advantage of the mouse routines presented in Chapter 7 and permits the user to "create" a target anywhere on the screen. If a target is created outside the limits of the arm's reach, the arm will extend as far as it can and then stop (see the code for the .MoveAxial method to see why this is so).

Listing 10-3

```
program List10_3;

uses Graph, Mouse, Crt, ProRobot, List10_2;

var
   Arm : RobotArm;
   P0 : Point;

   x, y : integer;

   GraphDriver : integer;
   GraphMode   : integer;
   ErrorCode   : integer;
   GlobalAnchorX,
   GlobalAnchorY,
   ArmLength : integer;

begin
     GraphDriver := Detect;
     InitGraph(GraphDriver, GraphMode, 'C:\TP');
     ErrorCode := GraphResult;
     if ErrorCode <> grOK then
        Writeln('Graphics error');

     GlobalAnchorX  := Round(GetMaxX/3);
     GlobalAnchorY  := Round(GetMaxY/2);
     ArmLength      := Round(GetMaxY/2.4);
```

```
    Graph.SetColor(white);
    SetTextStyle( DefaultFont, HorizDir, 2);
    OutTextXY( Round(GetMaxX/1.5), Round(GetMaxY*4/5),'Robot ''A''' );
    Arm.Init( GlobalAnchorX, GlobalAnchorY, ArmLength,
              0, true );
    Arm.ShowLimit;
    PO.Init( 0,0);
    if MouseInit = true then
       ; {do nothing}
    MouseShow;
    repeat
          repeat
          until MouseLPressed or KeyPressed;
          if not KeyPressed then
             begin
             PO.Hide;
             repeat
                   MouseCoords( x, y );
             until MouseLReleased;
             MouseHide;
             PO.Init( x, y );
             PO.Show;
             Arm.MoveTo( PO );
             PO.Show;  { in case any part of the box was trashed }
             MouseShow;
             end;
     until KeyPressed;
   end.
```

Robot B: Specification

Well, just as we were celebrating the creation of our robot arm, along comes a memo from the manager of the trade show demonstration project. It seems that the original plan for a single-segment robot arm has changed. Now, the demo is to show a two-segment arm. One of the arms moves only horizontally and is attached to the base, while the other arm is attached to the first and moves only vertically, as shown in Figure 10.3.

Figure 10.3 — Two-segment arm

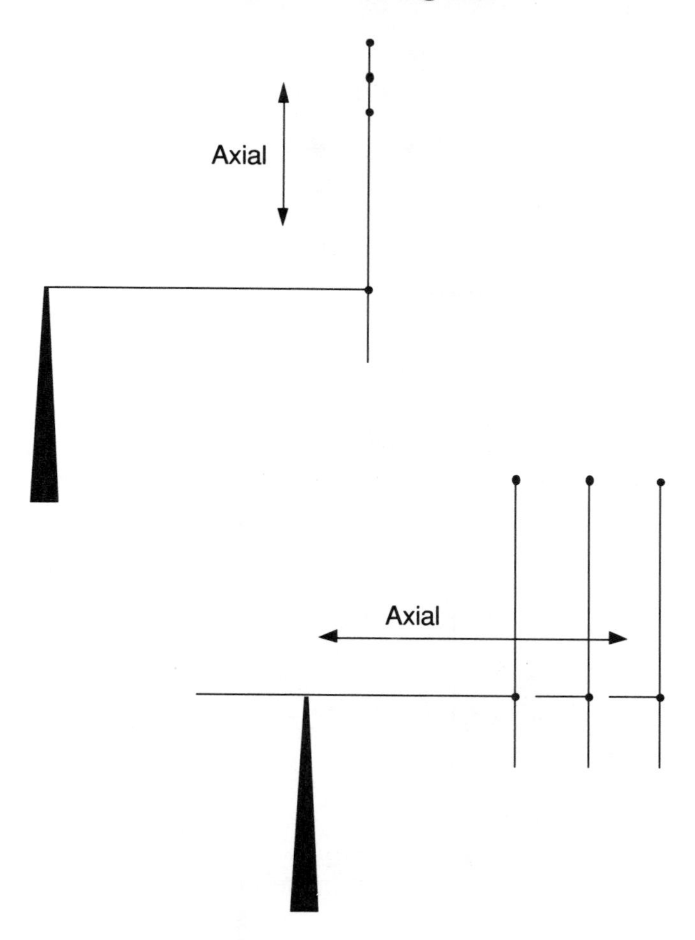

We are also told that if a target is on the side opposite to the end holding either the other segment or the gripper, the arms should "flip" on the screen after moving to the fully retracted ("in") position, and then reextend themselves as they move toward the target. Such a sequence is shown in Figure 10.4.

Figure 10.4 — Flip and reextend sequence of Robot arm

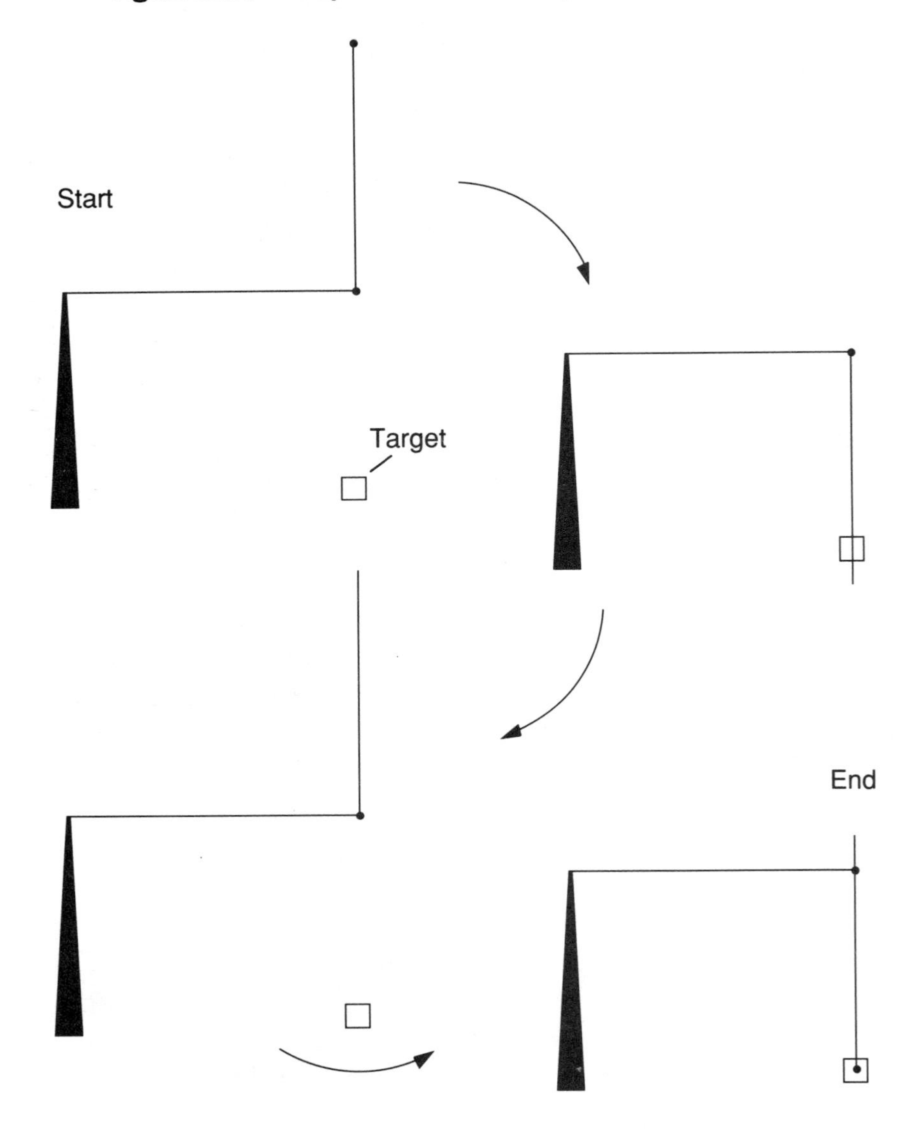

Robot B: Design

At this point, we must face a basic decision: Do we (1) scrap the software we've written and write something entirely new, or (2) attempt to retrofit a design that will allow the single- and double-segment robot arms to coexist? The resolution of this decision is another one of those "it depends" answers. If the effort for the trade show demo is a one-time deal, a better alternative might be (1), considering that the current `Segment` design is bare bones with no anticipated built-in flexibility. If the market for trade show animations looks good, however, it might make sense not only to pursue path (2), but you'd be well-advised to meet with the trade show group and find out as much as you can about their animation needs. OOP techniques work naturally from the general to the specific; being given a number of specific instances makes it very difficult to design intrinsically reusable OOP-based software.

Let's take a look at the second alternative, if only to see the types of issues we face in modifying existing code. An upgraded version of PROROBOT.PAS is presented as ROBOTSEG.PAS in Listing 10-4. Listing 10-2, which declares the `RobotArm` object type and its methods, has been upgraded, changed to be a unit, and is presented as ROBOT_A.PAS in Listing 10-5. The declaration of the new `RobotArm2` object type and its methods is presented in ROBOT_B.PAS in Listing 10-6.

<u>Listing 10-4</u>

```
unit RobotSeg;  { Listing 10-4 }

interface

uses Graph, Mouse, Crt;

const
     PI : real = 3.14159;
type

Degrees = 0..359;
```

```
Point = object
      X,Y : Integer;
      procedure Init(NewX,NewY : Integer);
      procedure Show;
      procedure Hide;
      end;


Segment = object
        Anchor      : Point;
        BusyEnd     : Point;
        Length      : integer;
        Orientation : Real;
        RotateStatus: Boolean;
        constructor Init( AnchorX, AnchorY, SegLen : Integer;
                         Position : Degrees;
                         Rotatable : Boolean );
        procedure MoveAxial( var i : integer ); virtual;
        procedure MoveAnchor( NewX, NewY : integer );
        procedure Rotate( i : integer );
        procedure Show;
        procedure Hide;
        function RotateQ : Boolean;
        end;

function Distance( P1, P2 : Point ) : real;


implementation

function Distance( P1, P2 : Point ) : real;
begin
     Distance :=
       Sqrt( Sqr( P1.X - P2.X + 0.01) + Sqr( P1.Y - P2.Y + 0.01) );
end;

procedure Point.Init( NewX, NewY : integer );
begin
     X := NewX;
     Y := NewY;
end;

procedure Point.Show;
begin
     Graph.Rectangle( X-8, Y-8, X+8, Y+8);
end;

procedure Point.Hide;
var TmpClr : integer;
begin
     TmpClr := Graph.GetColor;
```

```
     Graph.SetColor(GetBkColor);
     Show;
     Graph.SetColor(TmpClr);
end;

constructor Segment.Init( AnchorX, AnchorY, SegLen : Integer;
                        Position : Degrees;
                        Rotatable : Boolean );
var BX, BY : integer;
begin
     Anchor.Init( AnchorX, AnchorY );
     RotateStatus := Rotatable;
     Orientation := Position * PI / 180.0;
     Length := SegLen;
     BX := Round(Anchor.X + cos(Orientation)*SegLen);
     BY := Round(Anchor.Y - sin(Orientation)*SegLen);
     BusyEnd.Init( BX, BY );
end;

procedure Segment.MoveAxial( var i : integer );
var D : real;
begin
     Hide;
     D := Distance( Anchor, BusyEnd );
     if D-i >= Length then
        D := Length+i;
     BusyEnd.X := Round(Anchor.X + cos(Orientation)*(D-i));
     BusyEnd.Y := Round(Anchor.Y - sin(Orientation)*(D-i));
     Show;
end;

procedure Segment.MoveAnchor( NewX, NewY : integer );
var
   DeltaX, DeltaY : integer;
begin
     Hide;
     with Anchor do
          begin
          DeltaX := X - NewX;
          DeltaY := Y - NewY;
          X := NewX;
          Y := NewY;
          end;
     with BusyEnd do
          begin
          X := X + DeltaX;
          Y := Y + DeltaY;
          end;
     Show;
end;
```

```
procedure Segment.Rotate( i : integer );
begin
     Hide;
     Orientation := Orientation + ( i * ( PI / 90.0 ) ) ;
     Show;
end;

function Segment.RotateQ : Boolean;
begin
     RotateQ := RotateStatus;
end;

procedure Segment.Show;
var
    D : real;
    FX, FY : integer;
begin
     D := Distance( Anchor, BusyEnd );
     BusyEnd.X := Round(Anchor.X + cos(Orientation)*D);
     BusyEnd.Y := Round(Anchor.Y - sin(Orientation)*D);
     FX := Round(BusyEnd.X - cos(Orientation)*Length);
     FY := Round(BusyEnd.Y + sin(Orientation)*Length);
     Graph.Line( FX, FY, BusyEnd.X, BusyEnd.Y );
     Graph.Circle( BusyEnd.X, BusyEnd.Y, 2);
end;

procedure Segment.Hide;
var
   TmpClr : integer;
   LST : LineSettingsType;
begin
     TmpClr := Graph.GetColor;
     Graph.SetColor(GetBkColor);
     Show;
     Graph.SetColor(TmpClr);

end;

end.
```

Listing 10-5

```
unit Robot_A; { Listing 10-5 }

interface

uses Graph, Mouse, Crt, RobotSeg;

type

RobotArm = object( Segment )
           constructor Init( AnchorX, AnchorY, ArmLen : Integer;
                             Position : Degrees;
                             RotStat, DispQ : Boolean );
           procedure MoveTo( APoint : Point; ShowQ : boolean );
           procedure ShowBase;
           procedure ShowLimit; virtual;
           end;

implementation

constructor RobotArm.Init( AnchorX, AnchorY, ArmLen : Integer;
                           Position : Degrees;
                           RotStat, DispQ : Boolean );
begin
     Segment.Init( AnchorX, AnchorY, ArmLen, Position, RotStat );
     if DispQ = true then
        begin
        Show;
        ShowBase;
        end;
end;

procedure RobotArm.MoveTo( APoint : Point; ShowQ : boolean );

var D : real;
    RotDelta : integer;
    AxDelta  : integer;
begin
     if RotateQ = true then begin
          RotDelta := 1;
          D := Distance( APoint, BusyEnd );  { find distance }
          Rotate( RotDelta );                { rotate }
          if D < Distance( APoint, BusyEnd ) then begin
             { if new distance is greater than old distance }
             D := Distance( APoint, BusyEnd ); { set distance }
             RotDelta := -RotDelta;  { reverse direction of rotation }
             Rotate( RotDelta ); { rotate in opposite direction }
             end;
          while D > Distance( APoint, BusyEnd ) do begin
               { new distance should be less than old }
```

```
                D :=  Distance( APoint, BusyEnd );
                Rotate( RotDelta );
                end;
                { stops when Distance starts to get big again }
          RotDelta := -RotDelta;
          Rotate( RotDelta ); { go back one }
          end;
     AxDelta := 4;
     { set distance }
     D := Distance( APoint, BusyEnd );
     MoveAxial( AxDelta );  { move axially }
     if D < Distance( APoint, BusyEnd ) then begin
        D := Distance( APoint, BusyEnd );
        AxDelta := -AxDelta;
        MoveAxial( AxDelta );
        end;
     while D > Distance( APoint, BusyEnd ) do begin
        D :=  Distance( APoint, BusyEnd );
        MoveAxial( AxDelta );
        end;
     AxDelta := -AxDelta div 2;
     MoveAxial( AxDelta );  { should be here }
     if ShowQ = true then
        begin
        ShowLimit;
        ShowBase;
        end;
end;

procedure RobotArm.ShowBase;
begin
     with Anchor do
          Graph.PieSlice(X, Y, 268, 272, Round(GetMaxY/2.2));
end;

procedure RobotArm.ShowLimit;
begin
     SetColor( red );
     with Anchor do
          Circle( X, Y, Length );
     SetColor( white );
end;
end.
```

Listing 10-6

```
unit Robot_B; { Listing 10-6 }

interface

uses Graph, Mouse, Crt, RobotSeg, Robot_A;

type

RobotArm2Ptr = ^RobotArm2;

RobotArm2 = object( RobotArm )
            NextSeg : RobotArm2Ptr;
            constructor Init( AnchorX, AnchorY,
                              ArmLen, HandLen : Integer;
                              Position : Degrees;
                              RotStat, DispQ : Boolean;
                              pToNextSeg : pointer);
            procedure MoveAxial( var i : integer ); virtual;
            procedure MoveTo( APoint : Point; DispQ : boolean );
            procedure ShowLimit; virtual;
            end;

implementation

constructor RobotArm2.Init( AnchorX, AnchorY,
                            ArmLen, HandLen : Integer;
                            Position : Degrees;
                            RotStat, DispQ : Boolean;
                            pToNextSeg : pointer );
begin
    Segment.Init( AnchorX, AnchorY, ArmLen, Position, RotStat );
    NextSeg := pToNextSeg;
    if NextSeg <> nil then
       NextSeg^.Init( BusyEnd.X, BusyEnd.Y, HandLen, 0,
                      Round(Position + 90),
                      false, true, nil );
    if DispQ = true then
       begin
       if NextSeg <> nil then
          begin
          ShowLimit;
          ShowBase;
          end;
       Show;
       end;
end;
```

```
procedure RobotArm2.MoveAxial( var i : integer );
var D : real;
begin
     Hide;
     if NextSeg <> nil then
        NextSeg^.Hide;
     D := Distance( Anchor, BusyEnd );
     if D-i >= Length then
        D := Length+i;
     if (D <= i) and (Orientation > PI) then
        begin
        Orientation := Orientation - PI;
        D := -(D + i);
        i := -i;
        end
     else
        if D <= i then
           begin
           Orientation := Orientation + PI;
           D := -(D + i);
           i := -i;
           end;
     BusyEnd.X := Round(Anchor.X + cos(Orientation)*(D-i));
     BusyEnd.Y := Round(Anchor.Y - sin(Orientation)*(D-i));
     Show;
     if NextSeg <> nil then
        begin
        NextSeg^.MoveAnchor(BusyEnd.X,BusyEnd.Y);
        NextSeg^.Show;
        end;
end;


{ this insures that all segments (except the first one) will not
  have the base shown with them }
procedure RobotArm2.MoveTo( APoint : Point; DispQ : boolean  );
var D : integer;
    RotDir : integer;
    AxDir  : integer;
begin
     RobotArm.MoveTo( APoint, DispQ );
     if NextSeg <> nil then
        NextSeg^.MoveTo(APoint, false);
     ShowLimit;
end;

procedure RobotArm2.ShowLimit;
begin
     if NextSeg <> nil then
        begin
        Graph.SetColor( red);
```

```
        with Anchor do
             Rectangle( X - Length,
                        Y - NextSeg^.Length,
                        X + Length,
                        Y + NextSeg^.Length );
        Graph.SetColor(white);
        end;
end;
end.
```

Robot B: The RobotArm2 Object Type

The `RobotArm2` object type is a strange-looking bird. Its major distinction from the `RobotArm` type is the addition of a property that points to: another object of the `RobotArm2` type. This provides future flexibility for n- segment robot arms (where n > 2), but that's all theoretical. In fact, you may want to think about incorporating `List` behavior for many-segmented robot arms. For our case of a 2-segment robot, the segment attached to the base will be called the `Arm`, and the segment attached to the `Arm` will be called the `Hand`. The `.Init` procedure has been modified to include the lengths of the two segments, as well as the address of the `Hand` segment. You'll also notice that `.Init` is a constructor, which occurs as a result of the `.MoveAxial` method having to be a virtual method (more about which in a second).

`RobotArm2` is a direct descendant of the `RobotArm` object type, which means it also inherits the properties and methods of the `Segment` object type. However, it overrides all of the `RobotArm` methods (except for `.ShowBase`, which is not a crucial method by any means). The point, however, is this: `RobotArm2.MoveTo` calls the `RobotArm.MoveTo` method to move the `Arm`, after which it calls the `.MoveTo` method of the `Hand` to move the `Hand`'s `BusyEnd` to the target.

If you recall the code for `RobotArm.MoveTo`, you'll note that it makes numerous calls to `.MoveAxial`. (It also calls `.Rotate`, but this method is not accessible to `RobotArm2` objects, so we ignore it. If it were possible for `RobotArm2` objects to rotate, then `.Rotate` would have to be declared as a virtual method as well.) Since we want RobotArm.MoveTo to execute the appropriate (RobotArm or RobotArm2) .MoveAxial method, it must be declared to be a virtual method. The .ShowLimit method is in the same predicament, and thus must also be declared to be virtual.

The major difference between the RobotArm and RobotArm2 .MoveAxial methods lies in the ability of a RobotArm2 segment to "flip" after it retracts fully. Once the Distance between the Anchor and the BusyEnd becomes less than the distance moved axially, we flip the Orientation by 180 degrees, reverse the direction of motion, and then set the Distance to be a negative number so that the calculations for the BusyEnd coordinates works out correctly.

Robot B: Changes to Segment

The Segment object type now has a property RotateStatus (and associated method RotateQ) that identifies whether the segment can rotate or not. The property will be set to TRUE for two-segment robot arms, and FALSE for single-segment arms. The method will be called in the .MoveTo method to determine whether or not to execute the "phase 1" code. An added method, .MoveAnchor, erases the segment, moves it to a new position, and then redraws it. Owing to the interaction between the RobotArm and RobotArm2 object types, .Init has become a constructor and the .MoveAxial method is virtual.

Robot B: Changes to RobotArm

There are only a few relatively minor changes in the RobotArm object type. First, the rotation flag has been added to the list of parameters passed with the .Init constructor (again, caused by .MoveAxial's and .ShowLimit's need to be virtual). Second, an if statement that contains a call to the .RotateQ method has been "wrapped" around the phase 1 code in RobotArm.MoveTo. Third, RobotArm.MoveTo has a second parameter that indicates whether to show the limits of movement or the robot arm base after performing the move. This second parameter is TRUE when the method is called by the Hand; FALSE when called by the Arm.

Robot B: Implementation

A slightly modified version of Listing 10-3 is presented in Listing 10-7 to "exercise" our two-segment robot. Clicking the mouse anywhere inside the limits of action will send the robot arm to the target.

Listing 10-7

```
program List10_7; { Listing 10-7 }

uses Graph, Mouse, Crt, RobotSeg, Robot_B;
var
   Hand,Arm : RobotArm2;
   PO : Point;

   x, y : integer;

   GraphDriver : integer;
   GraphMode   : integer;
   ErrorCode   : integer;
   GlobalAnchorX,
   GlobalAnchorY,
   ArmLength,
   HandLength  : integer;
begin
     GraphDriver := Detect;
     InitGraph(GraphDriver, GraphMode, 'C:\TP');
     ErrorCode := GraphResult;
     if ErrorCode <> grOK then
        Writeln('Graphics error');

     GlobalAnchorX := Round(GetMaxX/3);
     GlobalAnchorY := Round(GetMaxY/2);
     ArmLength     := Round(GetMaxY/2.5);
     HandLength     := Round(GetMaxY/2.7);

     Graph.SetColor(white);
     SetTextStyle( DefaultFont, HorizDir, 2);
     OutTextXY( Round(GetMaxX/1.5), Round(GetMaxY*4/5),

          'Robot ''B''' );
     Arm.Init( GlobalAnchorX, GlobalAnchorY,
```

```
            ArmLength, HandLength,
            0, false, true, @Hand);
  P0.Init( 0,0);
  if MouseInit = true then
     :
  MouseShow;
  repeat
      repeat
      until MouseLPressed or KeyPressed;
      if not KeyPressed then
         begin
         P0.Hide;
         repeat
               MouseCoords( x, y );
         until MouseLReleased;
         MouseHide;
         P0.Init( x, y );
         P0.Show;
         Arm.MoveTo( P0, true );
         P0.Show;
         MouseShow;
         end;
  until KeyPressed;
end.
```

Postscript

So what have we learned? Well, when it comes to having to retrofit a design, you'll probably end up making a lot of small changes up and down the line (look at Figure 10.5, which compares the file and object hierarchies for Robots A and B). If you keep the functions performed by your methods simple and compartmentalized, you minimize the risk that a design change down the road will require you to abandon developed code. Your best defense, as always, is to extract as much information as possible before settling down to design a system.

Looking at two-dimensional stick figures is not really state-of-the-art in this day and age, but nevertheless demonstrates the capabilities of Turbo Pascal 5.5 given a nominal level of effort.

Figure 10.5 — Comparing the file and object hierarchies for Robots A and B

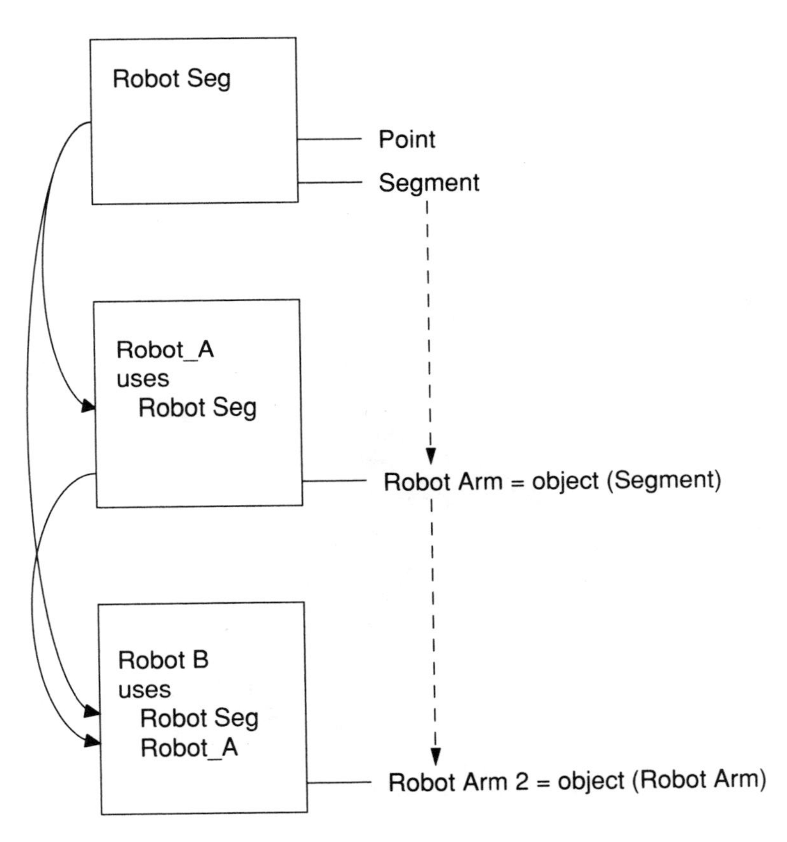

It might be interesting to "create" both types of robot on the screen and then modify their code so that they not only touch a target, but also "grab" it and move it from one spot to another, perhaps passing the target from one to the other. Alternatively, two (or however many) could "assemble" something on the screen by picking components up from bins and placing them on assemblies. There are a number of robotic programming languages that more advanced programmers might implement to work with the prototype robot arms developed in this chapter.

Appendix 1

PROGRAM FOR GENERATING MTEST5.OBJ

The following listing is for readers who did not buy the disk version of the book and who do not own a copy of Turbo Assembler. Running the program will create a file called MTEST5.OBJ that is byte-for-byte identical to the .OBJ file generated by Turbo Assembler. The file generated by this program can then be used with the rest of the programs presented in Chapter 7.

```
program MTEST5OB;

{ This program creates a copy of MTEST5.OBJ for those who
  do not yet own Turbo Assembler. }

const
 objfileary : array [0..225] of byte
                  = ($80, $0C, $00, $0A, $4D, $54, $45, $53,
                     $54, $35, $2E, $41, $53, $4D, $99, $88,
                     $1F, $00, $00, $00, $54, $75, $72, $62,
                     $6F, $20, $41, $73, $73, $65, $6D, $62,
                     $6C, $65, $72, $20, $20, $56, $65, $72,
                     $73, $69, $6F, $6E, $20, $31, $2E, $30,
                     $BA, $88, $12, $00, $40, $E9, $A1, $B3,
                     $46, $14, $0A, $4D, $54, $45, $53, $54,
                     $35, $2E, $41, $53, $4D, $B4, $88, $03,
                     $00, $40, $E9, $4C, $96, $02, $00, $00,
                     $68, $96, $06, $00, $04, $44, $41, $54,
                     $41, $46, $98, $07, $00, $48, $00, $00,
                     $02, $01, $01, $15, $96, $06, $00, $04,
                     $43, $4F, $44, $45, $45, $98, $07, $00,
                     $28, $15, $00, $03, $01, $01, $1F, $8C,
```

```
                    $19, $00, $04, $58, $50, $4F, $53, $00,
                    $04, $59, $50, $4F, $53, $00, $0A, $45,
                    $4E, $54, $52, $59, $50, $4F, $49, $4E,
                    $54, $00, $98, $90, $0D, $00, $00, $02,
                    $06, $4D, $53, $54, $41, $52, $54, $00,
                    $00, $00, $80, $88, $04, $00, $40, $A2,
                    $01, $91, $A0, $19, $00, $02, $00, $00,
                    $1E, $B8, $00, $00, $8E, $D8, $89, $0E,
                    $00, $00, $89, $16, $00, $00, $9A, $00,
                    $00, $00, $00, $1F, $CB, $4F, $9C, $14,
                    $00, $C8, $02, $54, $01, $C4, $08, $06,
                    $01, $01, $C4, $0C, $06, $01, $02, $CC,
                    $0F, $06, $02, $03, $9E, $8A, $02, $00,
                    $00, $74);
var
   i : integer;
   f : file of byte;
begin
     Assign( f, 'MTEST5.OBJ' );
     Rewrite( f );
     for i := 0 to 225 do
         write( f, objfileary[i] );
     Close( f );

end.
```

ABOUT THE AUTHOR

Alex Lane is a licensed professional engineer in Florida. He is currently employed as a knowledge engineer for an engineering-oriented expert systems consulting and development company. Alex has written numerous articles for various technical publications, including *BYTE* and *Dr. Dobb's Journal.*

INDEX

F

G

H

I

J

L

U

V

WXYZ

C Tools

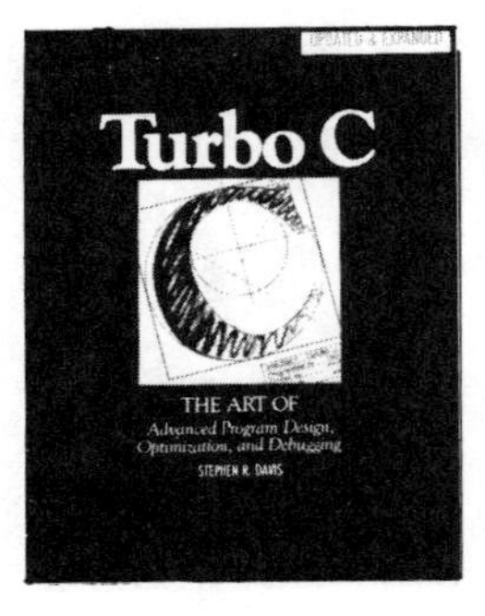

Turbo C

The Art of Advanced Program Design, Optimization, and Debugging

Stephen R. Davis

Packed with useful example programs, this book details the techniques necessary to skillfully program, optimize, and debug in Turbo C. Every topic and Turbo C feature is fully demonstrated in Turbo C source code examples.

Starting with an overview of the C language, the author advances to topics such as pointers, direct screen I/O, inline statements, and how to intercept and redirect BIOS calls, all of which are demonstrated in a RAM resident pop-up program written in Turbo C.

Fully outlined are the differences between UNIX C and Turbo C, the transition from Turbo Pascal to Turbo C, and the superset of K&R C features implemented in the proposed ANSI C standard.

Whether you are a C programmer who is interested in investigating this exciting new C environment or a Turbo Pascal programmer who is interested in learning more about this C långuage, **Turbo C** is invaluable reading!

Book & Disk (MS-DOS)
Item #45-3 **$39.95**
Book only
Item #38-0 **$24.95**

Dr. Dobb's Toolbook of C

by the Editors of *Dr. Dobb's Journal*

Over 700 pages of the best of C articles and source code from *Dr. Dobb's Journal* in a single volume! Not just a compilation of reprints, this comprehensive book contains new materials by various C experts, as well as updates and revisions of some classic articles.

The essays and articles contained in this virtual encyclopedia of information were designed to give the professional programmer a deeper understanding of C by addressing real-world programming problems and explaining how to use C to its fullest.

Some of the highlights include an entire C compiler with support routines, versions of various utility programs such as Grep, and a C program cross-referencer.

Dr. Dobb's Toolbook of C is an invaluable resource that you'll turn to again and again.

Book only
Item #599-8 **$24.95**

A Small C Compiler

Language, Usage, Theory, and Design

by James E. Hendrix

For anyone who uses or plans to use Small C, **A Small C Compiler** provides valuable information about the language and its compiler.

The design and operation theory of the Small C compiler and programming language are presented. In addition to a full, working Small C compiler, this book provides an excellent example for learning basic compiler theory. Here is a real compiler that is easy enough to be understood and modified by computer science students, and may be transformed into a cross-compiler or completely ported to other processors.

Features include code optimizing, internal use of pseudo-code, upward compatibility with full C, recursive descent parsing, a one-pass algorithm, and the generation of assembly language code. No other compiler available to the public has ever been so thoroughly documented.

The accompanying disk includes an executable compiler, fully documented source code, and many sample programs. A Microsoft or IBM Macro Assembler is required.

Book & Disk (MS-DOS)
Item #97-6 **$38.95**
Book only
Item #88-7 **$23.95**

Small-Tools User's Manual

by James E. Hendrix

This package of programs performs specific modular operations on text files such as editing, formatting, sorting, merging, listing, printing, searching, changing, transliterating, copying, and concatenating. **Small-Tools** is supplied in source code form. You can select and adapt these tools to your own purposes. Documentation is included.

Manual & Disk (MS-DOS)
Item #02-X $29.95

Small Assembler

An 80x86 Macro Assembler Written in Small C

by James E. Hendrix

Small Assembler is a full macro assembler that was developed primarily for use with the Small C compiler. In addition to being a full assembler that generates standard MASM compatible .OBJ files, the **Small Assembler** is written in Small C. It provides an excellent example for learning the basics of how an assembler works. The Small Assembler generates .OBJ files for all 80X86 processors, and will easily adapt to future Intel processors.

This manual presents an overview of the Small Assembler, documents the command lines that invoke programs, and provides appendixes and reference materials for the programmer. Included are the Small Assembler, linkage editor, CPU configuration utility, and a program to back up a file system. The accompanying disk includes both the executable assembler and full source code.

Manual & Disk (MS-DOS)
Item #024-9 $29.95

Small-Windows

A Library of Windowing Functions for the C Language

by James E. Hendrix

Small-Windows is an extensive library of C language functions for creating and manipulating display windows. This manual and disk package contains 41 windowing functions that allow you to clean, frame, move, hide, show, scroll, and push and pop windows. Also included are 18 video functions written in assembly language, and menu functions that support both static and pop-up menus.

A file directory illustrates the use of window menu functions and provides file selection, renaming, and deletion capability. Two test programs are provided as examples to show you how to use the library and the window, menu, and directory functions.

Small-Windows is available for MS-DOS systems, and Microsoft C Versions 4.0/5.0, Turbo C 1.5, Small C, and Lattice C 3.1 compilers. Documentation and full C source code are included.

Manual & Disk (MS-DOS)
(Microsoft C, Small C, Lattice C, or Turbo C Compiler)
Item #35-6 $29.95

The Small C Special Offer

Get *A Small C Compiler*, *Small Assembler*, *Small-Windows*, and *Small-Tools* all for only $99.99! That's like getting one package absolutely free! All disks are included. Item #007C

CALL TOLL FREE 1-800-533-4372
In CA CALL 1-800-356-2002

LANs

Blueprint of a LAN

by Craig Chaiken

Blueprint of a LAN provides a hands-on introduction to microcomputer networks. For programmers, numerous valuable programming techniques are detailed. Network administrators will learn how to build and install LAN communication cables, configure and troubleshoot network hardware and software, and provide continuing support to users. Included is a very inexpensive zero-slot, star topology network with remote printer and file sharing, remote command execution, electronic mail, parallel processing support, high-level language support, and more. Contained is the complete Intel 8086 assembly language source code that will help you build an inexpensive-to-install local area network. This complete reference is ideal for programmers and students experimenting with networking, and small businesses requiring a low-cost LAN. An optional disk containing all source code is available.

Book & Disk (MS-DOS)
Item #066-4 **$38.95**
Book only
Item #052-4 **$23.95**

LAN Troubleshooting Handbook

Mark A. Miller

Presenting a technical reference written for the systems analyst who needs to identify problems and maintain a LAN that is already installed. It is also ideal for users wanting to gain a better understanding of LAN problem resolution and to master LAN principles and troubleshooting techniques. Readers will gain knowledge that will enable them to install, troubleshoot, and maintain their LAN. Topics include LAN standards, the OSI model, network documentation, LAN test equipment, cable system testing, and more! Available December 1989.

Book & Disk (MS-DOS)
Item #056-7 **$39.95**
Book only
Item #054-0 **$24.95**

Building Local Area Networks with Novell's NetWare

by Patrick H. Corrigan and Aisling Guy

From the basic components to complete network installation, here is the practical guide that PC system integrators will need to build and implement PC LANs in this rapidly growing market. The specifics of building and maintaining PC LANs, including hardware configurations, software development, cabling, selection criteria, installation, and on-going management are described in a clear "how-to" manner with numerous illustrations and sample LAN management forms.

Building Local Area Networks gives particular emphasis to Novell's NetWare, Version 2.1. Additional topics covered include the OS/2 LAN Manager, Tops, Banyan VINES, internetworking, host computer gateways, and multisystem networks that link PCs, Apples, and mainframes.

Book & Disk (MS-DOS)
Item #025-7 **$39.95**
Book only
Item #010-9 **$24.95**

LAN SPECIAL OFFER!
Buy the *Building Local Area Networks with Novell's NetWare* book and disk set and *NetWare User's Guide* for only $52.95! You save 15%!
Item #026 **$52.95**

Dr. Dobb's Toolbook of 80286/80386 Programming

edited by Phillip Robinson

How much do you know about 80286/80386 programming? If it is not nearly enough, or you just want to learn more about it, then this book is for you. Editor Phillip Robinson has gathered the best 80286/80386 articles, updated and expanded them, and added new material to create this valuable resource for all 80X86 programmers.

This massive anthology contains a variety of ideas from experienced 386 programmers. Basic information has been compiled along with real-world solutions. New and previously published articles on programming the 80386 microprocessor and its relatives, the 80387 math coprocessor, the 82786 graphics coprocessor, and the 80286 16-bit processor are all included. You'll also find articles on moving old programs to the 32-bit 80386, reaping the benefits of the 386's memory-management abilities, creating and handling operating systems with multitasking and multiuser features, and optimizing graphics and floating-point operations. All source code is available on disk.

Book & Disk (MS-DOS)
Item #53-4 **$39.95**
Book only
Item #42-9 **$24.95**

Dr. Dobb's Toolbook of 68000 Programming

by the Editors of
Dr. Dobb's Journal

This complete collection of practical programming tips and techniques for the 68000 family includes the best articles on 68000 programming published in *Dr. Dobb's Journal*, along with new material. You'll learn about the most important features of the 68000 microprocessor from a full description of its history and design. Useful applications and examples will show you why computers using the 68000 family are easy to design, produce, and upgrade. Contents includes a comprehensive introduction to the 68000 family, development tools for the 68000 family, useful routines and techniques, a 68000 Cross Assembler, and The Worm Memory Test. All programs are available on disk.

Book & Disk (MS-DOS, CP/M 8" SS/SD, Osborne, Macintosh, Amiga, or Atari 520ST)
Item #75-5 **$49.95**
Book only
Item #216649-6 **$29.95**

X68000 Cross Assembler User's Manual

by Brian R. Anderson

In **Dr. Dobb's Toolbook of 68000 Programming**, a full chapter is devoted to the creation of a fully functional 68000 Cross Assembler written in Modula-2. Now, an executable version of this 68000 Cross Assembler is available separately, complete with source code and documentation.

A two-pass cross assembler for the Motorola MC68000 microprocessor, it accepts standard Motorola syntax and produces a formatted program listing file and an object file consisting of standard Motorola S-records, which is fully explained in this manual. In addition to the assembler program, the supplied software also includes OPCODE.DAT—a data file used to initialize the mnemonic lookup table for the assembler.

Manual & Disk (MS-DOS,CP/M: Osborne, 8" SS/SD)
Item #71-2 **$25.00**

CALL TOLL FREE 1-800-533-4372
In CA CALL 1-800-356-2002

UNIX-Like Features

On Command

Writing a UNIX-Like Shell for MS-DOS

by Allen Holub

On Command and its ready-to-use program demonstrate how to write a UNIX-like shell for MS-DOS, with techniques applicable to most other programming languages as well. The book and disk include a detailed description and working version of the Shell, complete C source code, a thorough discussion of low-level MS-DOS interfacing, and significant examples of C programming at the system level.

Supported features include: read, aliases, history, redirection and pipes, UNIX-like command syntax, MS-DOS compatible prompt support, C-like control-flow statements, and a Shell variable that expands to the contents of a file so that a program can produce text that is used by Shell scripts.

The ready-to-use program and all C source code are included on disk. For IBM PC and direct compatibles.

Book & Disk (MS-DOS)
Item #29-1 **$39.95**

/Util

A UNIX-Like Utility Package for MS-DOS

by Allen Holub

When used with the Shell, this collection of utility programs and subroutines provides you with a fully functional subset of the UNIX environment. Many of the utilities may also be used independently. You'll find executable versions of cat, c, date, du, echo, grep, ls, mkdir, mv, p, pause, printevn, rm, rmdir, sub, and chmod.

The **/Util** package includes complete source code on disk. All programs and most of the utility subroutines are fully documented in a UNIX-style manual. For IBM PCs and direct compatibles.

Manual & Disk (MS-DOS)
Item #12-7 **$29.95**

NR

An Implementation of the UNIX NROFF Word Processor

by Allen Holub

NR is a text formatter that is written in C and is compatible with UNIX's NROFF. Complete source code is included in the **NR** package so that it can be easily customized to fit your needs. **NR** also includes an implementation of how -ms works. NR does hyphenation and simple proportional spacing. It supports automatic table of contents and index generation, automatic footnotes and endnotes, italics, boldface, overstriking, underlining, and left and right margin adjustment. The **NR** package also contains: extensive macro and string capability, number registers in various formats, diversions and diversion traps, and input and output line traps. NR is easily configurable for most printers. Both the ready-to-use program and full source code are included. For PC compatibles.

Manual & Disk (MS-DOS)
Item #33-X **$29.95**

UNIX-LIKE SPECIAL! SAVE 15%
Receive *On Command*, */Util*, and *NR* all for only $89.95!
Get the convenience of UNIX-like features and save 15%!
Item #167

Operating Systems

The Programmer's Essential OS/2 Handbook

by David E. Cortesi

For writers of OS/2 programs, **The Programmer's Essential OS/2 Handbook** provides the OS/2 technical information that will enable you to write efficient, reliable applications in C, Pascal, or assembler. Two indexes and a web of cross-referencing provide easy access to all OS/2 topic areas. There's even detailed technical information that is not included in the official OS/2 documentation. Equal support for Pascal and C programmers is provided.

Inside you'll find an overview of OS/2 architecture and vocabulary, including references to where the book handles each topic in depth: a look at the 80286 and a description of how the CPU processes data in real and protected mode; an overview of linking, multiprogramming, file access, and device drivers; and an in-depth discussion of important OS/2 topics, including dynamic linking, message facility, the screen group, inputs, outputs, the queue, the semaphore, and more.

The Programmer's Essential OS/2 Handbook is written in precise language and is a resource no programmer developing in the OS/2 environment can afford to be without.

Book & Disk (5-1/4" & 3-1/2" OS/2)
Item #89-5 **$39.95**
Book only
Item #82-8 **$24.95**

UNIX Programming on the 80286/80386, Second Edition

by Alan Deikman

UNIX Programming on the 80286/80386, 2nd Edition provides experienced system programmers with an overview of time-saving UNIX features and a detailed discussion of the relationship between UNIX and DOS. Included are many helpful techniques specific to programming under the UNIX environment on a PC.

This is where you will find complete coverage of the UNIX program environment, file system shells and basic utilities, C programming under UNIX, mass storage problems, 80286 and 80386 architecture, segment register programming, and UNIX administration and documentation.

UNIX Programming on the 80286/80386, 2nd Edition contains many practical examples of device drivers necessary to communicate with PC peripherals. Also included is useful information on how to set up device drivers for AT compatibles, such as cartridge tape drives and raster scan devices. Many examples of actual code are provided and are available on disk.

Book & Disk (UNIX 5-1/4")
Item #91-7 **$39.95**
Book only
Item #83-6 **$24.95**

DESQview

A Guide to Programming the DESQview Multitasking Environment

by Stephen R. Davis

DESQview is currently the most sophisticated and versatile multitasking software integrator. This new book provides users with the information needed to get the most out of DESQview. Discussed are the object-oriented DESQview 2.0 API (Application Program Interface) and the multitasking concepts necessary to program the DESQview environment. These concepts are applied by creating example programs that control and interact with DESQview's API. These sample programs demonstrate such concepts as windowing, intertask communication, memory management (including EMS-type "expanded" memory), software objects, and subtask control. **DESQview: A Guide to Programming the DESQview Multitasking Environment** is fully endorsed by Quarterdeck Office Systems, publisher of DESQview.

Book & Disk (MS-DOS)
Item #006-0 **$39.95**
Book only
Item #028-1 **$24.95**

Tele Operating System

SK

The System Kernel of the Tele Operating System Toolkit

by Ken Berry

SK includes the most crucial part of the Tele Operating System: the preemptive multitasking algorithm. This package provides you with complete documentation for installing and using the Tele kernel on personal computers utilizing an 8086-compatible processor. Though the code is designed specifically for a standard IBM PC, it can be easily modified for a wide range of architectures. **SK** also contains an initialization module, general purpose utility functions for string and character handling, format conversion, terminal support and machine interface, and a real-time task management system.

Manual & Disk (MS-DOS)
Item #30-5 **$49.95**

DS

Window Display

by Ken Berry

DS contains the programs necessary to control the operator console in the Tele Operating System and will work with any memory-mapped hardware. It features BIOS-level drivers for a memory-mapped display, window management support, and communication coordination between the operator and tasks in a multitasking environment. **DS** includes functions to create and delete virtual displays, and functions to overlay a portion of a virtual display on the physical display. An unlimited number of virtual displays can belong to any particular task, and an unlimited number can be in the system at any time. Information necessary to use **DS** on standard personal computers and install it on nonstandard machines is provided. Requires **SK: The System Kernel.**

Manual & Disk (MS-DOS)
Item #32-1 **$39.95**

FS

The File System

by Ken Berry

This package provides you with complete documentation for installing and using **FS**. **FS** supports MS-DOS disk file structures and serial communication channels. It manages the storage of information on disks with a UNIX-like file allocation method, and is compatible with both UNIX and MS-DOS. The code can be easily modified for a wide range of architectures. **FS** also features a telecommunications support facility that allows a common set of functions to handle both disk files and communications. Requires **SK: The System Kernel.**

Manual & Disk (MS-DOS)
Item #65-8 **$39.95**

Demonstration Disk

Give the Tele Operating System a try! For just $5 you can get a demo disk that includes a working sample of the Tele Operating System. Demo Disk (MS-DOS) Item #70-4

XS

The Index System

by Ken Berry

XS implements a tree-structured, free-form database. **XS** allows names and data of variable length with no practical limitation on data size. The algorithm used optimizes access for different processors and disk speeds, thus minimizing the time required to access the data associated with a particular name. Besides locating a given name, **XS** allows names to be inserted, updated, and deleted. Applications can also dynamically adjust memory usage and ensure that the physical device has an up-to-date copy of the index. All C and assembler source code, as well as precompiled libraries, are included. Requires **SK: The System Kernel** and **FS: The File System.**

Manual & Disk (MS-DOS)
Item #66-6 **$39.95**

Public-Domain Software
& Shareware
Untapped Resources for the PC User
2ND EDITION

Dr. Dobb's Journal
VOLUME
13
Software
Tools
1988

Special Offers

SMALL C SPECIAL
Get **A Small C Compiler**, **Small Assembler**, **Small-Windows**, and **Small-Tools** all for only $99.99! Disks are included.
Item #007C

MIDI SPECIAL
Order both **C Programming for MIDI** and **MIDI Sequencing in C** book and disk packages for $69.95! You save 10%!
Item #90-M

FORTH SPECIAL
Save over $10 by ordering both volumes of **Dr. Dobb's Toolbook of Forth** for only $74.95! Disks are included.
Item #57-X

UNIX-Like SPECIAL
On Command, **/Util**, and **NR** all for only $89.95 Save 15%!
Item #167

dBASE III SPECIAL
Get **Time & Task Management** and **Sales Management** for only $75! Disks are included.
Item #025

BOUND VOLUMES SPECIAL
The entire 13-volume set of **Dr. Dobb's Bound Volumes** is available for only $376.55. You save 15% off the regular price of $443! If you don't need the entire set, you can still save by ordering four or more volumes. Simply deduct 10% off the Bound Volume subtotal!
Item #041-9

VIDEOTAPES SPECIAL
Get all seven **Software Engineering Forum Videotapes** for $450 postage paid! You save over $200!
Item #012V

LAN SPECIAL
Buy the ***Building Local Area Networks With Novell's NetWare*** book and disk set and ***NetWare User's Guide*** for only $52.95. Save 15%!
Item #026

Our books can be found at fine bookstores near you including B. Dalton, Egghead Discount Software, Software Etc., WaldenBooks, and Waldensoftware Stores.

TO ORDER: CALL TOLL-FREE 1-800-533-4372. In CA call 1-800-356-2002. Mail to **M&T BOOKS**, 501 Galveston Drive, Redwood City, CA 94063 or FAX to (415) 366-1685.

ORDERED BY (Please print):
Name: ______________________
Address: ______________________
City: ____________ State: ____ Zip: ________
Daytime phone: ______________________

METHOD OF PAYMENT
☐ Check enclosed, payable to M&T Books.
☐ Visa ☐ MC ☐ AmEx
Acct. # ______________ Exp. Date ______
Signature ______________________

Note: For disk orders, indicate format and/or compiler. Refer to ad for standard format availability for each product.

Qty	Item #	Description	Format	Unit Price	Total

Subtotal	
CA residents add sales tax	
Shipping	
Total	

NG:
ping on domestic orders of $75 or more.
ing on foreign orders of $150 or more.
Add $2.99 per item for books and disks, $4.50 per
nd Volumes.
$7.60 per item for surface mail, $10.60 per Bound Volume
d $12.00 surface mail for special offer packages.
e: If you are not satisfied with your order for any
o us within 15 days of receipt for a full refund!

M&T BOOKS